IMAGES
of America

TANEYTOWN

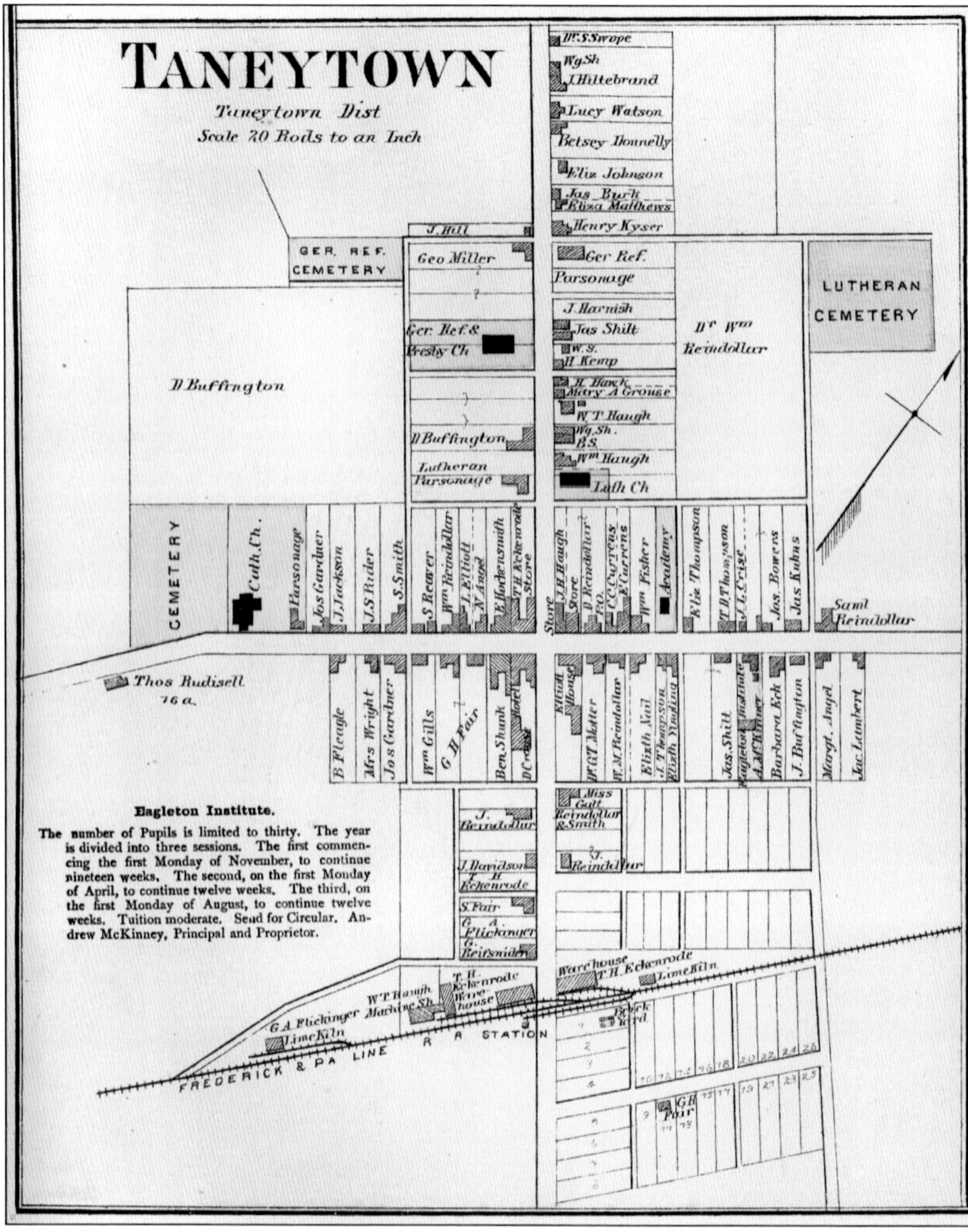

Pictured is a map of Taneytown from the 1877 *Illustrated Atlas of Carroll County, Maryland.*

IMAGES
of America

TANEYTOWN

Historical Society of Carroll County
Compiled and Edited by Tyler J. Boone

ARCADIA
PUBLISHING

ISBN 978-0-7385-1634-9

Published by Arcadia Publishing
Charleston, South Carolina

Printed in the United States of America

Library of Congress Catalog Card Number: 2004100624

For all general information contact Arcadia Publishing at:
Telephone 843-853-2070
Fax 843-853-0044
E-mail sales@arcadiapublishing.com
For customer service and orders:
Toll-Free 1-888-313-2665

Visit us on the Internet at www.arcadiapublishing.com

Dedicated to the people of Taneytown, yesterday and today.

Contents

ACKNOWLEDGMENTS

Compiling and editing this work on behalf of the Historical Society of Carroll County has proven to be an amazing experience. Originally planned as a tribute to Taneytown on the occasion of its 250th birthday, the project soon took on a life of its own.

From my earliest days, Taneytown and its rich history have fascinated me. The buildings, the people, and the oral traditions have all influenced and shaped my life. Listening is my greatest pleasure. I treasure the stories and memories that have been passed on to me and I am forever thankful to those who have shared their reminiscences and friendship.

This volume is in no way meant to be a definitive history of Taneytown. Rather, it is a pictorial representation intended to provide some small insight into the rich tradition of Taneytown.

For their moral and technical support, special thanks must be given to the staff of the Historical Society of Carroll County, president and CEO, Barbara Lilly, and curator of collections, Cathy Baty.

I wish to gratefully acknowledge the following people who so generously shared their photographs and memories: Jean Brown, Brenda Clapsaddle, Shirley Clem, Barry Garner, Helen Gorman, Ginny Henderson, Joe Hill, Anna Motter, George Motter, George Naylor, Robert Neal, Dean Reindollar, Mike Reifsnider, Susan Reifsnider, Mildred Stine, and the Taneytown Volunteer Fire Co. No. 1. Without their assistance, this project would not have been possible.

The research and writings of the following individuals proved invaluable in the compilation of this text: Miss Elizabeth Annan, Catherine Baty, Dr. Clotworthy Birnie, Basil Crapster, Joe Getty, Helen Gorman, Jay Graybeal, J. Leland Jordan, Ken Short, and Chris Weeks.

Lastly, I thank my mother Barbara R. Boone for her constant support and encouragement.

Tyler J. Boone
February 2004

INTRODUCTION

Nestled at the foothills of the rolling Catoctin Mountains in central Maryland, Taneytown has been witness to two-and-a-half centuries of American history. The town's founding in 1754 coincides with one of the earliest land grants in the area—a 7,900-acre tract of land patented as the "Resurvey on Brothers Agreement." By the late 18th century, Taneytown was a bustling village of about 250 people. The burgeoning hamlet supported a number of craftsmen of various trades, and on each of the four corners of the town square stood a tavern.

In 1791, Taneytown played host to a most distinguished guest—George Washington. He lodged overnight at the Adam Good Tavern and is said to have dined on "mush and milk." Washington noted in his diary, "Tawneytown is but a small place with only the street through which the road passes built on. The buildings are principally of wood . . . ."

Francis Scott Key, lawyer, poet, and author of "The Star Spangled Banner," is undoubtedly Taneytown's most famous native son. Key was born on August 1, 1779, at Terra Rubra, his family's plantation just outside of town, and he made frequent visits to the area throughout his life.

At the outbreak of the Civil War, Taneytown, a community of just 500, sent more than 75 men to battle. During the Gettysburg Campaign, thousands of Union soldiers passed through Taneytown to and from the battle. Union general George Meade, commander of the Army of the Potomac, established his field headquarters at a farm just outside of town, where he developed his Pipe Creek Line plan. The steeple of the Lutheran church was used as a signal tower and local legend maintains that the cupola of the magnificent plantation Antrim was used to observe troop movement.

On July 14, 1871, the railroad arrived in Taneytown, creating an economic boon, increasing business, and allowing easier transportation of the region's agricultural products. By the late 19th century, the town's population had grown to about 700 and supported myriad businesses, including three cigar factories, a carriage maker shop, two warehouses, a steam flour mill, and two banks.

With such newfound prosperity, many of the 18th and early 19th century buildings in town were replaced with fashionable Victorian edifices. In 1884, the third effort to incorporate the town was successful. In 1885, the first telephone service was installed, and by 1918 the town was wired for electricity—clearly Taneytown was on its way!

One

STREET SCENES

Located at the intersection of two important 18th-century roads, Taneytown maintained a commercially advantageous location. York and Frederick Streets developed more rapidly than did East and West Baltimore Streets (known in the 18th century as "Second Street" and in the early 19th century as "Church Street.") Only later, with improvements to the roads from Westminster, did the roads east and west develop.

With the expansion of the railroad to Taneytown in the 1870s, the town enjoyed economic prosperity, which greatly influenced the architectural appearance of the main streets. Older buildings were remodeled with fashionable Victorian ornamentation and new commercial and residential structures were built, creating the quintessential 19th-century streetscape.

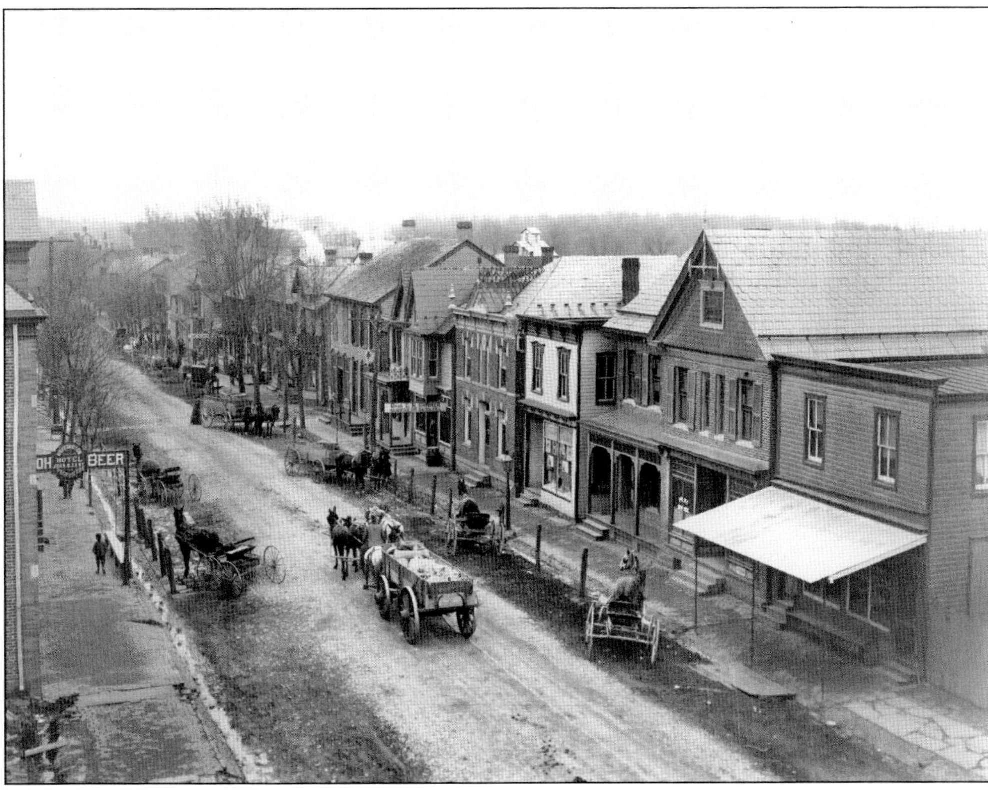

Photographer Edward P. Zepp worked in Taneytown at the turn of the century. His studio on the second floor of the Central Hotel provided him with the vantage point for this street scene of East Baltimore Street. (Courtesy of the Historical Society of Carroll County.)

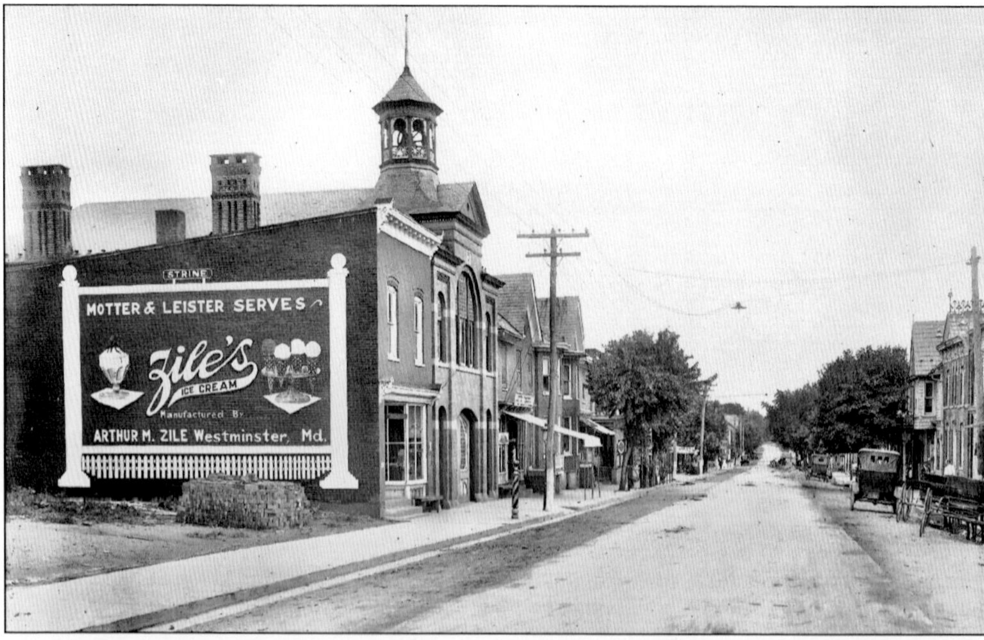

A view of East Baltimore Street from the town square in the 1920s shows the fire engine house with its fanciful cupola, which towers above the other buildings. The sign painted on the side of Burke's Barber Shop (note the barber's pole on sidewalk) advertises Zile's Ice Cream, which was served in the restaurant of the nearby Central Hotel. (Courtesy of the Historical Society of Carroll County.)

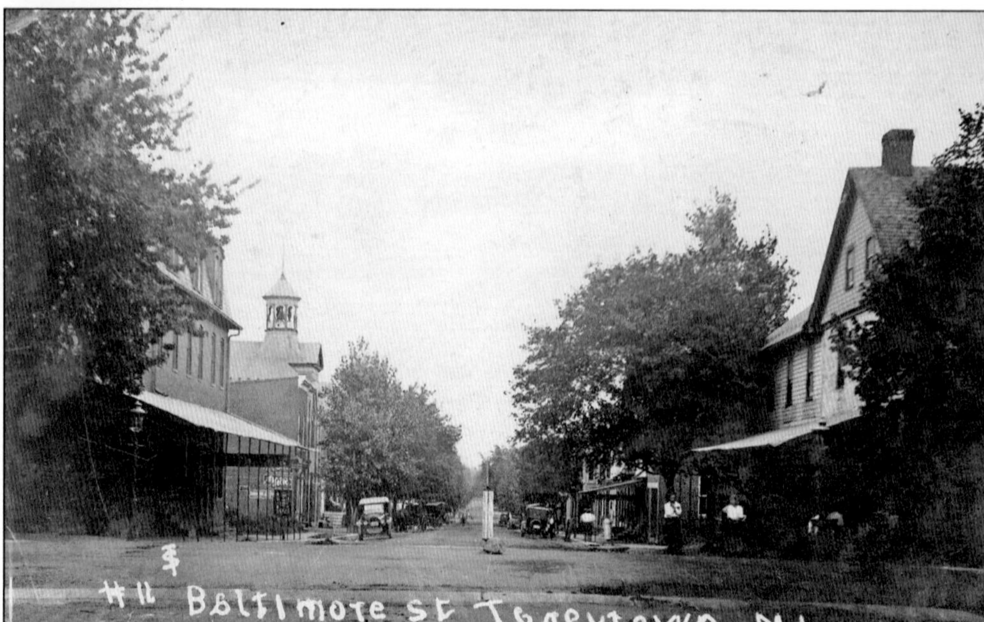

An early 20th century postcard shows East Baltimore Street from the square. Note the directional signpost planted in the middle of the square; fondly referred to as "The Dummy," the signpost was the forerunner of the modern day traffic light that currently occupies the square. (Courtesy of the Historical Society of Carroll County.)

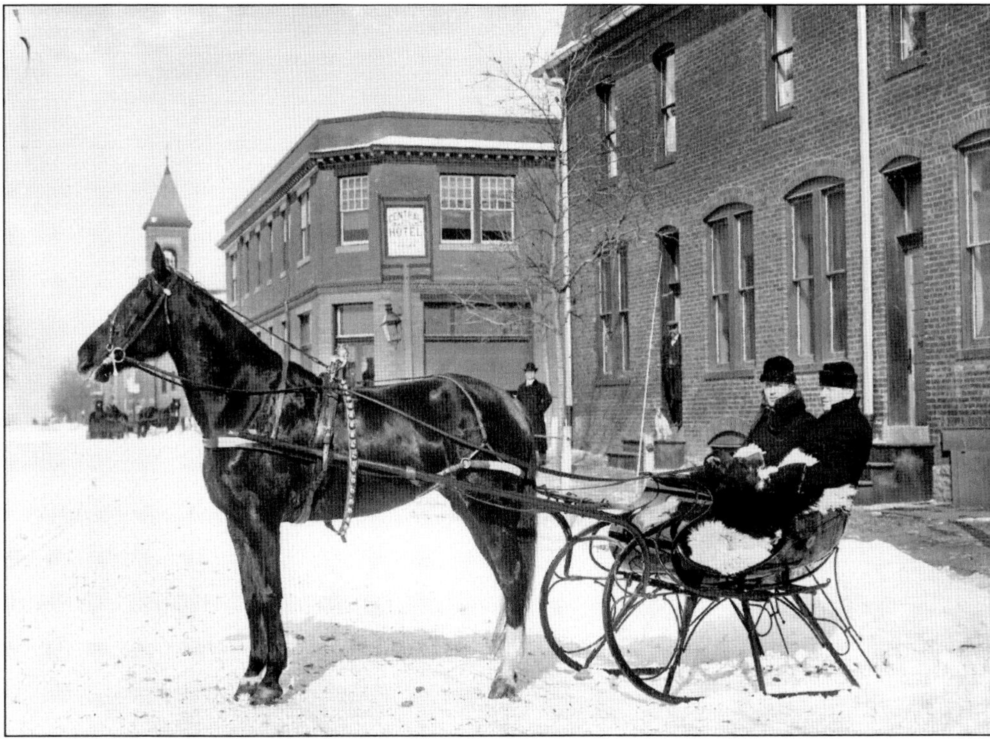

Two gentlemen sleighing pause for photographer Ed Zepp near the Central Hotel in the early 1900s. Perhaps the man in the doorway observing the scene with his dog is hotel proprietor Elias Fissel. (Courtesy of the Historical Society of Carroll County.)

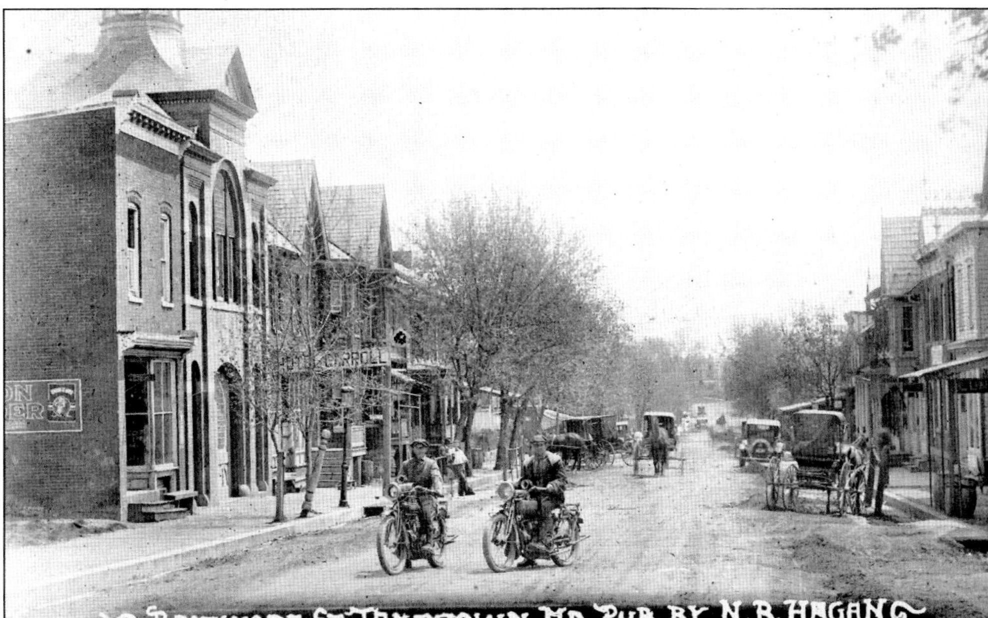

Motorcycles, buggies, and automobiles mingle on East Baltimore Street c. 1920. (Courtesy of the Historical Society of Carroll County.)

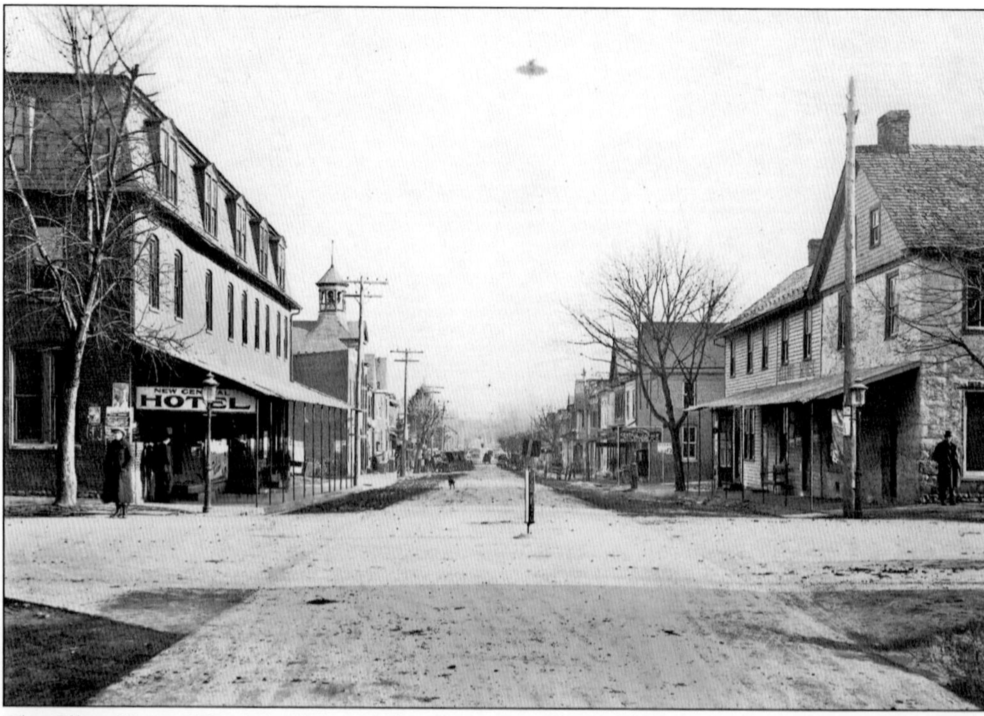

The Elliot House Hotel (right) and the New Central Hotel (left) anchor the corners of East Baltimore Street at the square. (Courtesy of the Historical Society of Carroll County.)

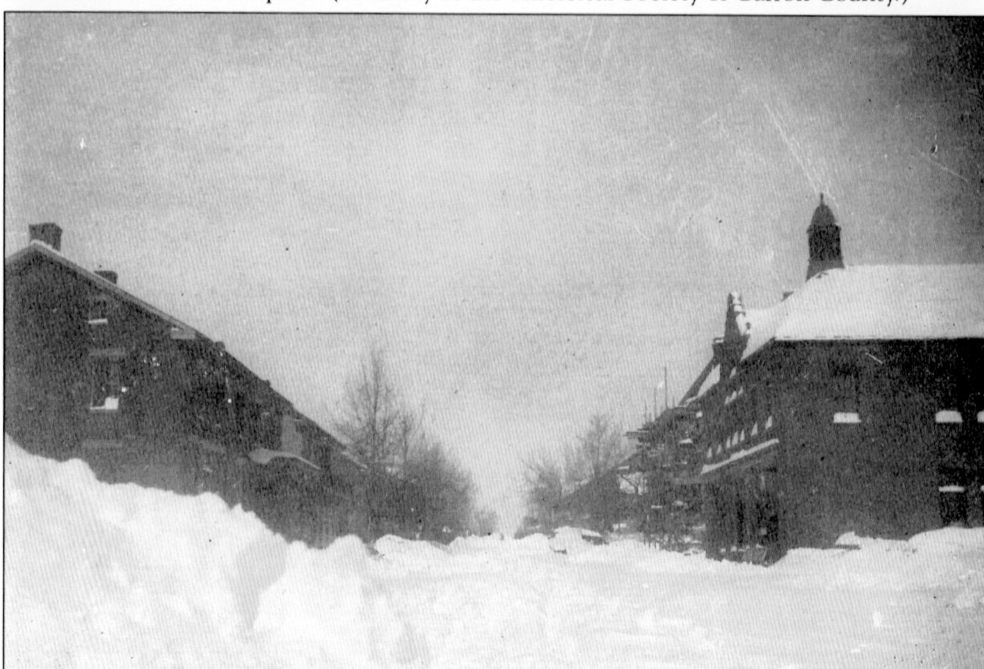

This photograph, which looks down East Baltimore Street toward the square, may have been taken during the great blizzard of February 11, 1895, after which it took four locomotives to clear the railroad track. (Courtesy of George and Anna Motter.)

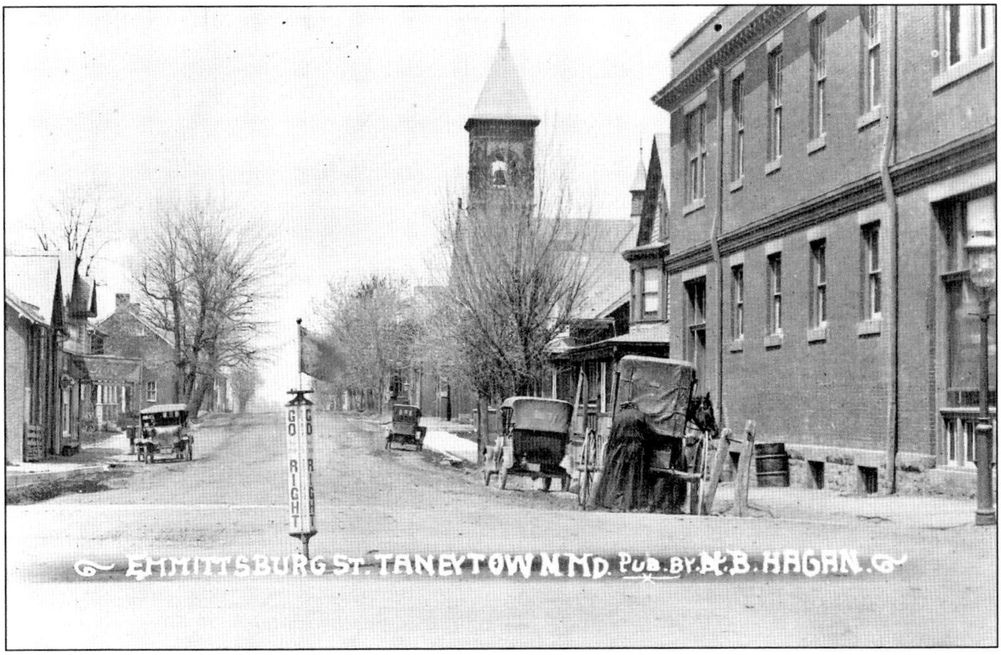

In this early 20th century postcard published by N.B. Hagan, automobiles and a buggy line unpaved Emmitsburg Street, currently West Baltimore Street. (Courtesy of the Historical Society of Carroll County.)

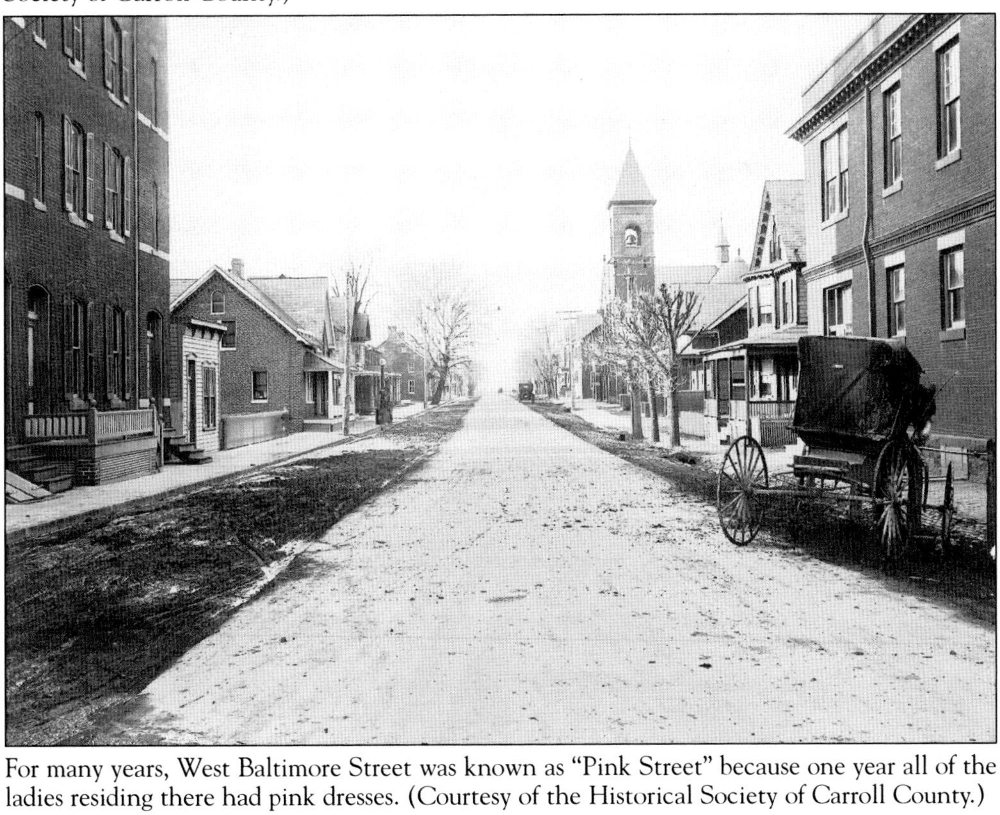

For many years, West Baltimore Street was known as "Pink Street" because one year all of the ladies residing there had pink dresses. (Courtesy of the Historical Society of Carroll County.)

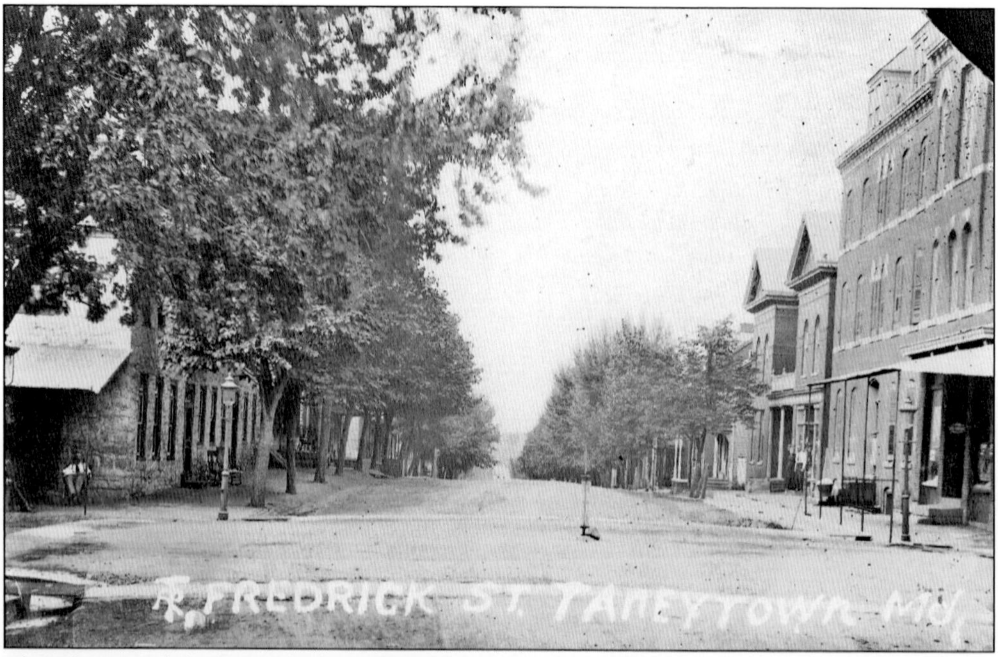

This photograph looks south down Frederick Street from the square, *c.* 1900. (Courtesy of the Historical Society of Carroll County.)

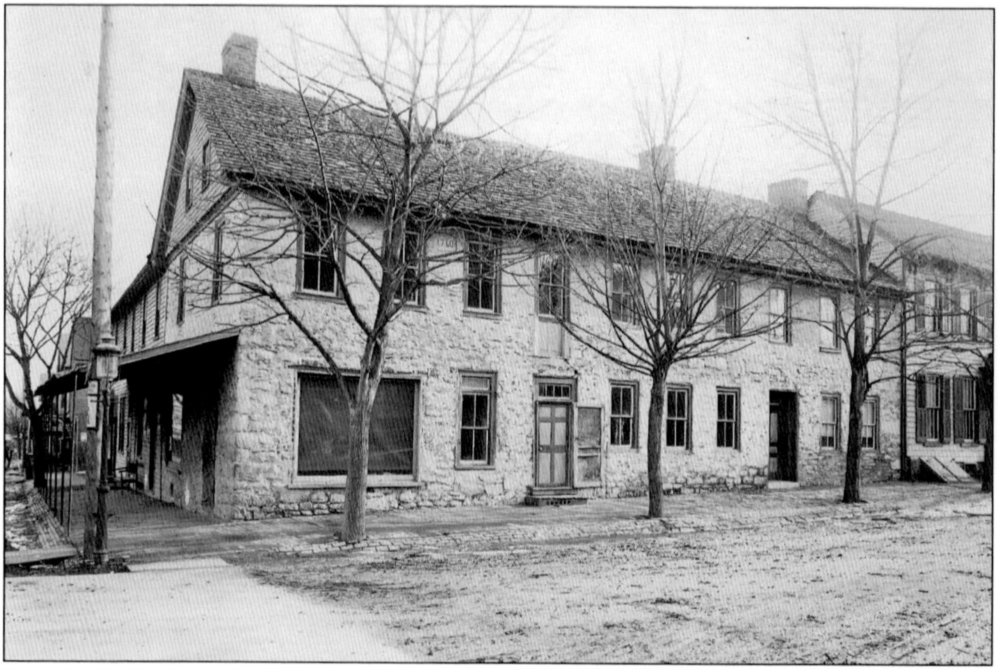

Built in 1760, the old stone tavern on Frederick Street is believed to be the oldest existing structure in town. It was operated under various names, including Elliot House and Hotel Bankard. Part of the tavern was torn down in the 20th century. (Courtesy of the Historical Society of Carroll County.)

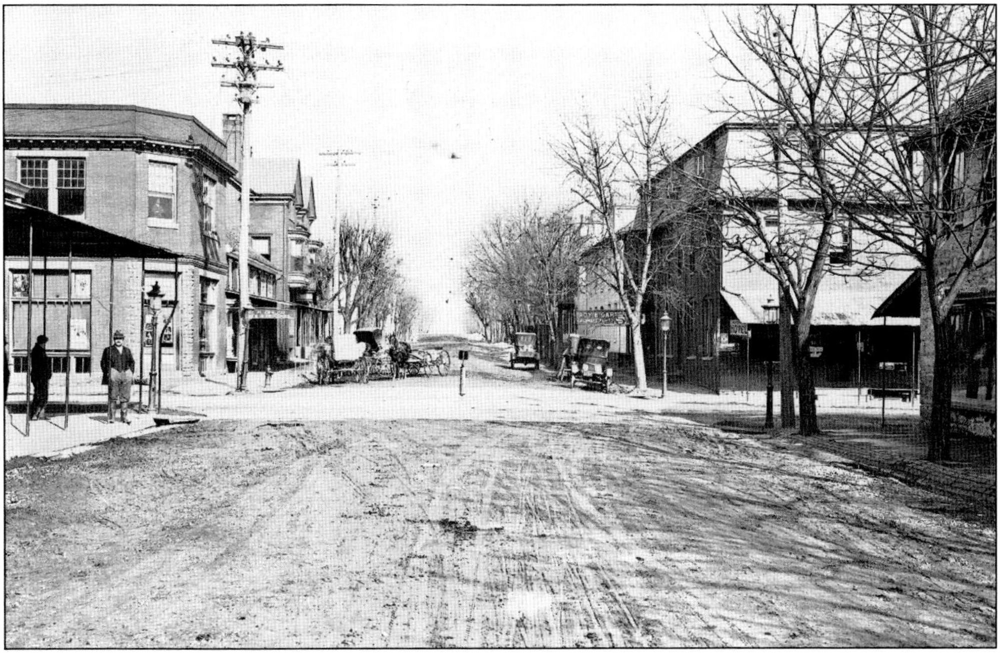

This is a view of York Street looking north from the square, *c.* 1900. (Courtesy of the Historical Society of Carroll County.)

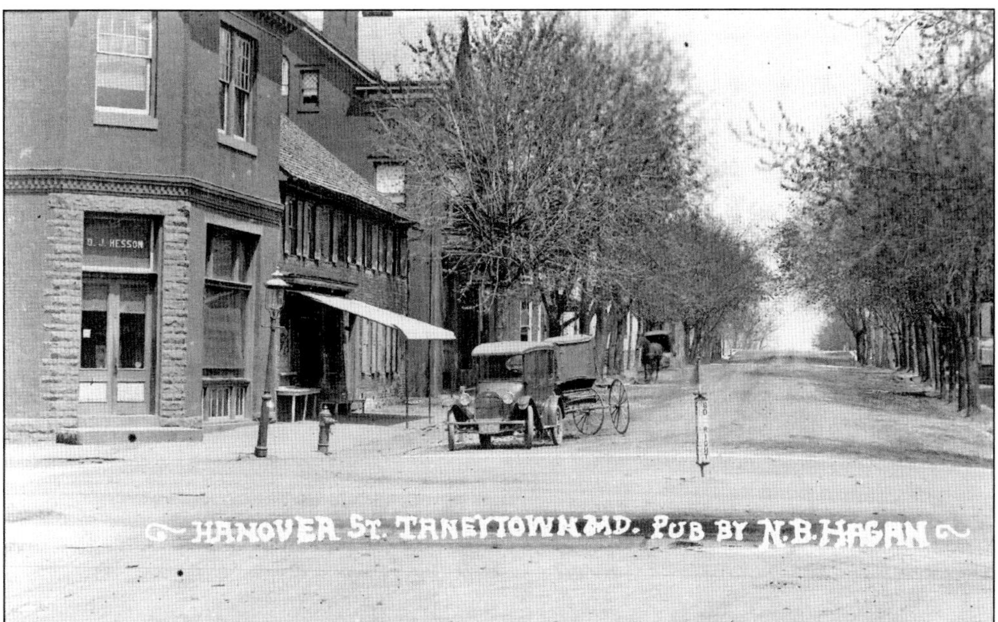

Another postcard published by Hagan shows Hanover Street (the current York Street); on the right is Hesson's Department Store and an 18th-century building that housed Reindollar's Store. (Courtesy of the Historical Society of Carroll County.)

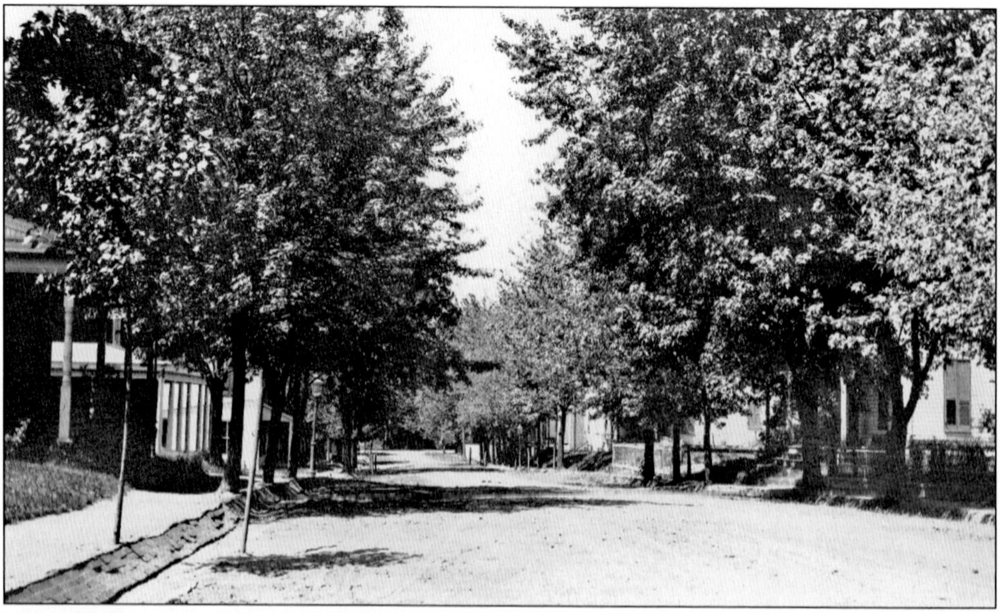

Large shade trees once lined Middle Street, as seen in this view looking toward East Baltimore Street. (Courtesy of the Historical Society of Carroll County.)

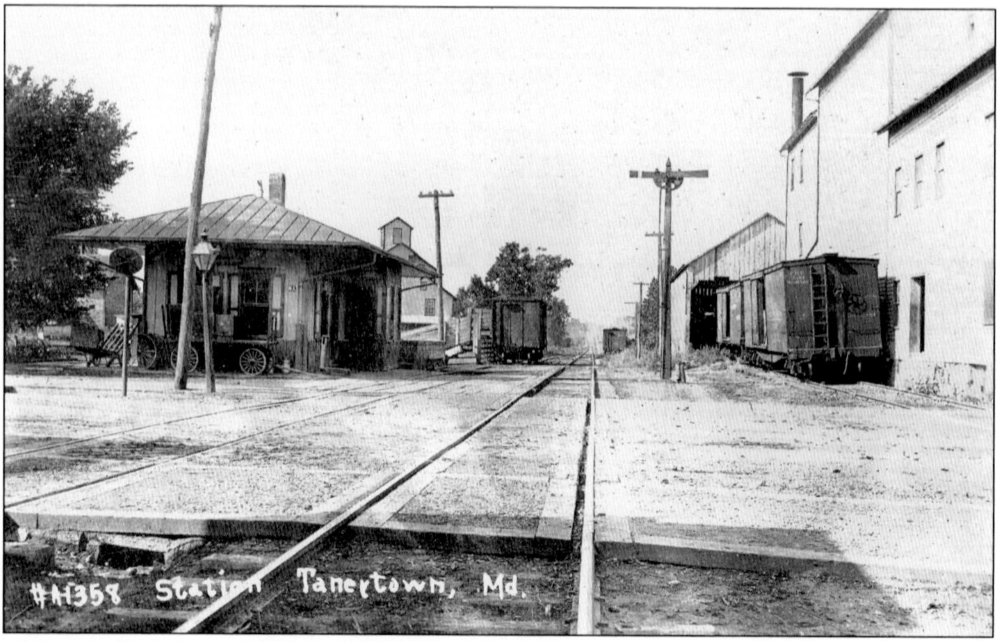

The arrival of the railroad in Taneytown on July 14, 1871, created an economic boom. Transportation of the region's agricultural products was made easier, allowing for substantial economic development. In August 1948, all passenger service was discontinued, but freight service remained. (Courtesy of Mildred Stine.)

Two

BUSINESS AND INDUSTRY

A major reason for Taneytown's existence was as a center for commerce. By the late 1700s, the town was bustling with taverns, inns, and myriad craftsmen. Among them were silversmith and clockmaker Eli Bentley, tanner and blacksmith Tobias Rudisill, brewer Abraham Krise, stocking weaver Hugh Bigham, and many more. For some years prior to 1799, Matthias Shroyer manufactured firearms, which he supplied to the United States government.

By the late 1800s, Taneytown had become a commercial center of Piedmont Maryland. Hotels, restaurants, bakeries, and department stores all lined the unpaved streets. Business continued to boom well into the 20th century with the addition of larger factories and enterprises. Despite a lull in business in the last half of the 20th century, Taneytown's main street is currently experiencing a rebirth.

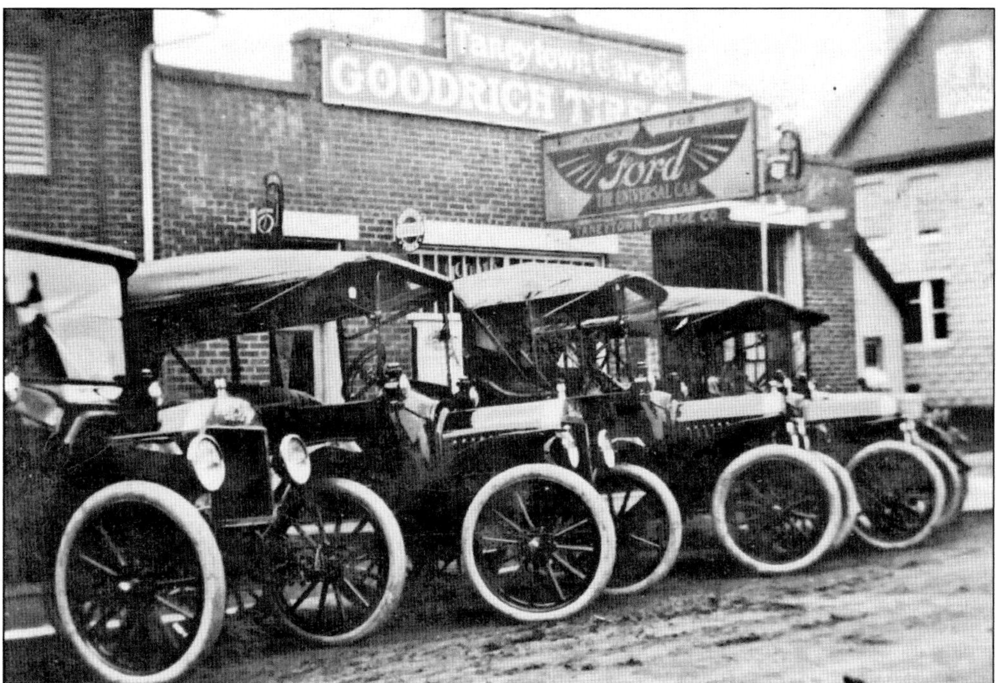

Established in 1914, the Taneytown Garage on West Baltimore Street sold Ford automobiles and Goodrich tires. (Courtesy of George and Anna Motter.)

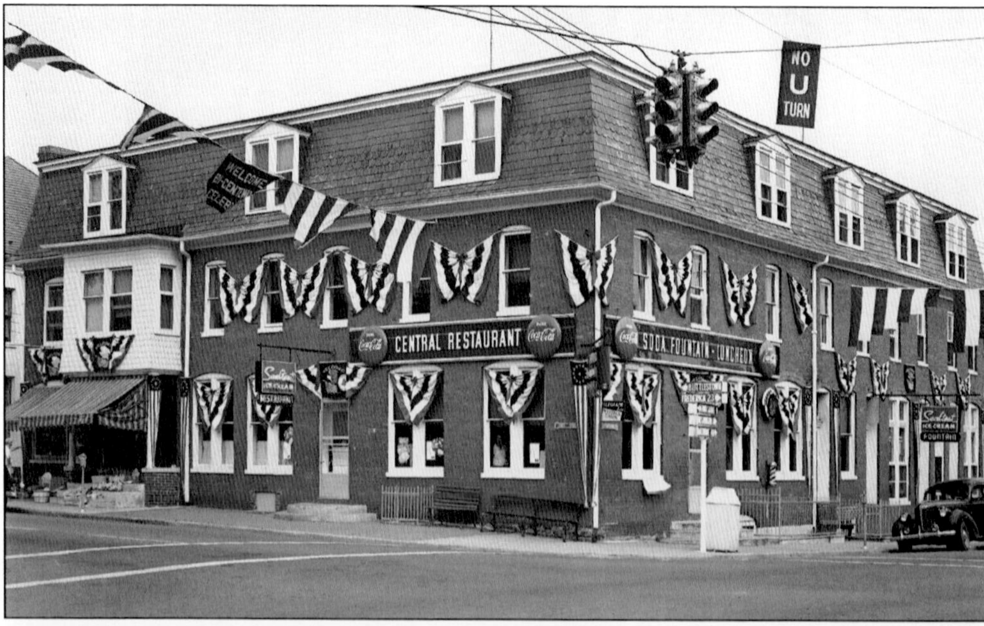

David Mehring erected Central Hotel on the northeast corner of the town square in 1902. A bustling marketplace, the hotel housed within its three stories accommodations for guests, a restaurant, barbershop, dry goods store, dentist's office, photographer's studio, and meat market. Adjacent to the hotel was the livery stable, where horse and carriages were housed. This photograph shows the hotel bedecked in patriotic splendor for Taneytown's bicentennial celebration in July 1954. (Courtesy of the Clem family.)

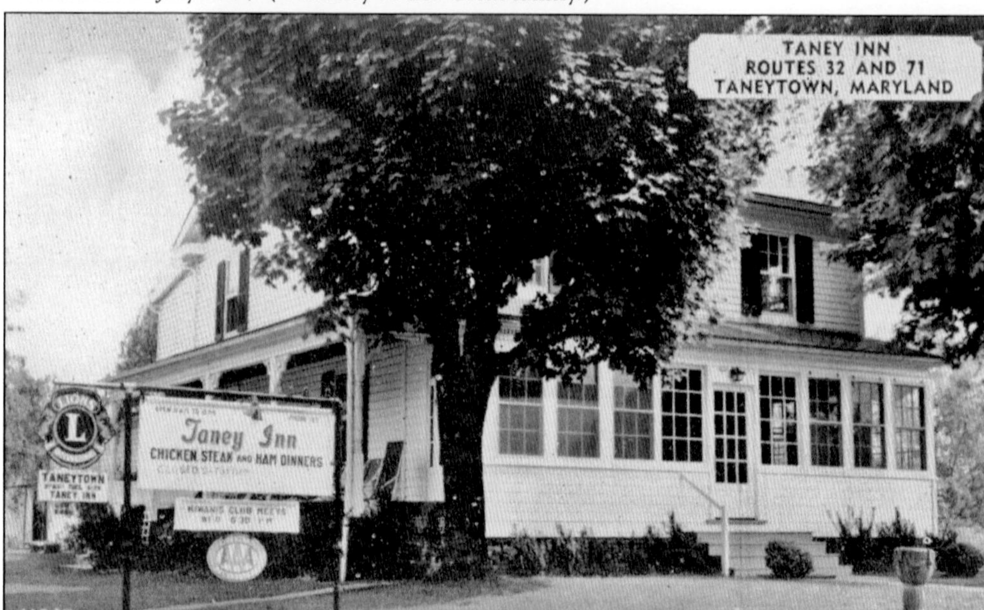

The Taney Inn was a popular restaurant for many years and offered chicken, steak, and ham dinners. Opened in 1946 by Tom and Harmon Albaugh, the restaurant stood at the junction of East Baltimore Street and Trevanion Road. (Courtesy of the Historical Society of Carroll County.)

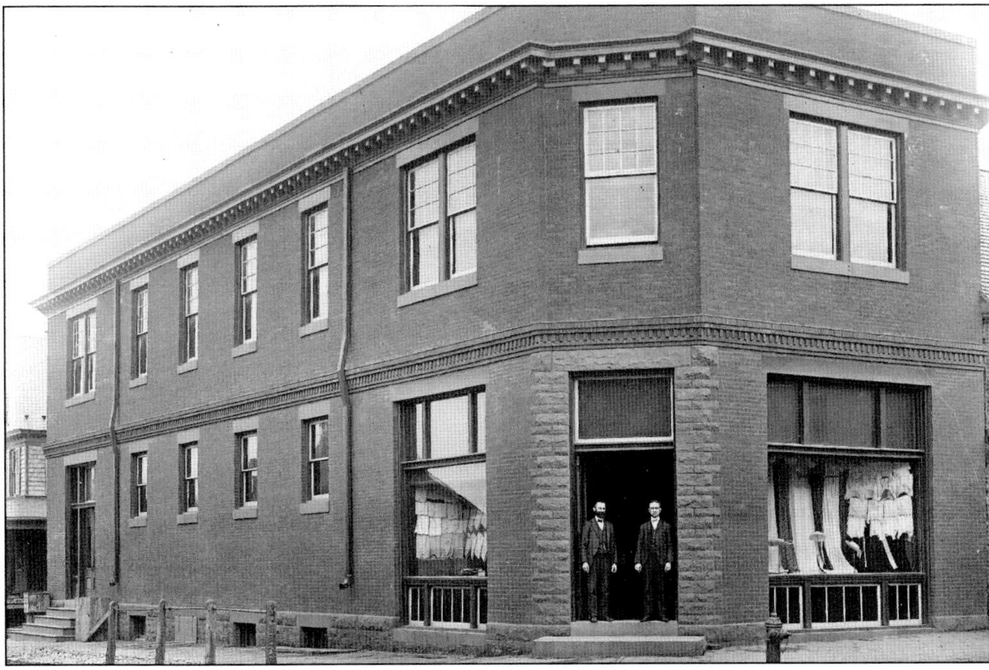

In November 1903, D.J. Hesson opened a department store on the northwest corner of the square. Mr. Hesson and his son Clyde are pictured standing in the doorway. (Courtesy of the Historical Society of Carroll County.)

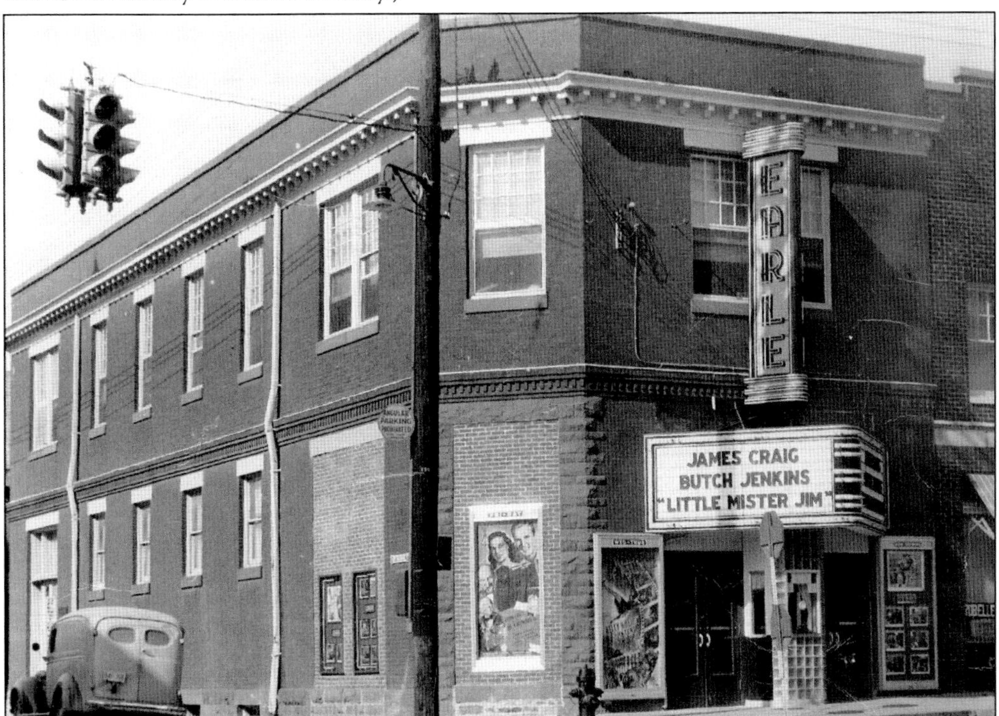

Years later, the building constructed by Hesson was transformed into the Taneytown Movie Theater. Manager Kenneth Clem took this photograph in 1946. (Courtesy of the Clem family.)

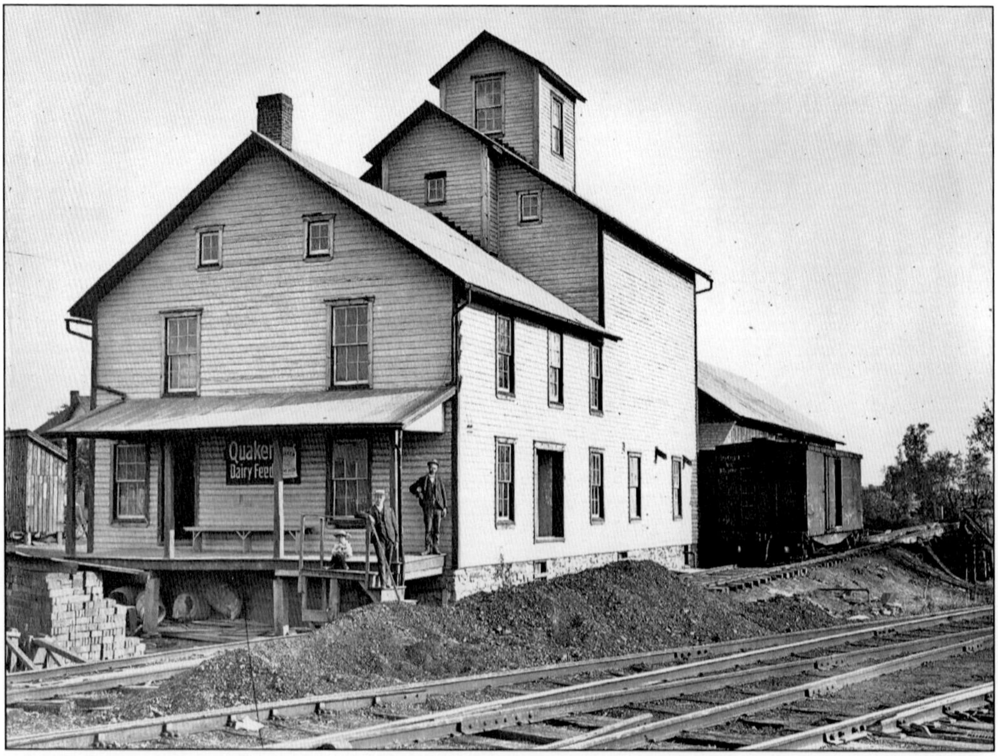

The grain elevator in this photograph was built in 1899 by the Farmer's Warehouse Company. Later leased to the Taneytown Elevator Company, it eventually became the Taneytown Grain and Supply Company. The original board of directors consisted of Samuel Stover, Edward Kemper, G.W. Baumgardner, Joseph Roelky, and Calvin Fringer. In this photograph, Laverne Zepp sits on the steps and Joseph Roelky and Frank Crouse stand. (Courtesy of the Historical Society of Carroll County.)

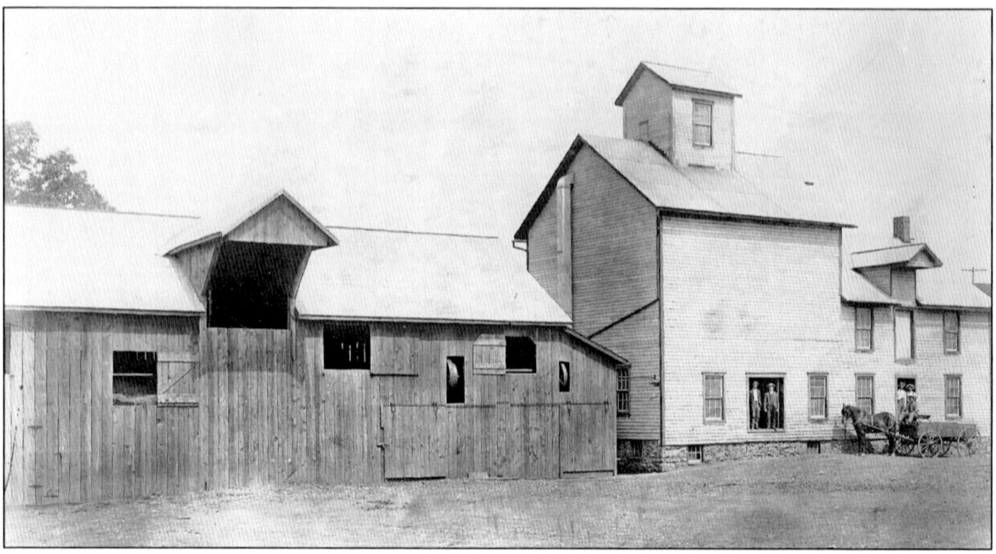

This photograph offers a view of the side of the Grain and Supply Company, c. 1900. (Courtesy of the Historical Society of Carroll County.)

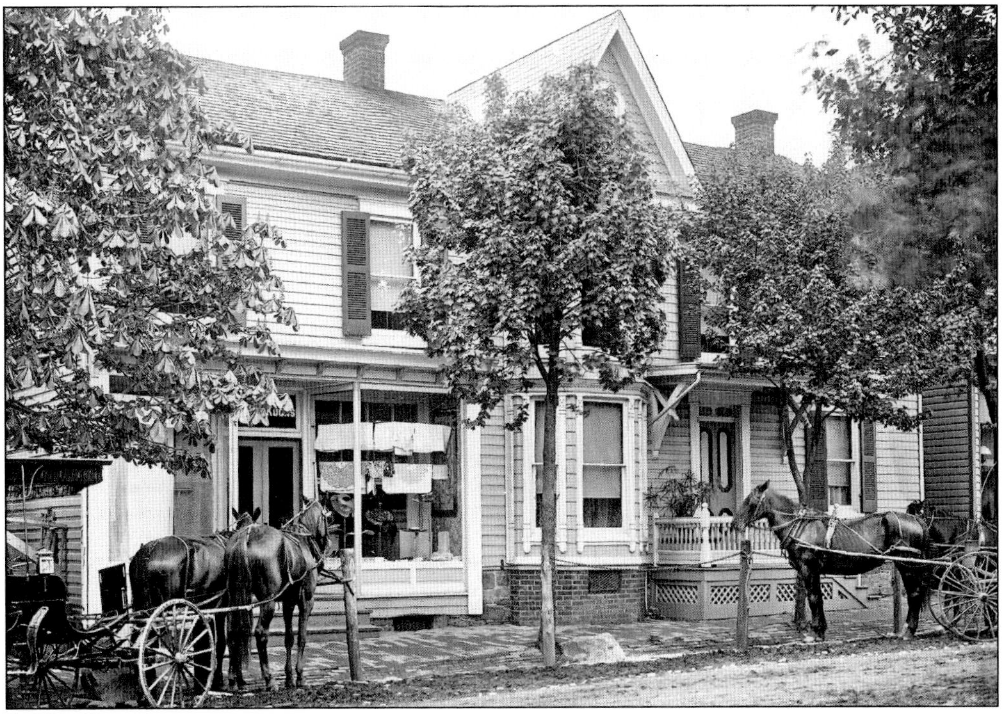

Founded on East Baltimore Street in 1896 as Weant & Koons, the store became known as Koons Bros. in 1903. Koons Bros. Department Store was "Taneytown's Leading Fashion Store." Dry goods, men's and women's clothing, floor coverings, and leather goods were all offered within its walls. (Courtesy of the Historical Society of Carroll County.)

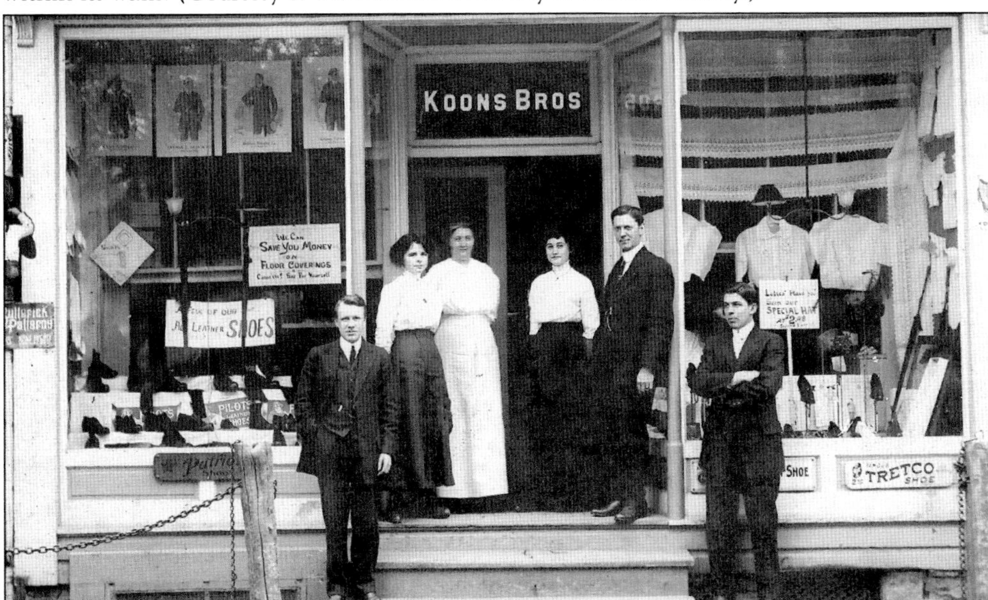

The staff of Koons Bros. Department Store stands ready to assist customers. Selling the latest in fashions, Koon's Bros. offered W.B. and American Lady corsets, Zerfing and Lightner and Fleisher Brothers clothing, and Walk-Over and Star Brand Shoes. (Courtesy of Mildred Stine.)

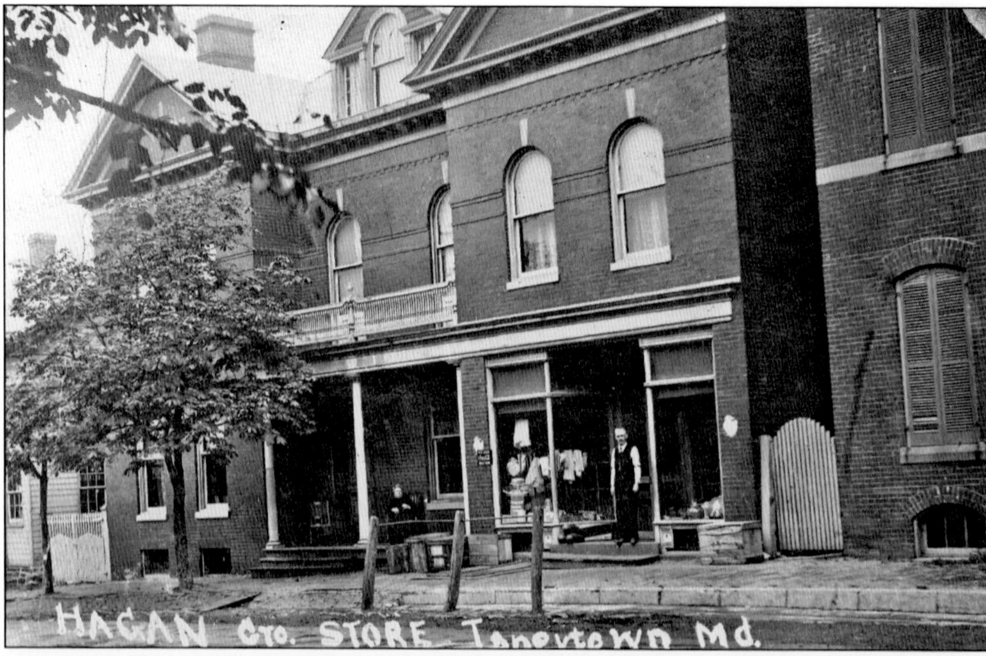

Norman B. Hagans stands in front of his store on Frederick Street while his wife sits on the porch of their impressive home built in the 1890s on the site of the Adam Good Tavern. (Courtesy of the Historical Society of Carroll County.)

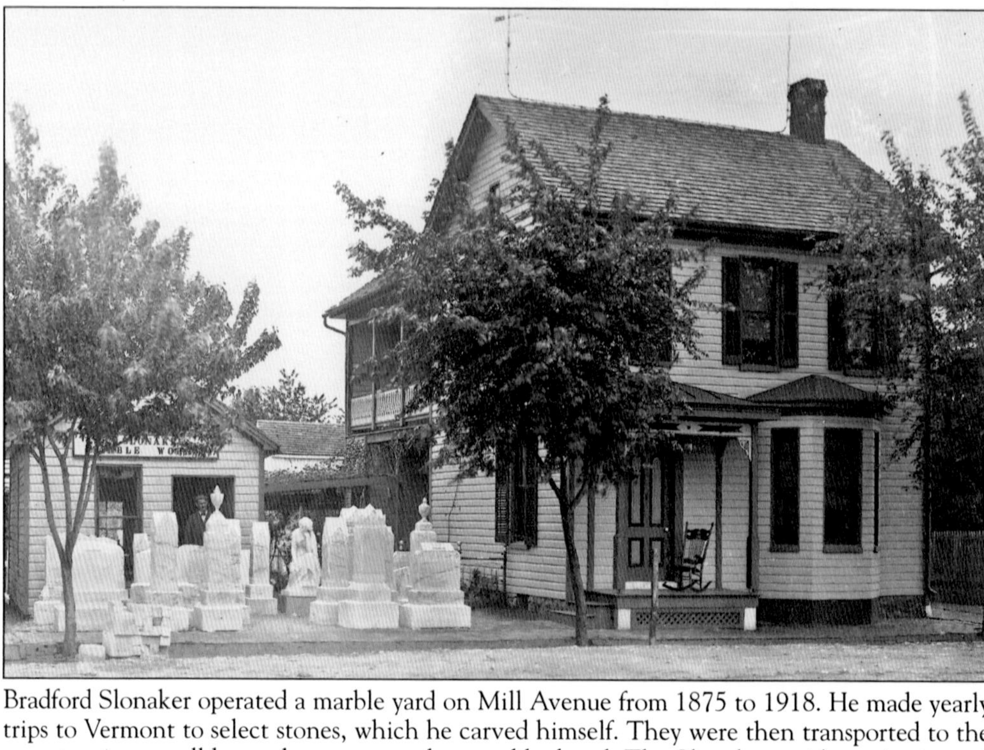
Bradford Slonaker operated a marble yard on Mill Avenue from 1875 to 1918. He made yearly trips to Vermont to select stones, which he carved himself. They were then transported to the cemetery in a small horse drawn cart and erected by hand. The Slonaker residence is pictured to the right. (Courtesy of the Historical Society of Carroll County.)

With its stained glass windows and louvered shutters, the residence of P.B. Englar, which also doubled as the post office, made a pretty picture for photographer Ed Zepp in 1905. The following people are pictured standing on the steps, from left to right: (front row) Harry Baumgardner, Charles Baumgardner, and Kurg Eyler (all mail carriers); (back row) Stanley Reaver (postmaster), Arthur Combs (assistant postmaster), and John Yingling (mail carrier). (Courtesy of the Historical Society of Carroll County.)

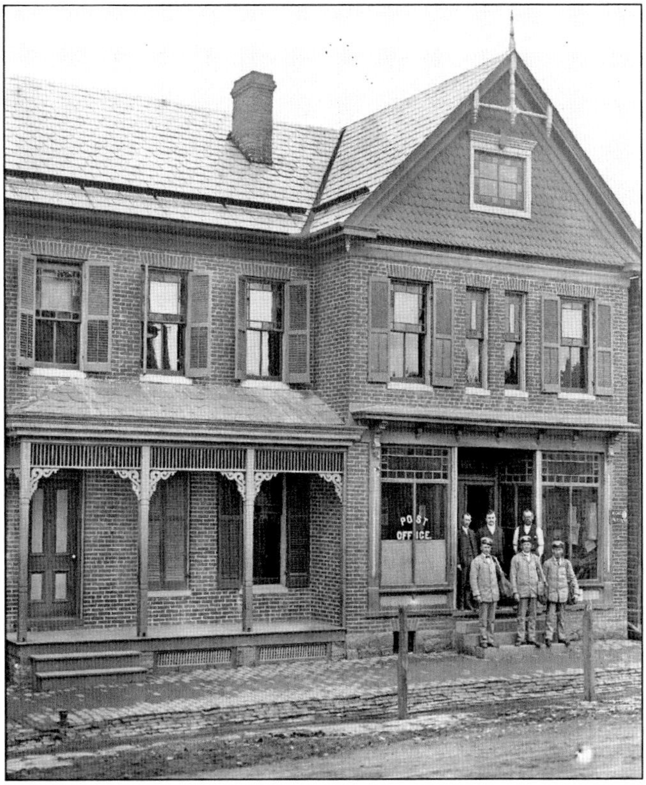

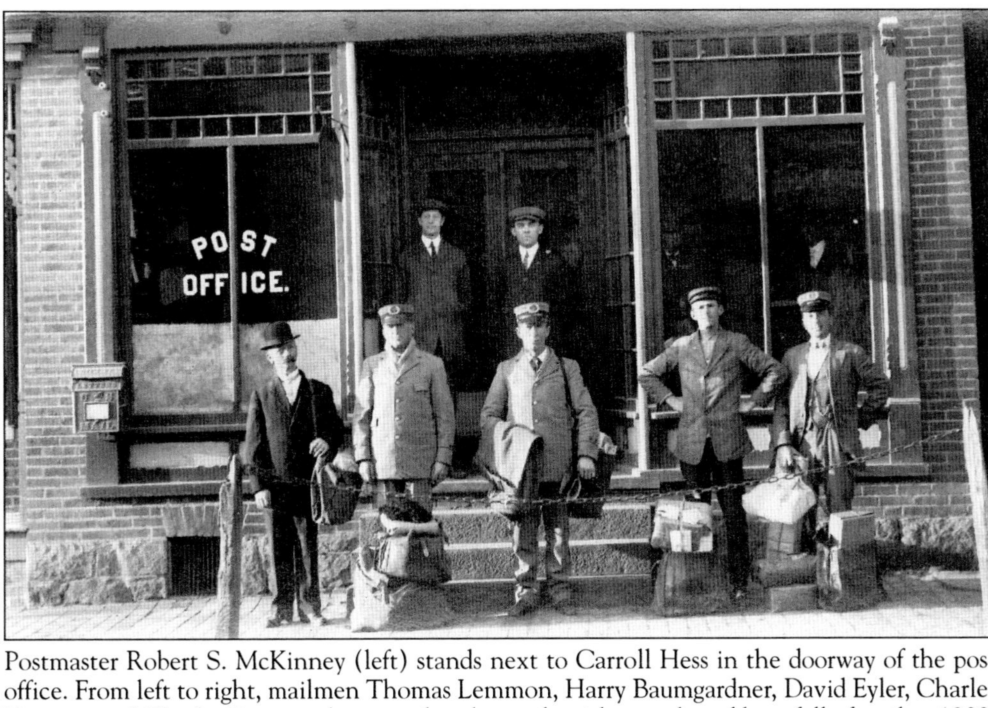

Postmaster Robert S. McKinney (left) stands next to Carroll Hess in the doorway of the post office. From left to right, mailmen Thomas Lemmon, Harry Baumgardner, David Eyler, Charles Kemper, and Charles Baumgardner stand at the ready with parcels and bags full of mail, *c*. 1900. (Courtesy of Mildred Stine.)

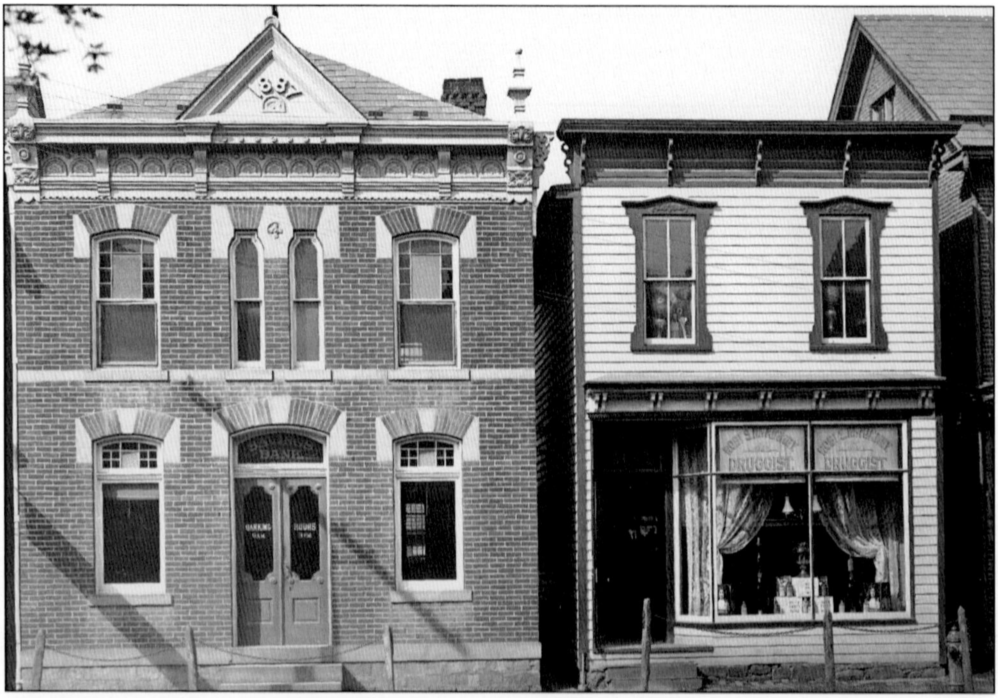

The Taneytown Savings Bank (left) and the neighboring McKinney Drug Store are shown as they appeared in the early 1900s. Robert S. McKinney established his drug store in 1890, and in 1895 he "remodeled and refitted his store with every facility for the compounding of drugs . . . ." He continued to operate his business until his death in 1946. (Courtesy of the Historical Society of Carroll County.)

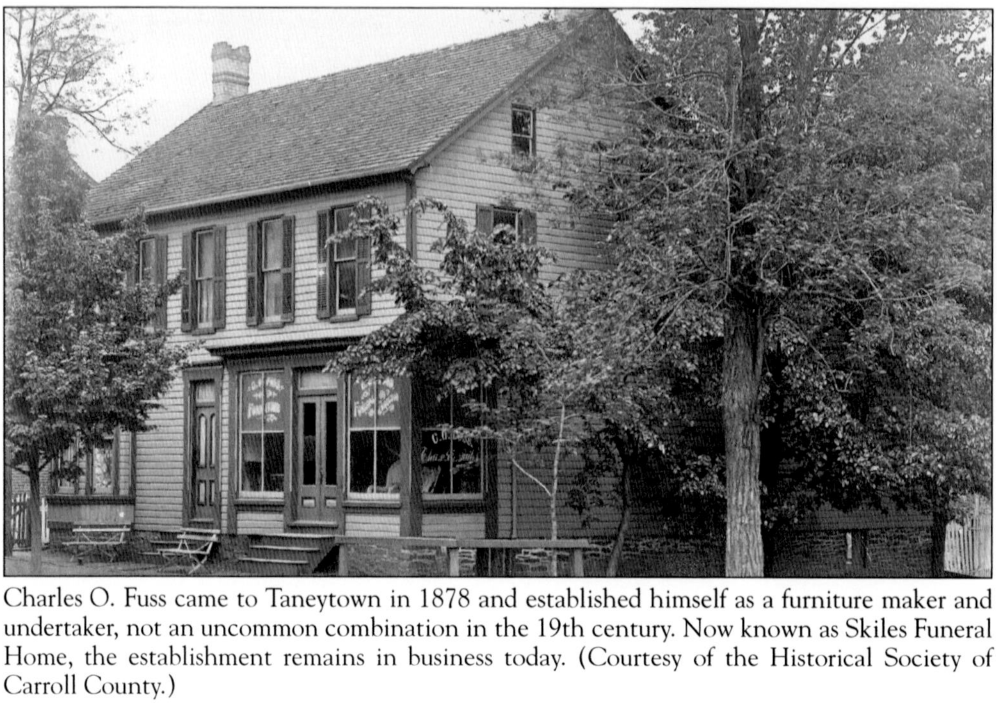

Charles O. Fuss came to Taneytown in 1878 and established himself as a furniture maker and undertaker, not an uncommon combination in the 19th century. Now known as Skiles Funeral Home, the establishment remains in business today. (Courtesy of the Historical Society of Carroll County.)

Established by James Buffington in the 19th century, the Buffington Hotel was known in the early 20th century as Kane's Hotel. (Courtesy of the Historical Society of Carroll County.)

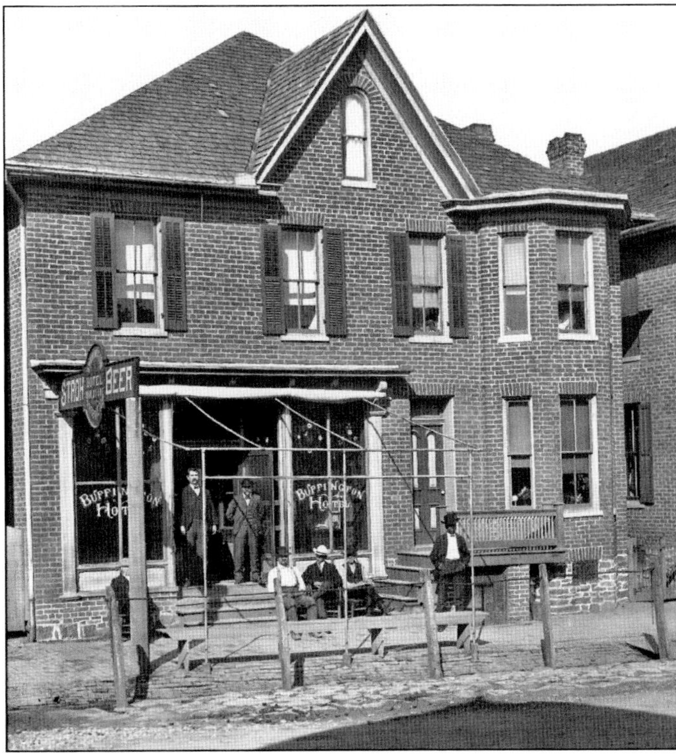

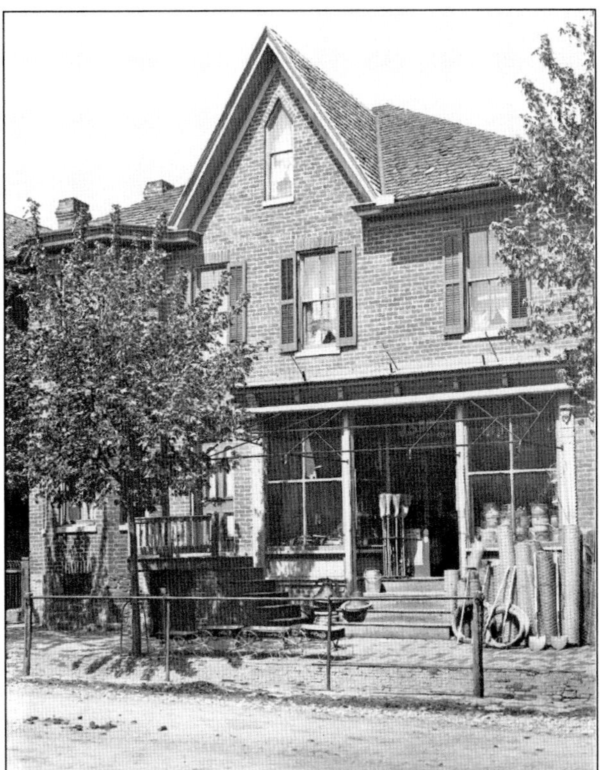

Rolls of wire, shovels, brooms, and toy wagons clearly identify John Bower's establishment as a hardware store. (Courtesy of the Historical Society of Carroll County.)

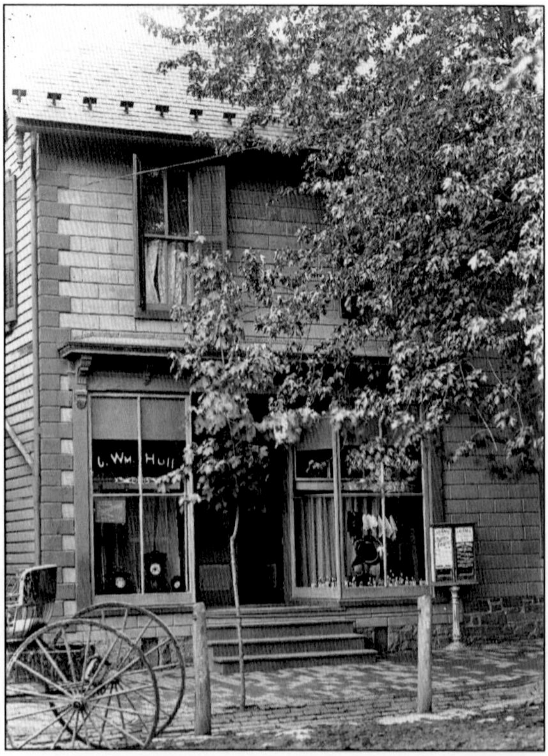

In November 1898, J. William Hull succeeded H.E. Slagenhaup as Taneytown's jeweler. Hull repaired and sold jewelry, watches, and clocks. He also offered "talking machines." The Reindollar Hardware Company later occupied the building that housed Hull's jewelry store. (Courtesy of the Historical Society of Carroll County.)

McKellip's Pharmacy on Frederick Street was established in 1853 by John McKellip. The drug store at left, famous for its diarrhea syrup, was torn down in the early 20th century, but the McKellip residence at right remains today. (Courtesy of the Historical Society of Carroll County.)

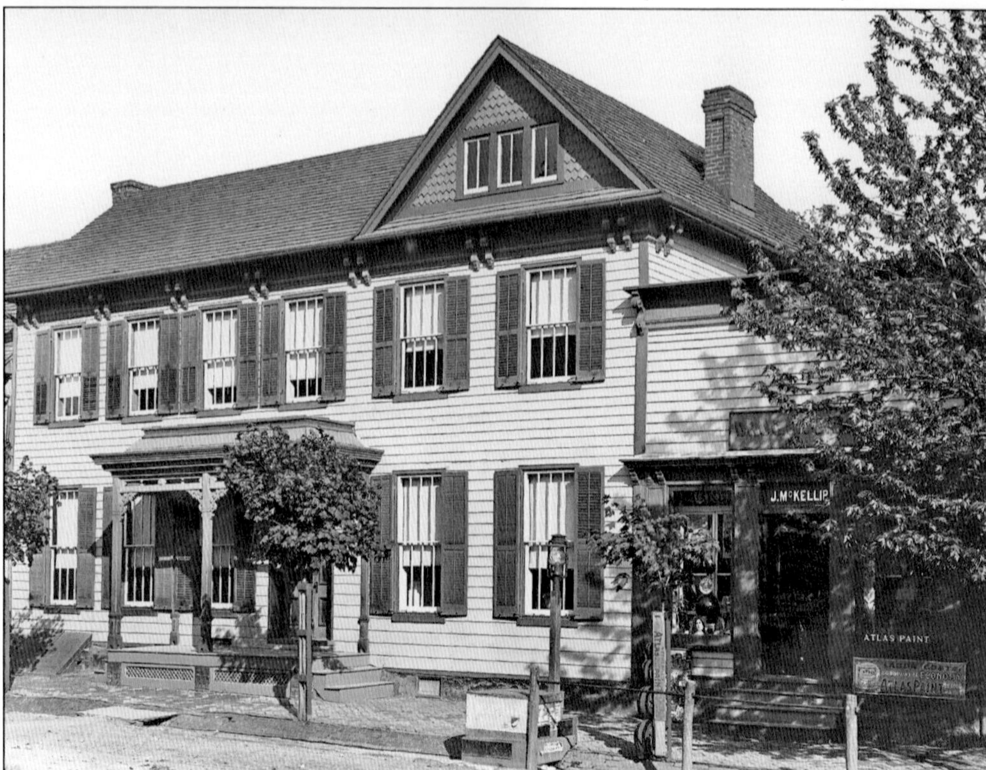

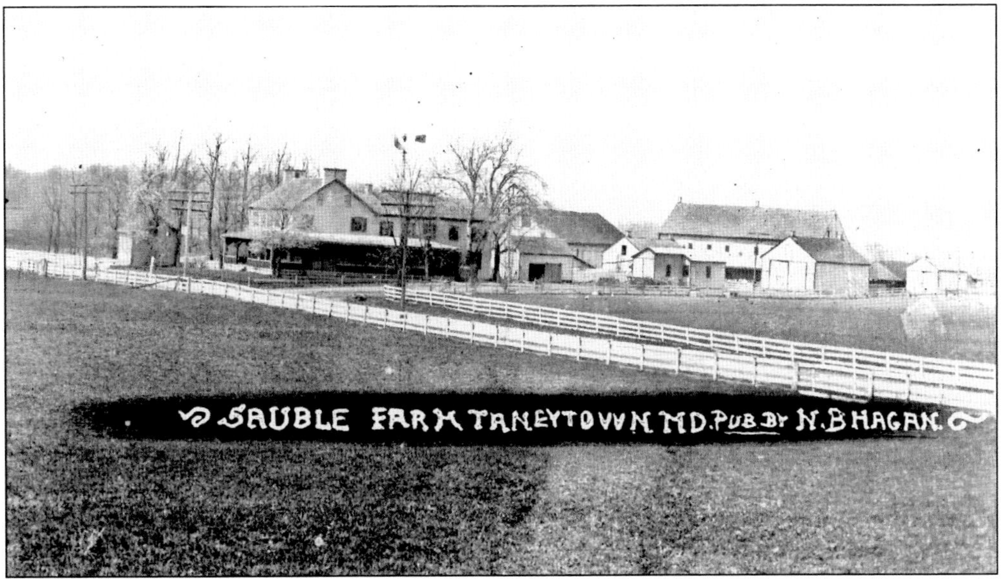

Locust Grove, at the western edge of town, was originally owned by the Crapster family, who operated a stagecoach inn and tavern there. George and Irene Sauble purchased the farm in 1912. In 1918, the Saubles opened their home to boarders who were delighted with the home-cooked meals they received. Word soon spread and Sauble's Inn became known far and wide for its huge country meals, which might have featured as many as 32 different items on the table. The inn closed on August 1, 1943. (Courtesy of the Historical Society of Carroll County.)

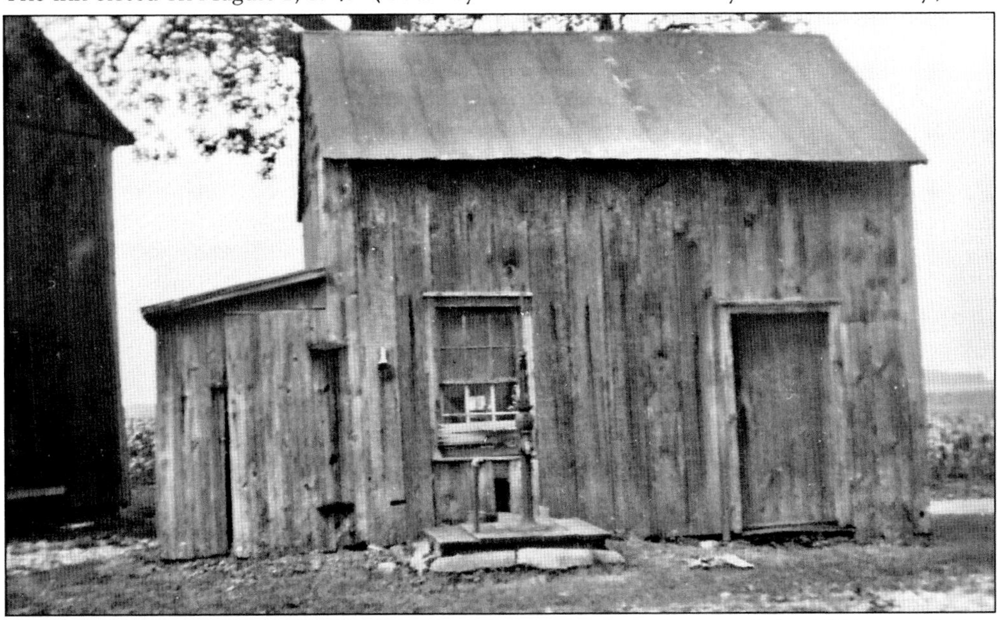

This photograph of John Slagenhaupt's chair shop was taken in July 1954, just before the building was razed. The shop was located off of Trevanion Road, near the Otterdale Schoolhouse. John Slagenhaupt and his father, Samuel, made ladder back chairs and rockers in Taneytown in the first half of the 19th century. Often made of maple, Slagenhaupt chairs are characterized by their delicate turnings, fine proportions, and "shrunk joint" construction. (Courtesy of the Historical Society of Carroll County.)

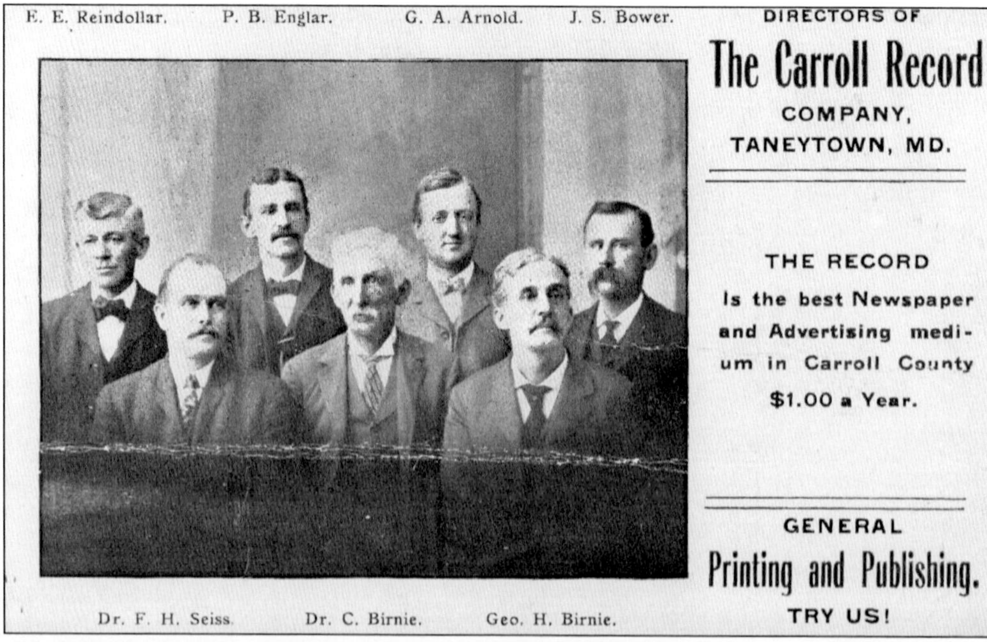

This business card from 1910 advertises the Taneytown newspaper *The Carroll Record* with a photograph of the board of directors. Note that subscriptions cost just $1 per year. (Courtesy of the Historical Society of Carroll County.)

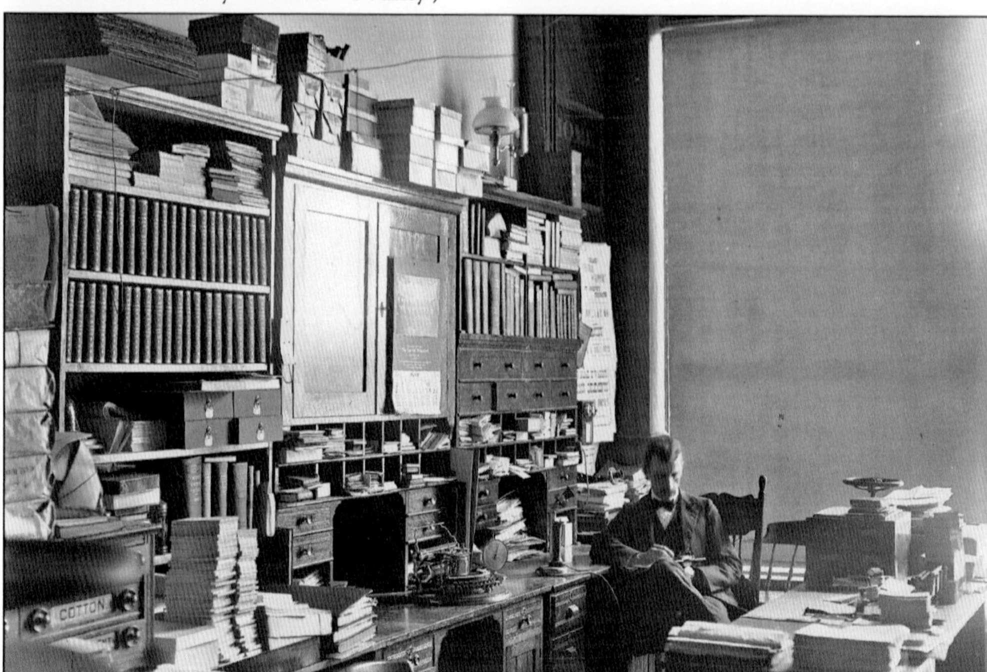

Editor P.B. Englar sits at his desk in *The Carroll Record* business office. Preston B. Englar was a founder of the newspaper and served as editor until his death in 1945. *The Carroll Record* premiered on July 7, 1894, and continued to be published in Taneytown until 1971. (Courtesy of the Historical Society of Carroll County.)

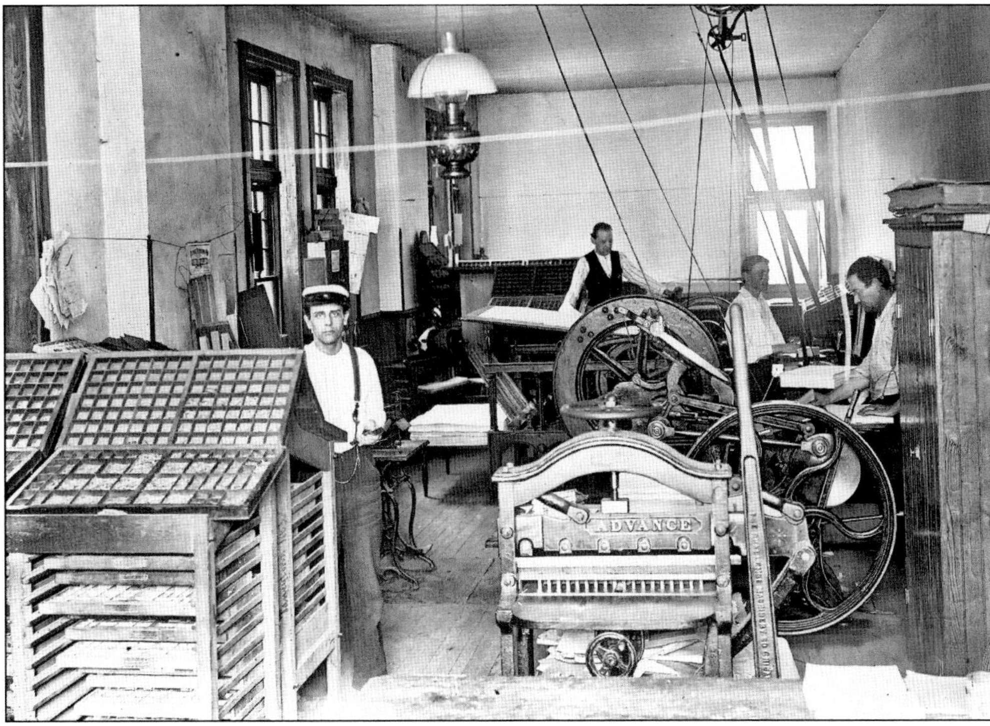

During the early 20th century, *The Carroll Record* printing plant operated by a line shaft powered by a one-cylinder gasoline engine. Ross Fair, who served as the typesetter, is shown in the left foreground of this photograph. (Courtesy of the Historical Society of Carroll County.)

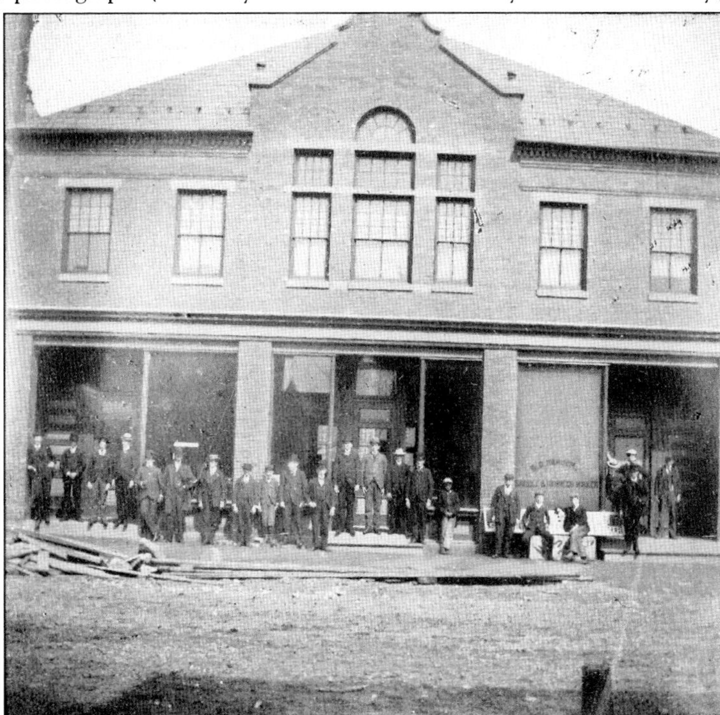

The Opera House in Taneytown served as the offices and plant of *The Carroll Record*. Aside from being a venue for plays and minstrel shows, the ground floor of the Opera House contained the shop of saddle and harness maker S.C. Reaver, the cigar shop of F.S. Staley, and *The Carroll Record* Printing Company. (Courtesy of the Historical Society of Carroll County.)

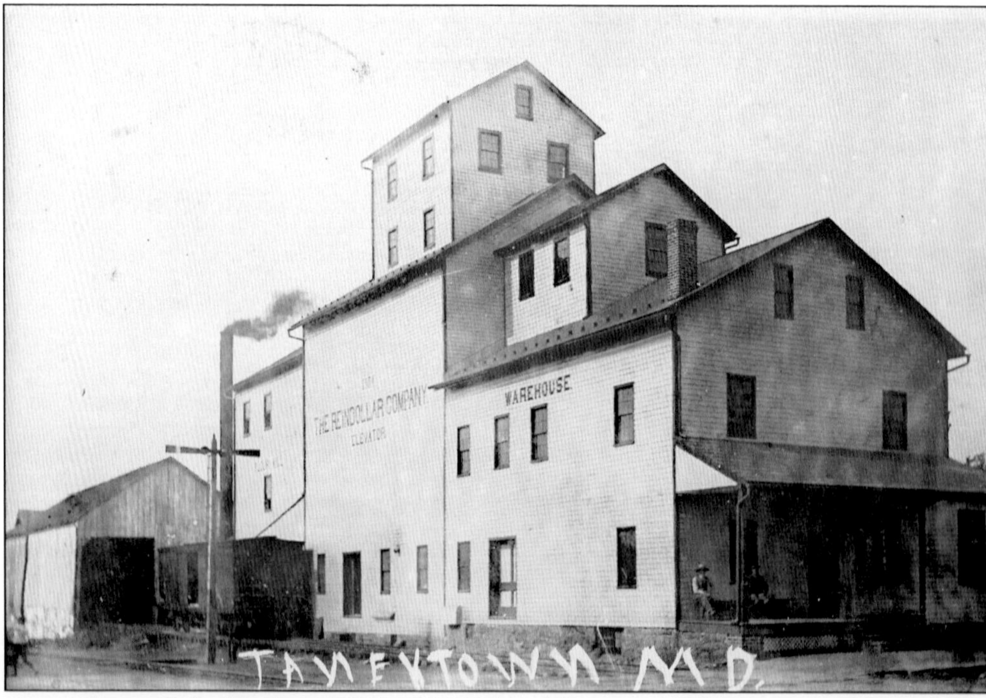

Originally established in the 1870s by T.H. Eckenrode as a grain, lumber, and coal warehouse situated along the railroad tracks, the Reindollar Company was purchased by E.E. Reindollar in 1892. (Courtesy of George and Anna Motter.)

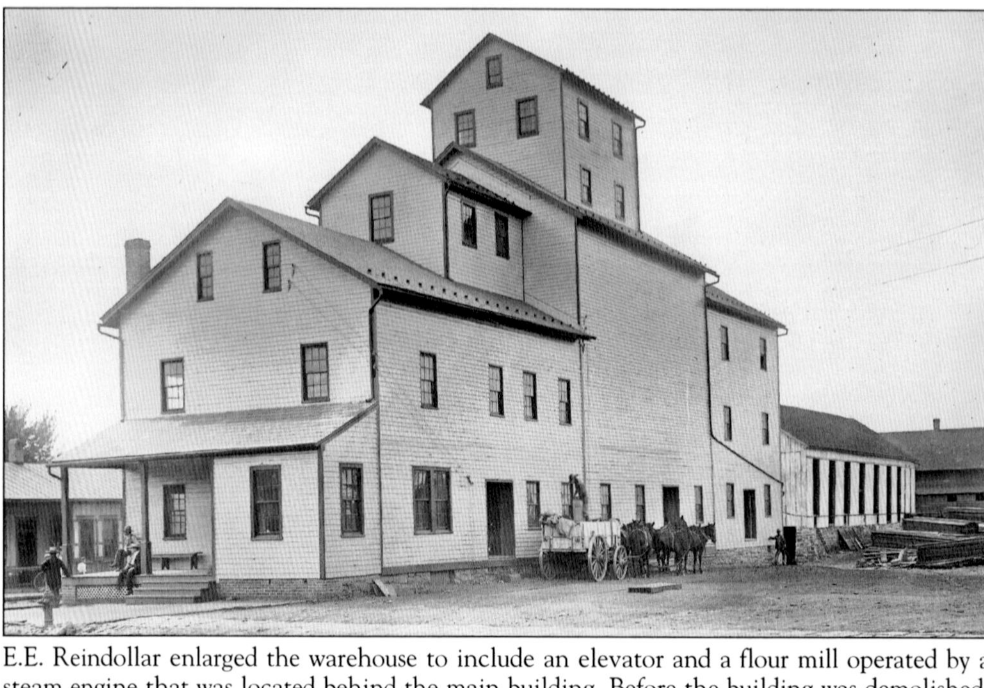

E.E. Reindollar enlarged the warehouse to include an elevator and a flour mill operated by a steam engine that was located behind the main building. Before the building was demolished, it housed Southern States Taneytown Cooperative, Inc. for many years. (Courtesy of the Historical Society of Carroll County.)

A corn meal bag from the Glen Dale Roller Mills is pictured at right. (Courtesy of the Historical Society of Carroll County.)

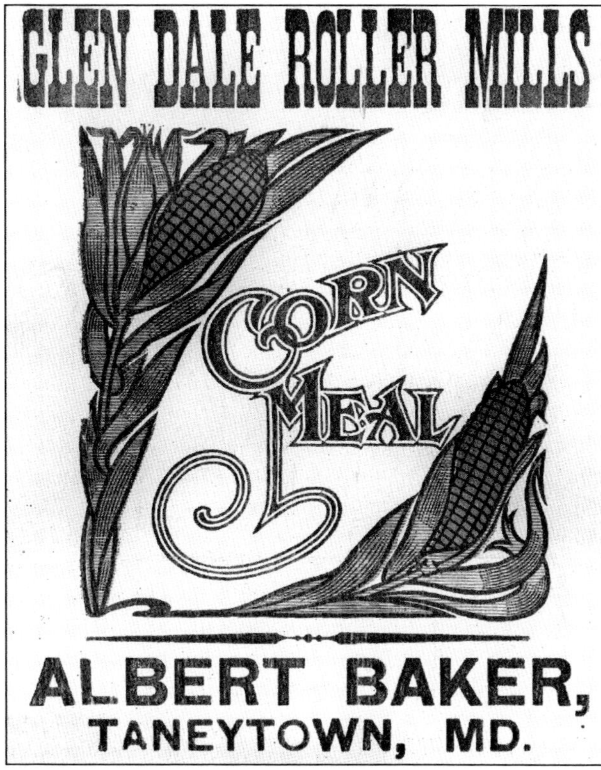

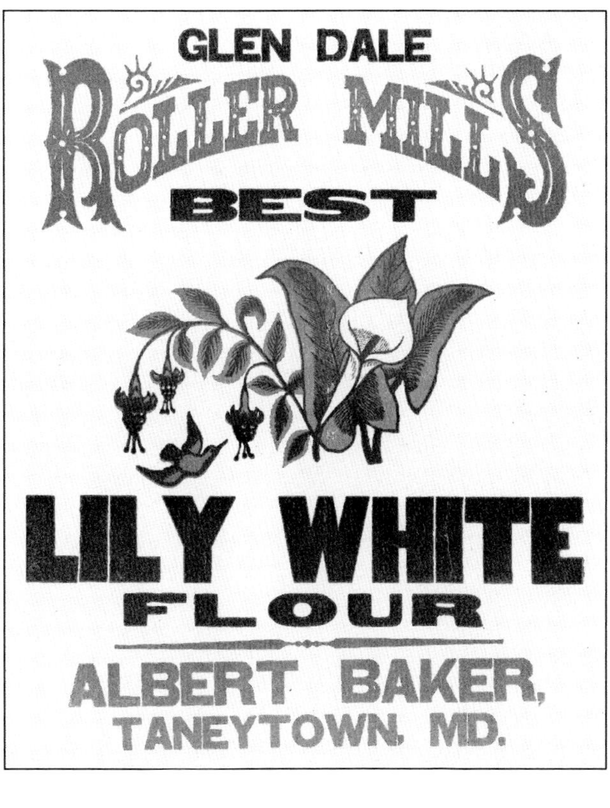

At left is a Lily White flour bag from the Glen Dale Roller Mills. (Courtesy of the Historical Society of Carroll County.)

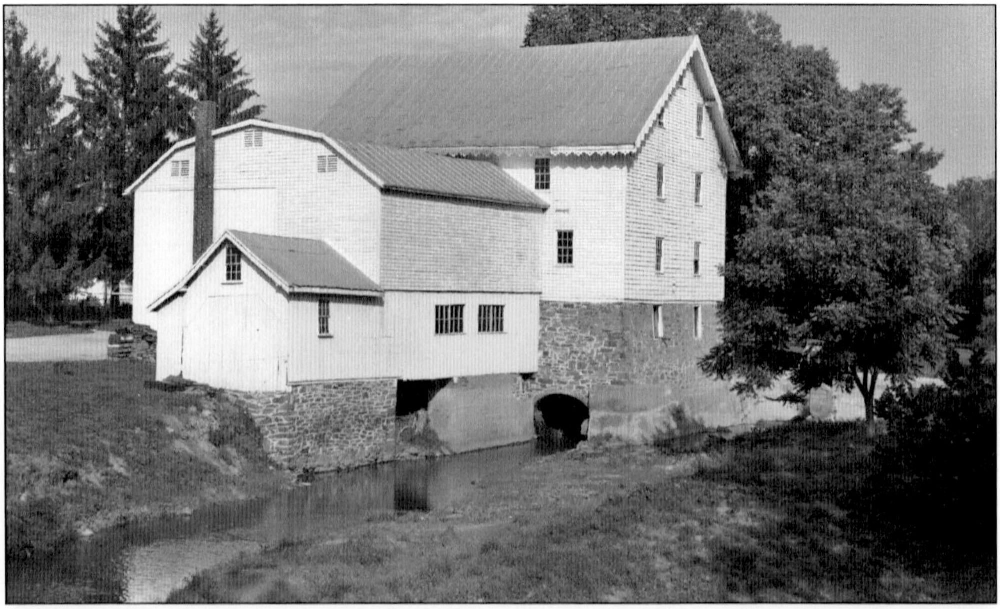

Although there has been a gristmill at Otterdale since the late 18th century, the present Otterdale Mill was built in the late 1860s by James Bostian. Though once used to grind grain, the mill has housed frozen food lockers for many years. (Courtesy of the Historical Society of Carroll County.)

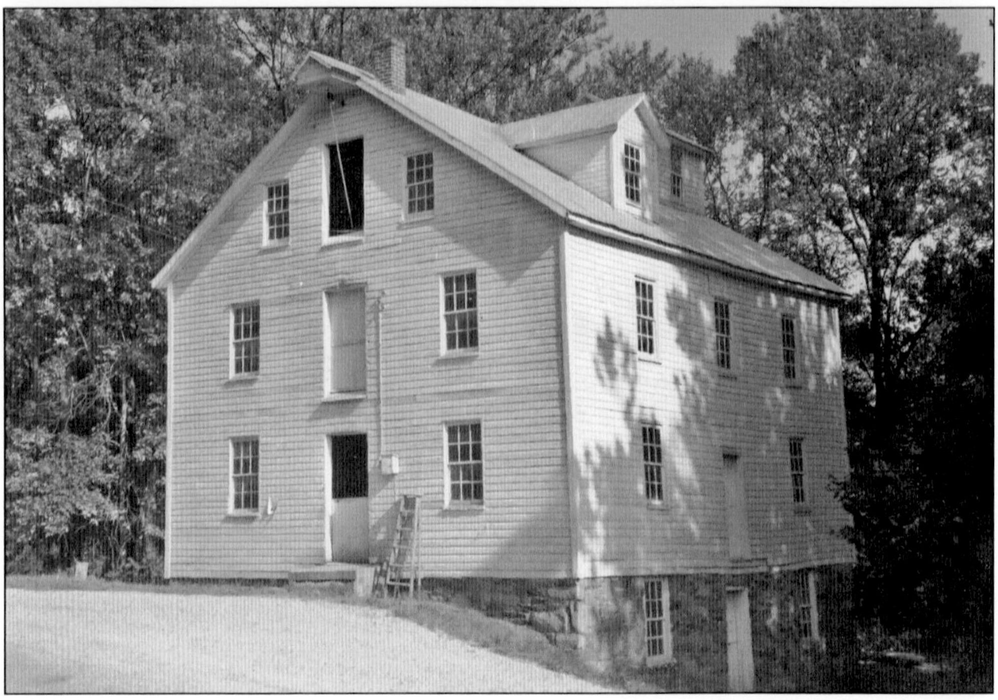

Built along Big Pipe Creek in 1887 as a gristmill and sawmill, Crouse Mill was purchased by the Crouse family in 1889 and continued to operate until 1978. Sandwiched between the creek and present-day Crouse Mill Road, its setting is typical of many area mills of the 19th century. (Courtesy of the Historical Society of Carroll County.)

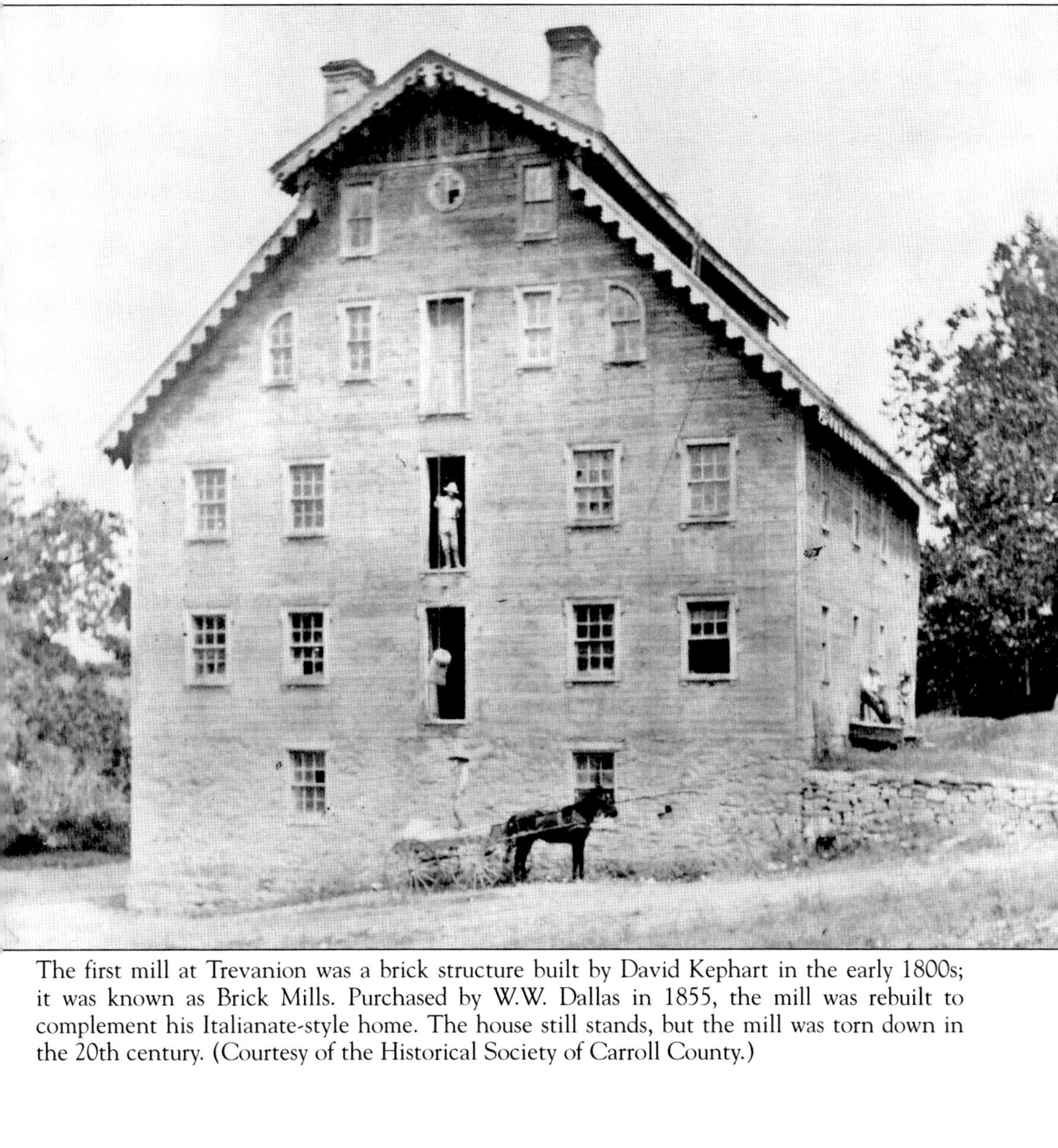

The first mill at Trevanion was a brick structure built by David Kephart in the early 1800s; it was known as Brick Mills. Purchased by W.W. Dallas in 1855, the mill was rebuilt to complement his Italianate-style home. The house still stands, but the mill was torn down in the 20th century. (Courtesy of the Historical Society of Carroll County.)

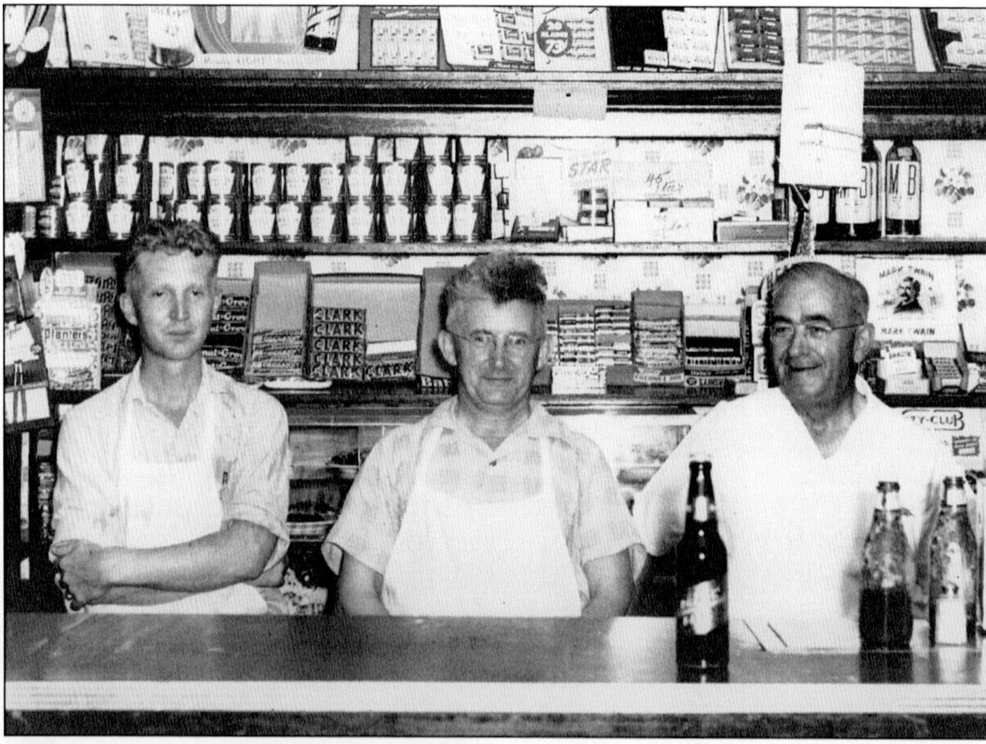

Anxiously waiting to serve their customers, the staff of the restaurant at Baumgardner's Bakery stands behind the counter. Pictured from left to right are Harry Shirk, Clarence Legore, and Merle Baumgardner. (Courtesy of the Clem family.)

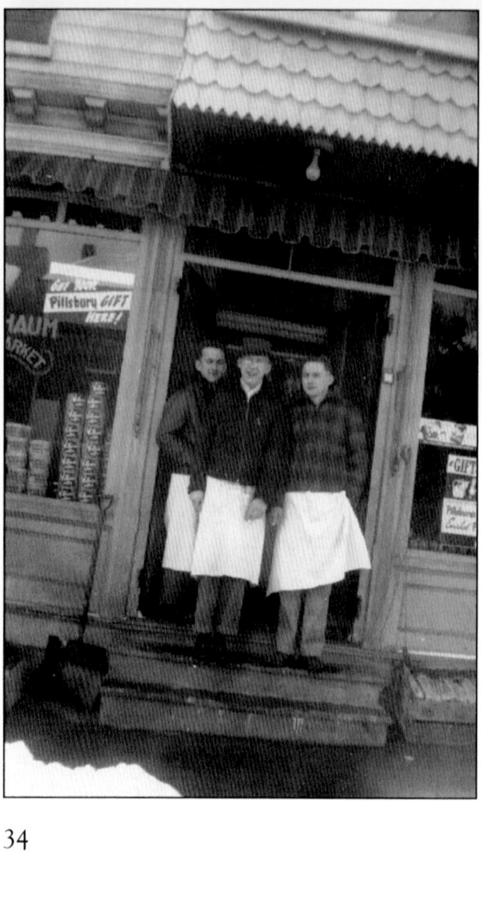

After the snow has been shoveled off of the front steps, Shaum's Meat Market is open for business. Standing in crisp, white aprons from left to right are Joe Shaum, Frank Shaum, and Richard Myers. (Courtesy of the Clem family.)

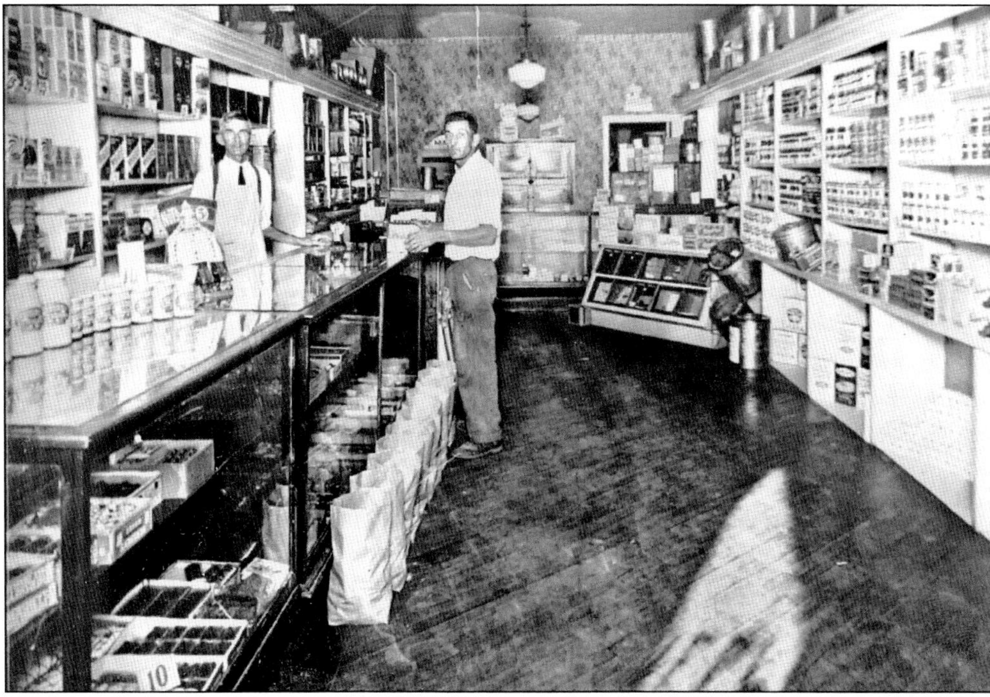

This is an interior view of Riffle's Store, which sold groceries and housed a soda fountain. (Courtesy of Alice Riffle Ecker.)

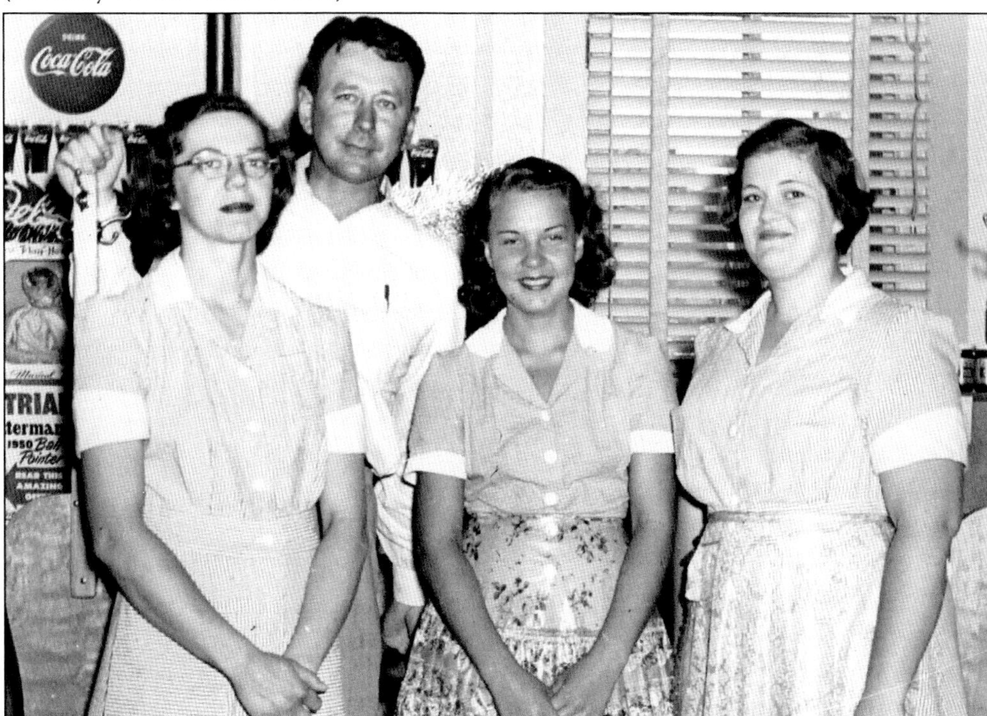

The staff of Riffle's Restaurant, pictured from left to right, are Shirley Welk, Delmar Riffle, Mary Stansberry, and Nancy Heiner. (Courtesy of the Clem family.)

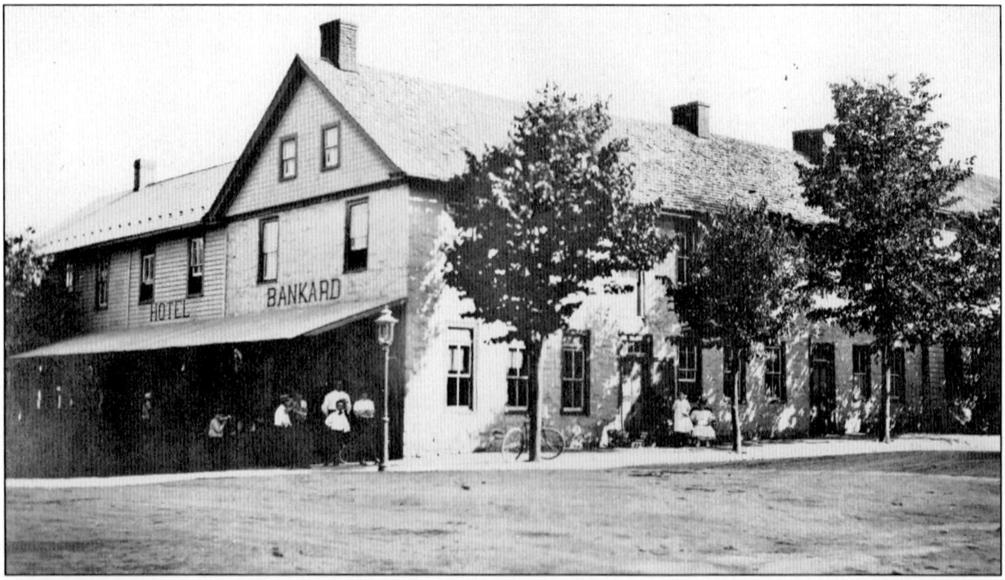

By 1790, Taneytown, a village of just 250 people, had a tavern on each of the four corners of the square. Under the ownership of Mr. and Mrs. A.H. Bankard, the Old Stone Hotel offered "The Best of Accommodations." Commenting on the hotel's bar, a 1910 newspaper article said, "The best beverages . . . meet the demands of those who appreciate high class products." (Courtesy of the Historical Society of Carroll County.)

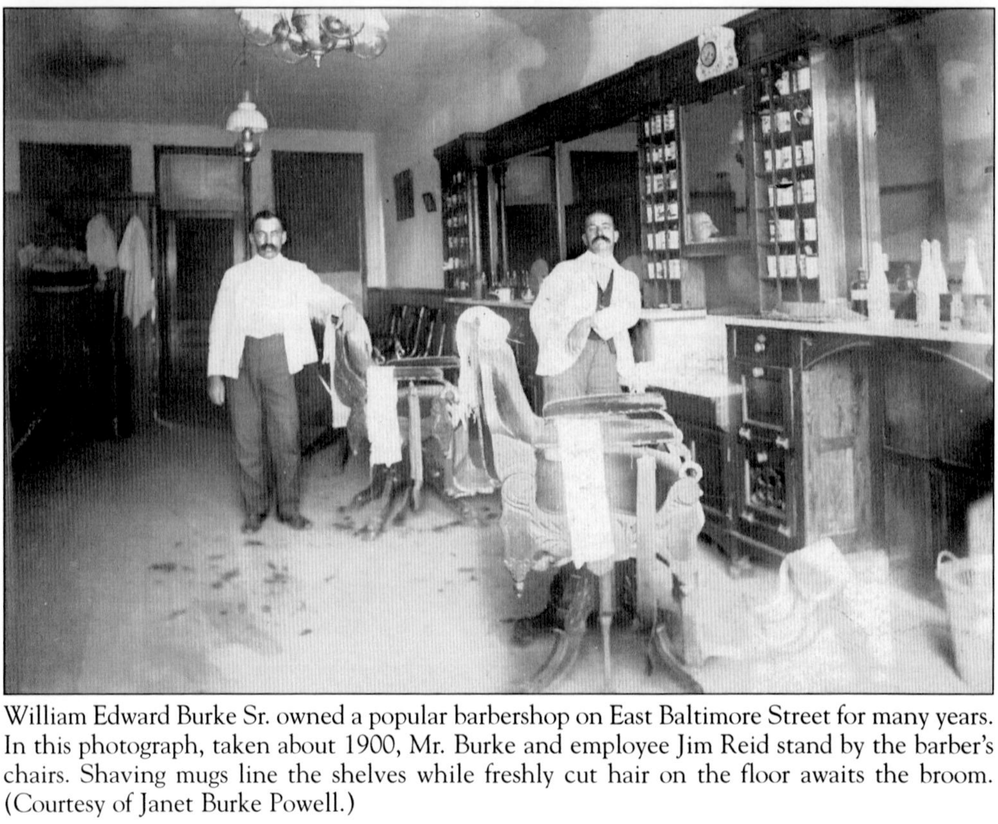

William Edward Burke Sr. owned a popular barbershop on East Baltimore Street for many years. In this photograph, taken about 1900, Mr. Burke and employee Jim Reid stand by the barber's chairs. Shaving mugs line the shelves while freshly cut hair on the floor awaits the broom. (Courtesy of Janet Burke Powell.)

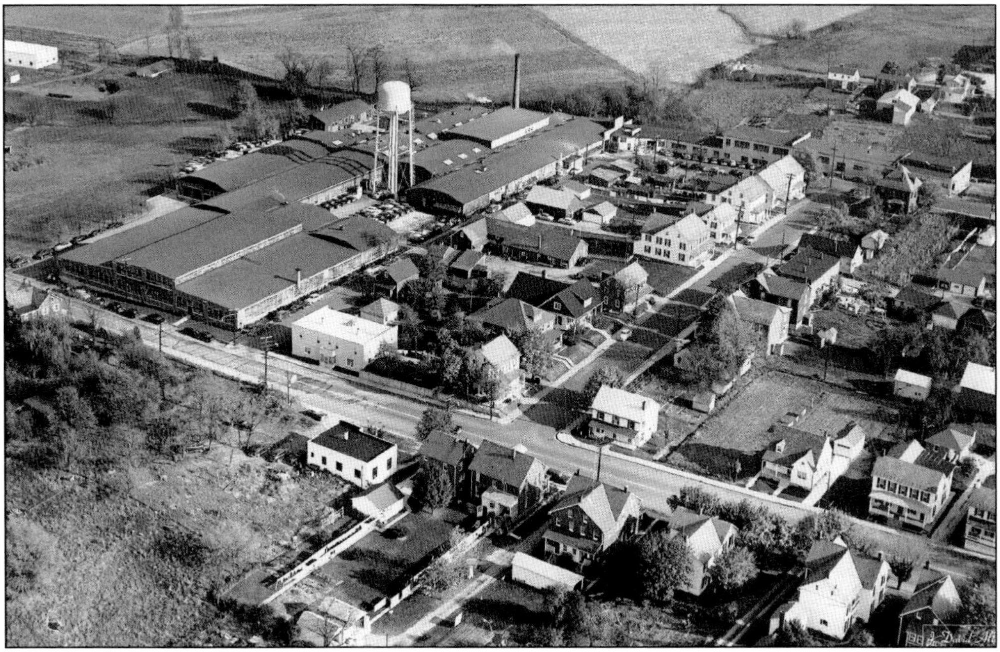

The Blue Ridge Rubber Company opened in Taneytown in 1936 and produced casual and waterproof footwear. After a devastating fire burned the factory to the ground in 1942, the plant was rebuilt and resumed production the following year as the Cambridge Rubber Company. After World War II, nearly 1,000 people were employed there. One would be hard-pressed to find a Taneytown native who did not have some connection to the rubber factory. Production stopped in 1986, and the plant was closed. (Courtesy of George W. Naylor Jr.)

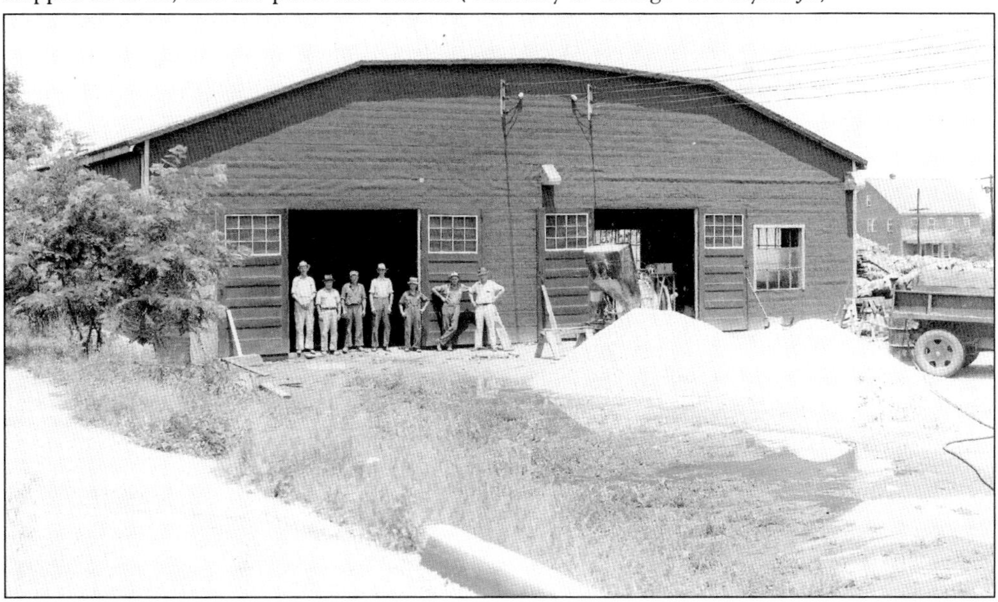

Employees stand in front of the first building constructed at the rubber factory. Ground was broken for the 36,000-square-foot building on February 26, 1936; construction was completed by August. The Taneytown Chamber of Commerce paid for the cost of construction. (Courtesy of George W. Naylor Jr.)

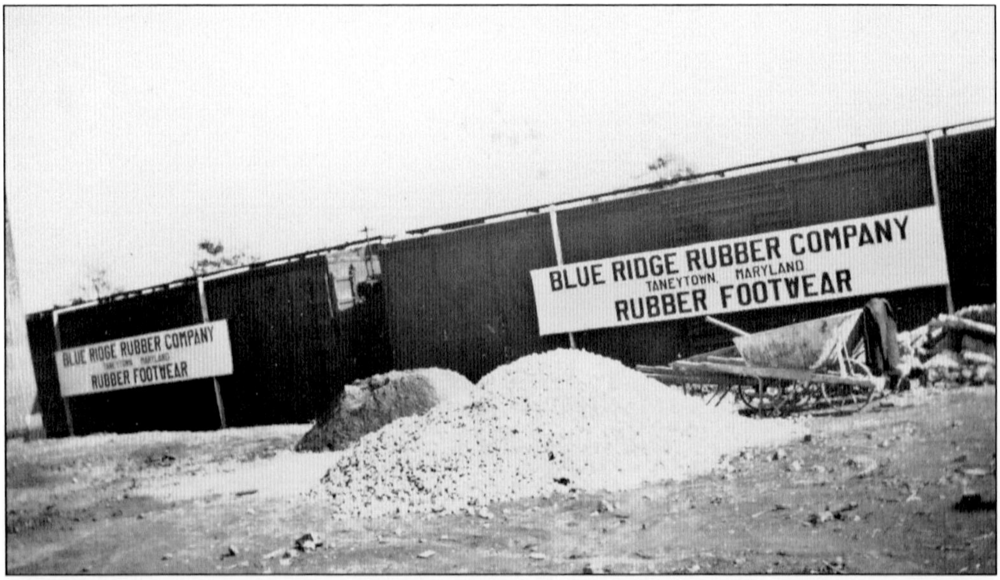

The first shipment of shoes was sent by rail from the Blue Ridge Rubber Company on October 19, 1936. (Courtesy of George and Anna Motter.)

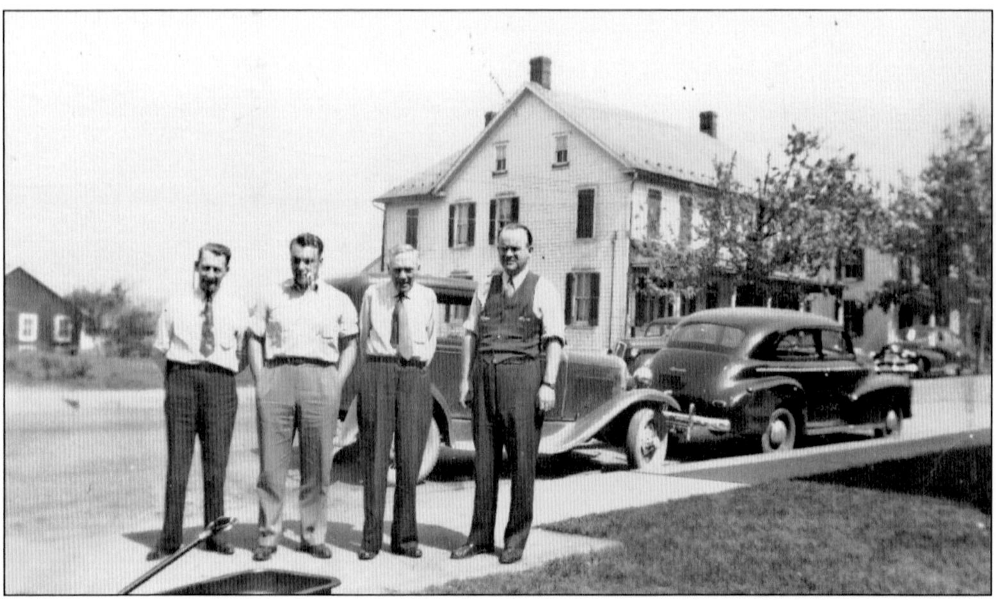

Rubber factory employees pose for a picture on Fairview Avenue in the late 1930s. The following are pictured from left to right: unidentified, Robert Kenworthy, Rein Motter, and George Smith. (Courtesy of George and Anna Motter.)

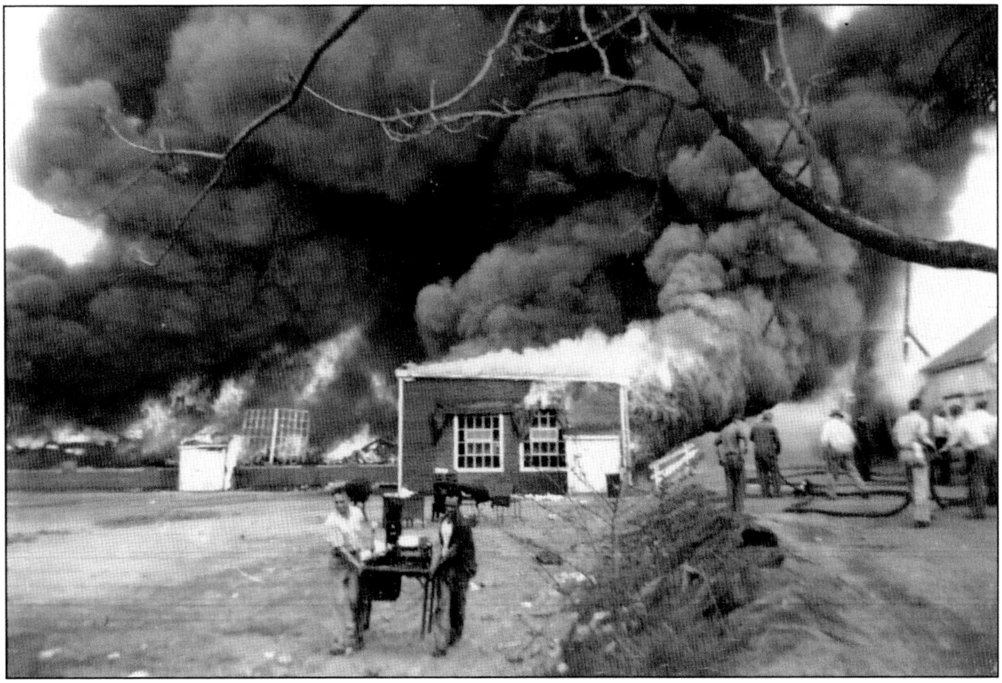

On April 25, 1942, a disastrous fire destroyed the Blue Ridge Rubber Company. In this photograph, billowing clouds of black smoke cover the sky as workers carry equipment to safety. (Courtesy of Dean Reindollar.)

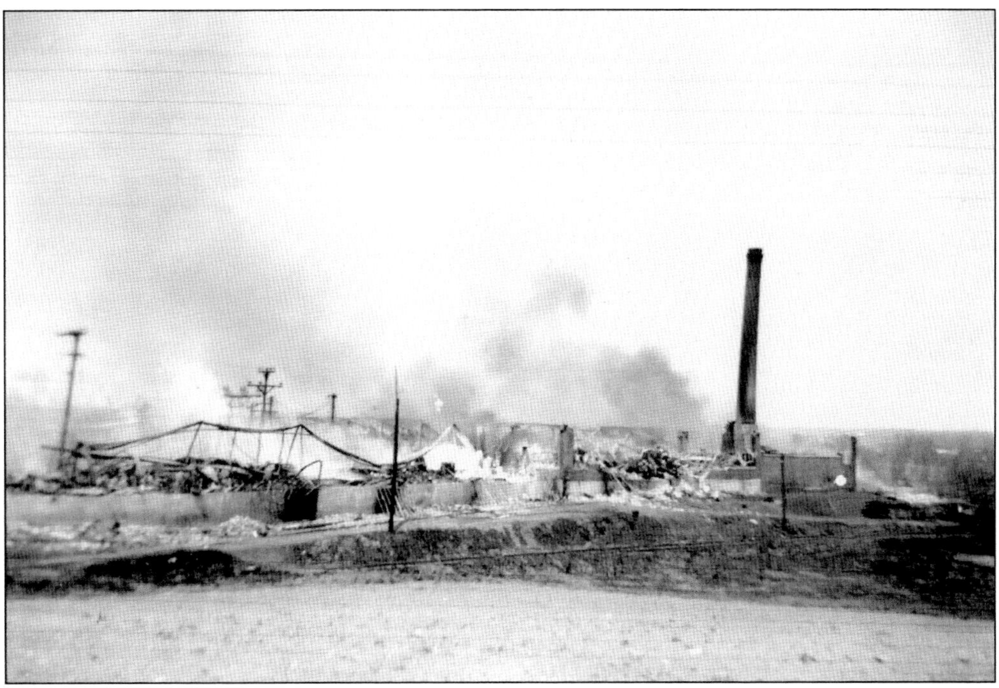

The smoldering ruins of the Blue Ridge Rubber Company are shown above. The factory was rebuilt in 1943 under the new name, Cambridge Rubber Company. (Courtesy of Dean Reindollar.)

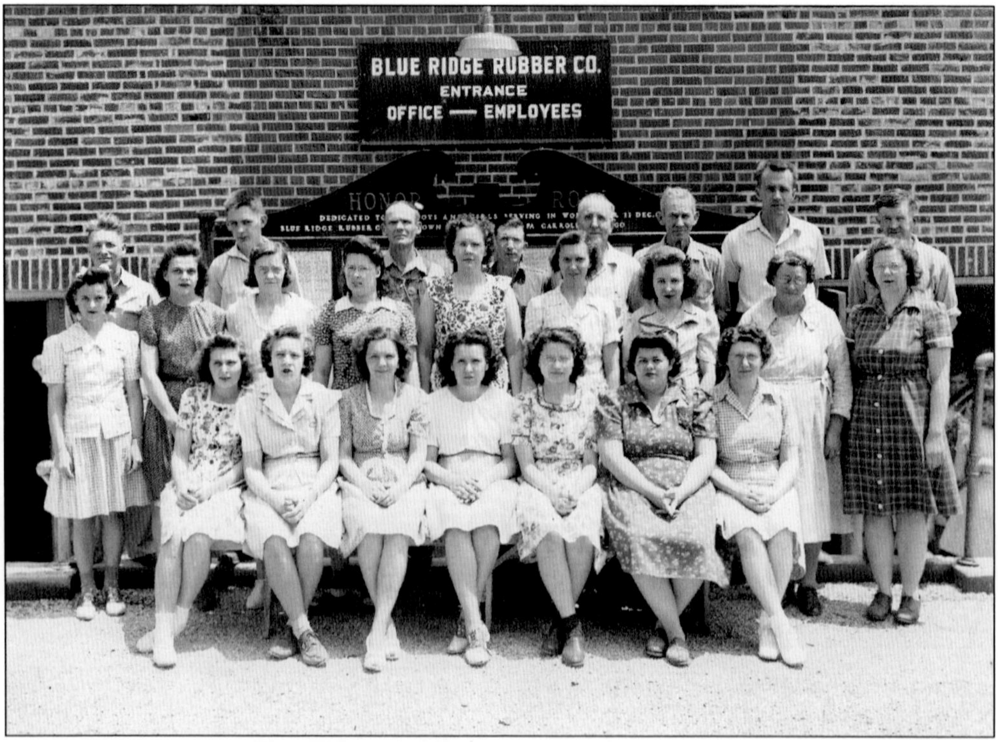

Since most men were called off to duty during World War II, it was up to the female employees to keep things running smoothly at the rubber factory. (Courtesy of the Clem family.)

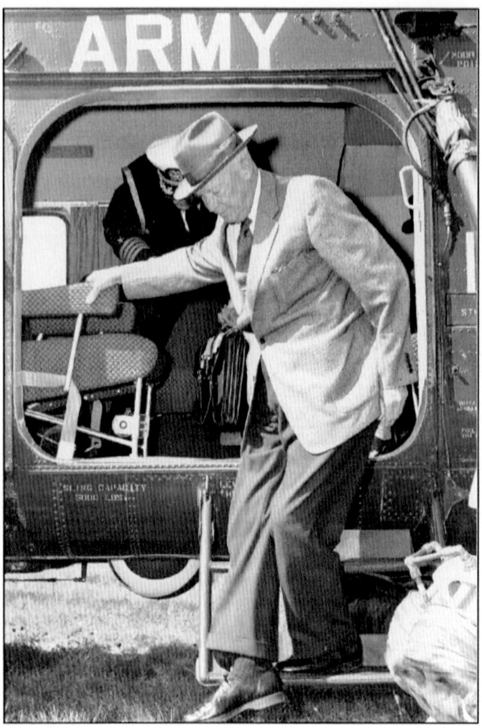

President Dwight D. Eisenhower, wearing Cambridge-made shoes, steps out of a helicopter to visit the Cambridge Rubber Company. (Courtesy of George W. Naylor Jr.)

Three

PRIVATE ARCHITECTURE

In 1762, the first lots in Taneytown were offered for sale. By purchasing a lot, the buyer obligated himself to build a 20 feet by 24 feet house with a brick or stone chimney within one year; he was subject to losing his land if he did not comply. Constructed of log, stone, and brick, these early houses reflected the Vernacular architectural traditions of the Pennsylvania Germans who settled the area.

As Taneytown grew and developed, new architectural trends and techniques were embraced, resulting in houses that reflected nationally popular design ideals.

Today the houses in and around Taneytown run the gamut from grand country mansions, to Victorian townhouses, to post-World War II bungalows. While many lovely old homes have been demolished or "remuddled," there is now a renewed interest in the timeless craftsmanship and beauty of these unique structures that have sheltered many over the past 250 years.

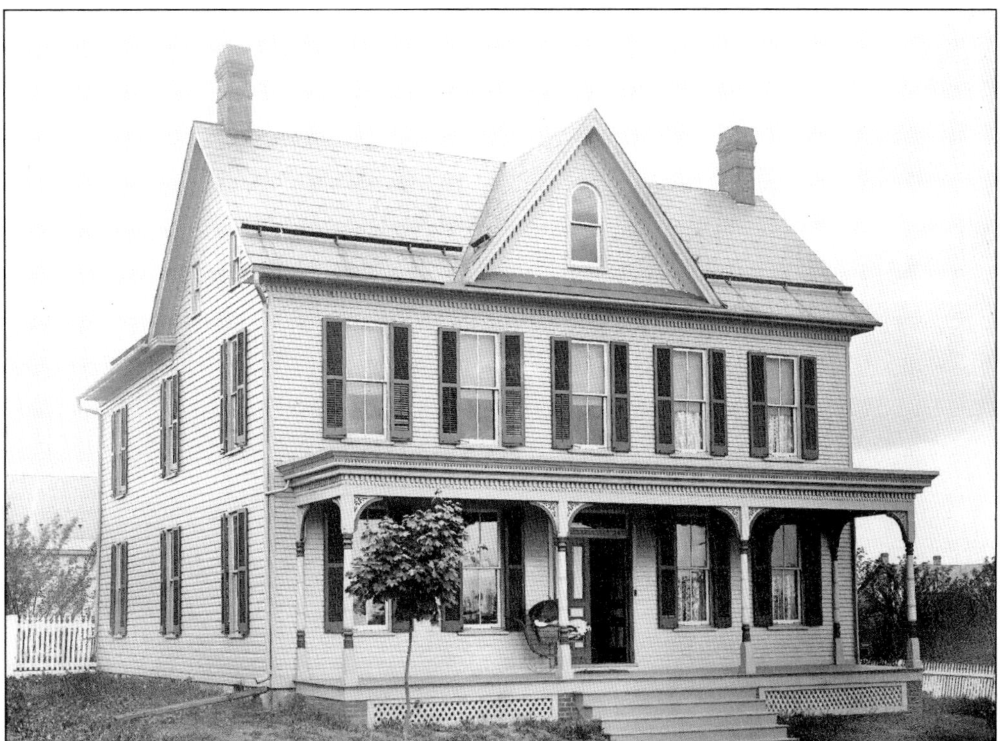

Based on the tradition of the regional farmhouse, this house on Middle Street was embellished with Victorian ornamentation. Note the baby carriage on the porch. (Courtesy of Michael and Susan Reifsnider.)

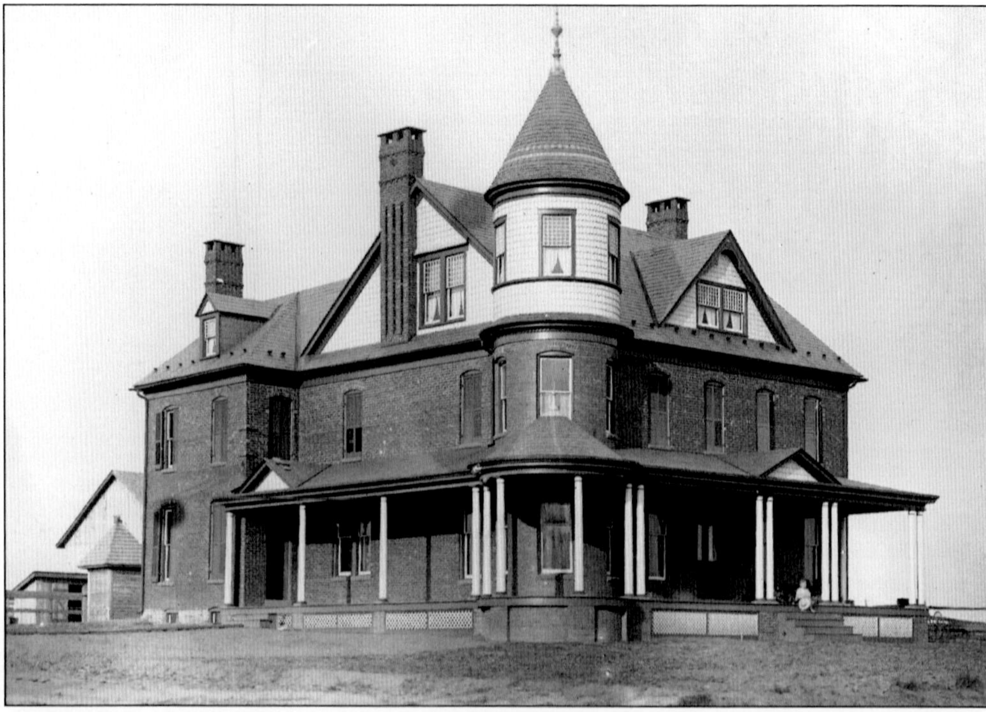

Dr. Nelson A. Hitchcock built this grand Victorian house in the late 1800s. Purchased by the Hesson-Snider Post 59 of the American Legion in 1947, it served as the legion headquarters. Sadly, the building was demolished *c.* 1960 to make way for a gas station. (Courtesy of Michael and Susan Reifsnider.)

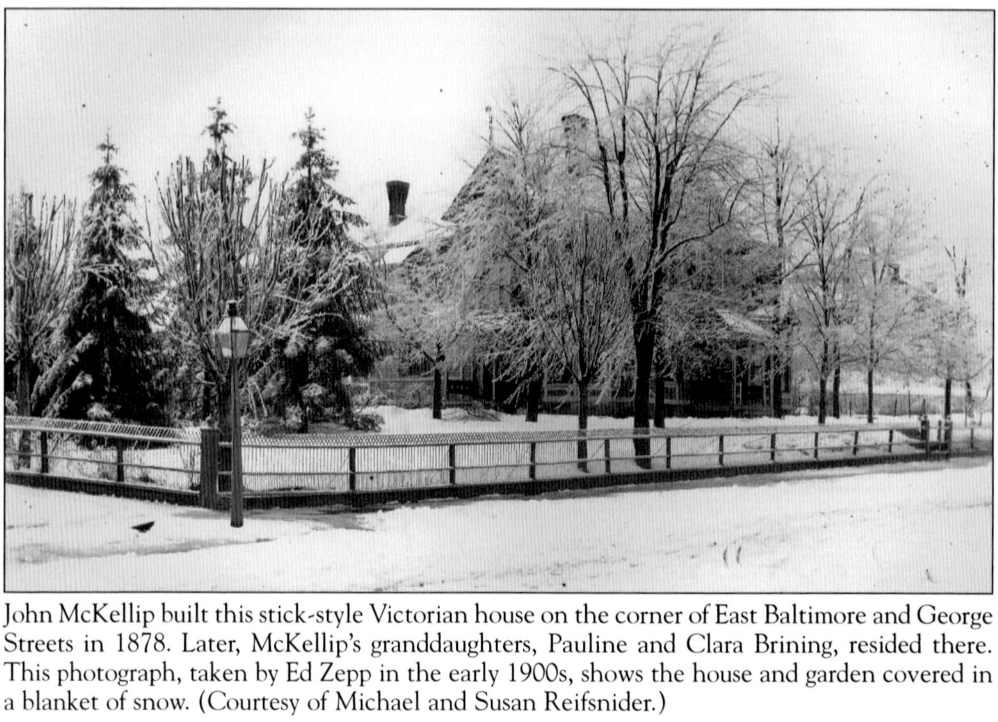

John McKellip built this stick-style Victorian house on the corner of East Baltimore and George Streets in 1878. Later, McKellip's granddaughters, Pauline and Clara Brining, resided there. This photograph, taken by Ed Zepp in the early 1900s, shows the house and garden covered in a blanket of snow. (Courtesy of Michael and Susan Reifsnider.)

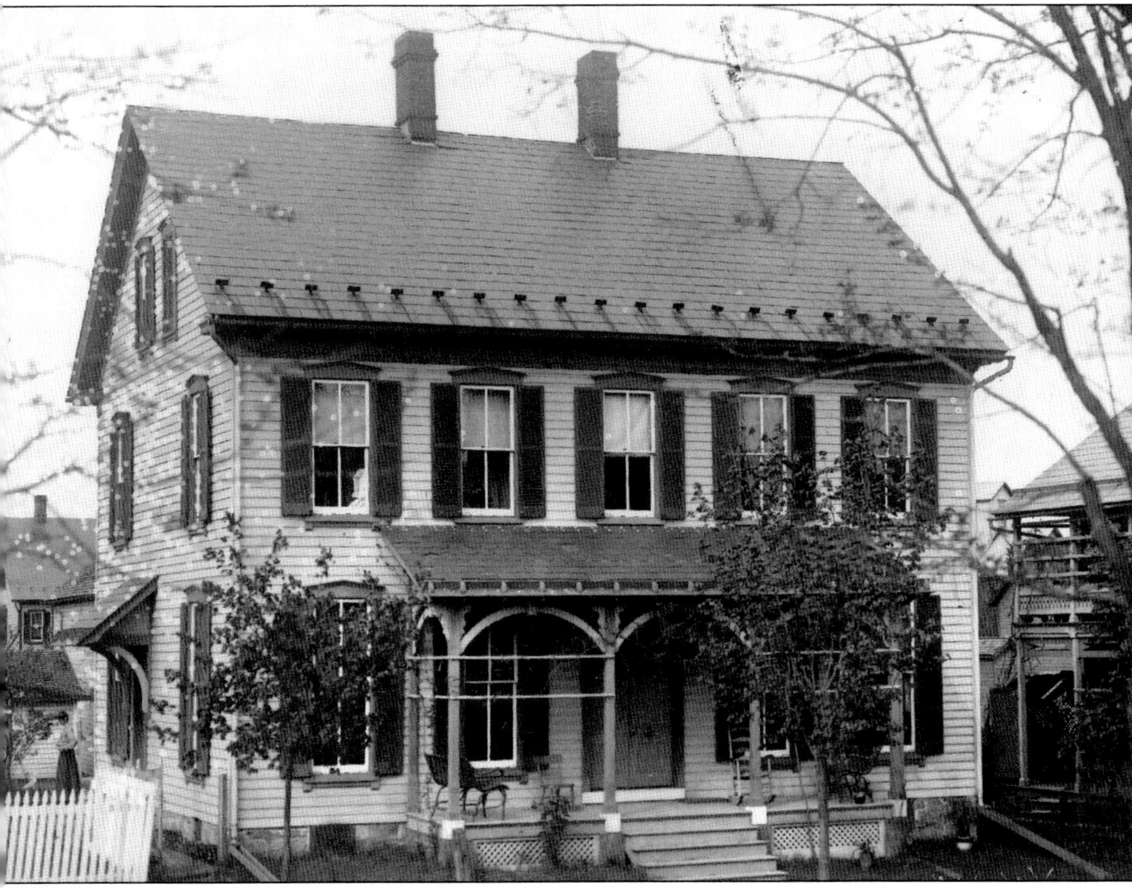

This photograph, taken about 1900, shows the home of Dr. Clotworthy Birnie, a prominent Taneytown physician. Born in 1843 at his family farm, Glenburn, Dr. Birnie was the son of Rogers Birnie, the grandson of Clotworthy Birnie of Thorndale, and the great-grandnephew of Dr. Upton Scott of Annapolis. Dr. Birnie served as president of the Medical and Chirurgical Faculty of Maryland and represented Carroll County in the Maryland House of Delegates. His nieces, Amelia and Elizabeth Annan, later resided at the Birnie residence. (Courtesy of Michael and Susan Reifsnider.)

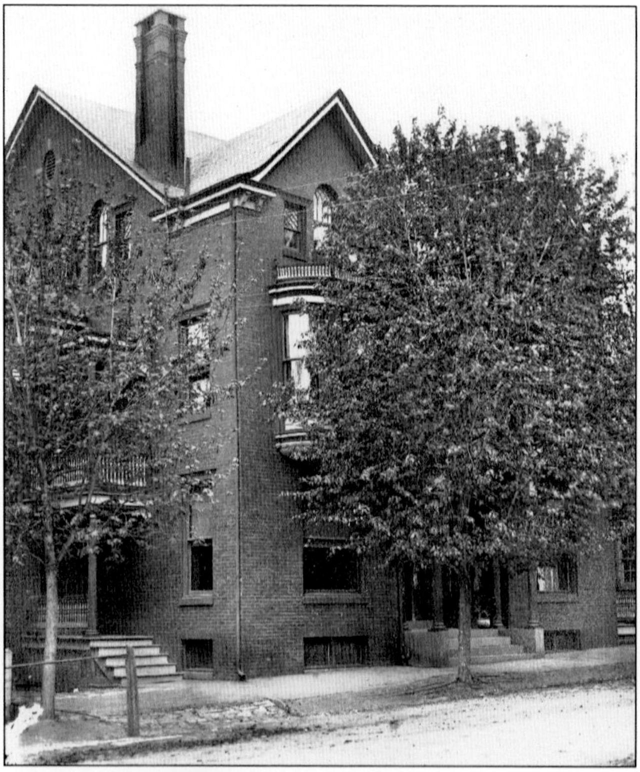

Prominent Taneytown businessman Edward E. Reindollar built this imposing brick house on York Street in 1896. In 1921, it was purchased by the Alexander family and remains in the possession of a descendant today. (Courtesy of Michael and Susan Reifsnider.)

The home and office of Dr. F.H. Seiss was located on East Baltimore Street. In this photograph, two ladies lean against the elaborate wrought iron balcony on the second floor. (Courtesy of Michael and Susan Reifsnider.)

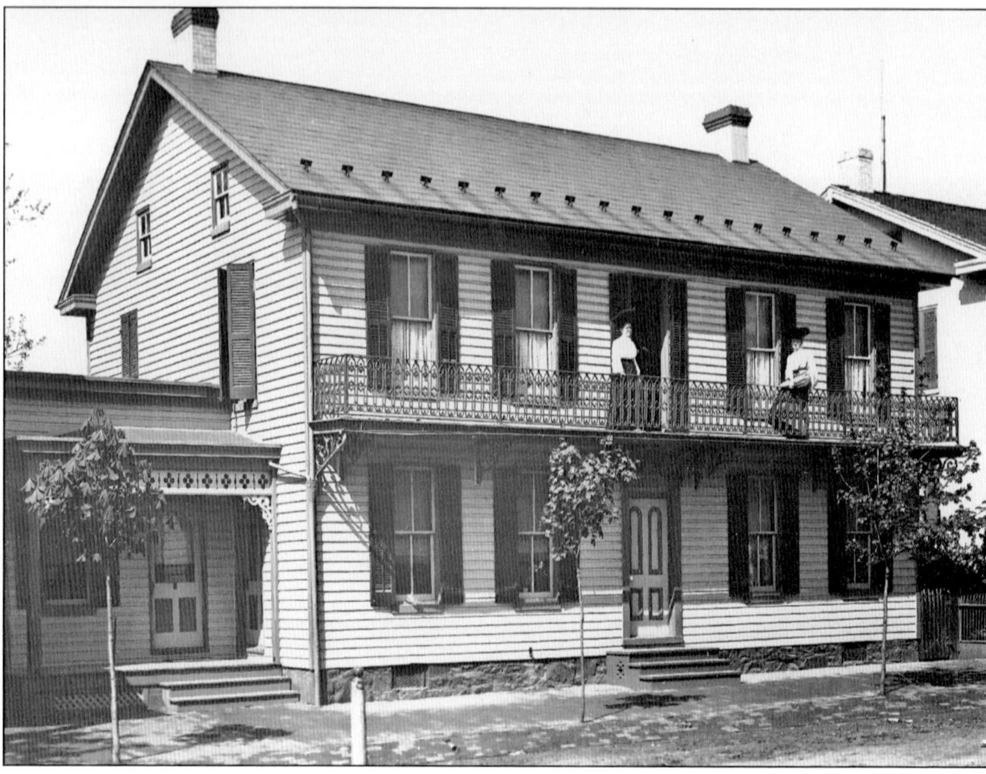

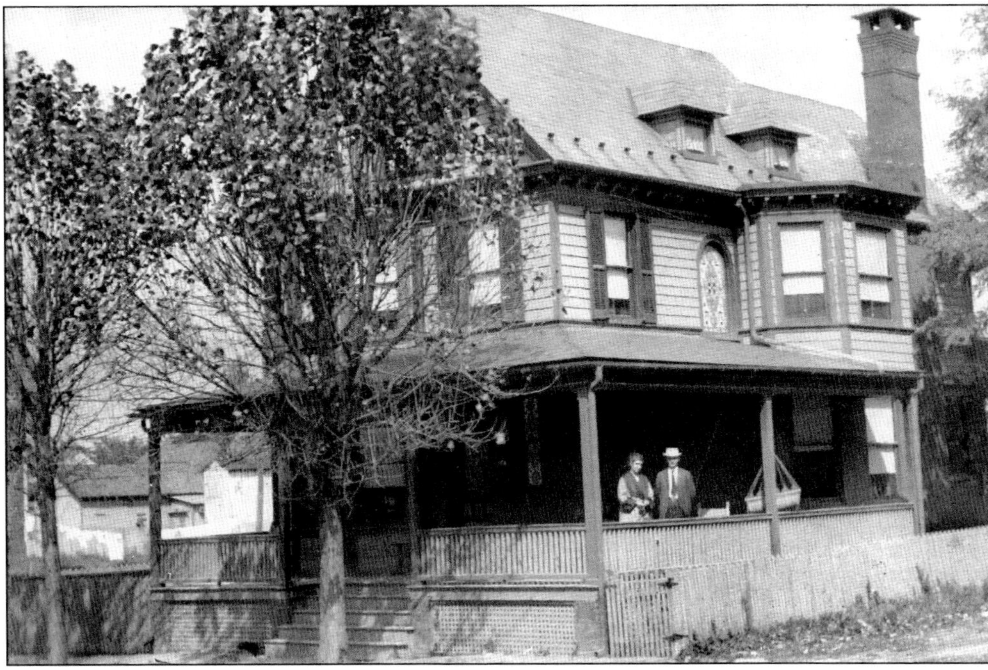

Sam and Rose Ott stand on the porch of their charming West Baltimore Street home in this photograph from about 1910. Sam Ott owned a popular store on East Baltimore Street that offered a variety of merchandise. Their daughter, Virginia Sanders, later resided at the home. (Courtesy of Tyler J. Boone.)

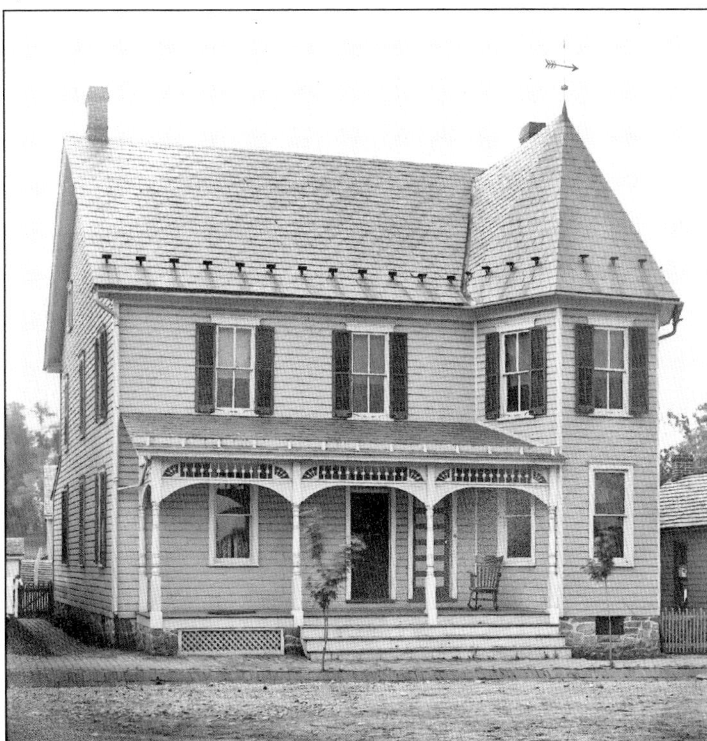

This house on Mill Avenue was the residence of famed Taneytown photographer, Edward P. Zepp. He took this photograph and many others featured throughout this book, in the early 1900s. (Courtesy of Michael and Susan Reifsnider.)

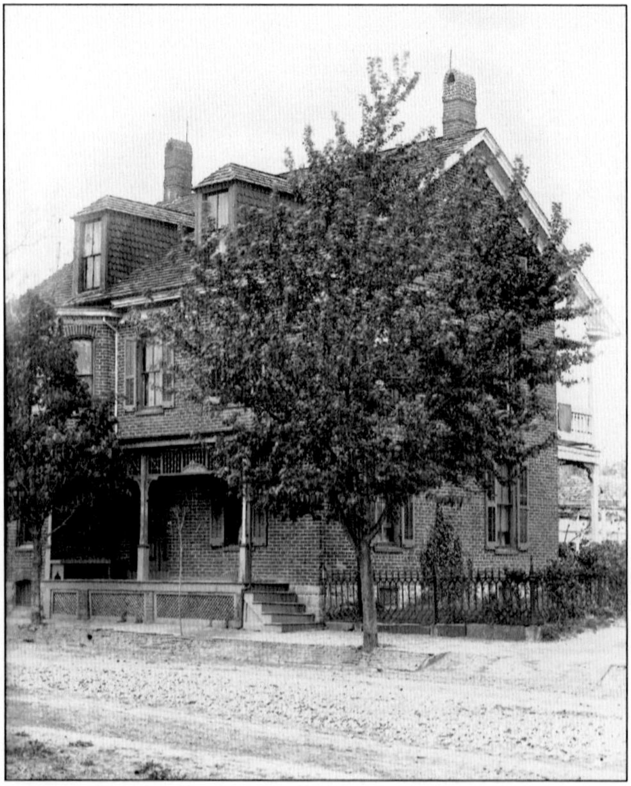

Originally a private residence, this building on West Baltimore Street currently houses the office of Trinity Lutheran Church. Of special note is the elaborate fretwork featured on the porch. (Courtesy of Michael and Susan Reifsnider.)

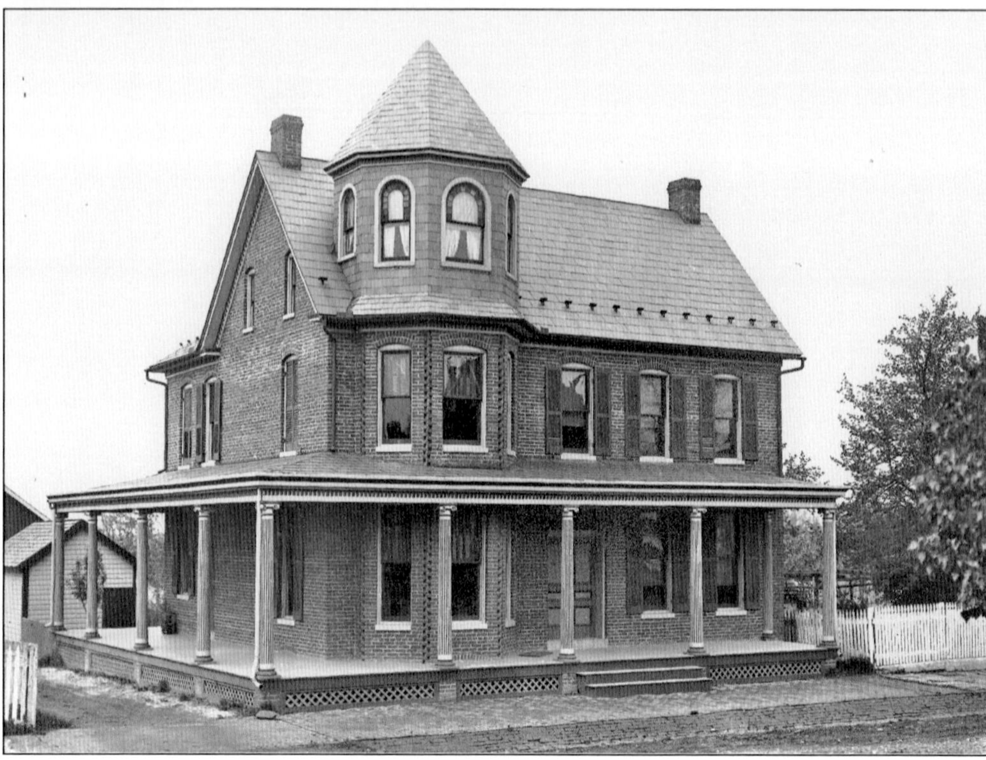

Fluted Ionic columns line the wrap-around porch of this West Baltimore Street home. Arched windows with stained glass panels embellish the top of the turret. (Courtesy of Michael and Susan Reifsnider.)

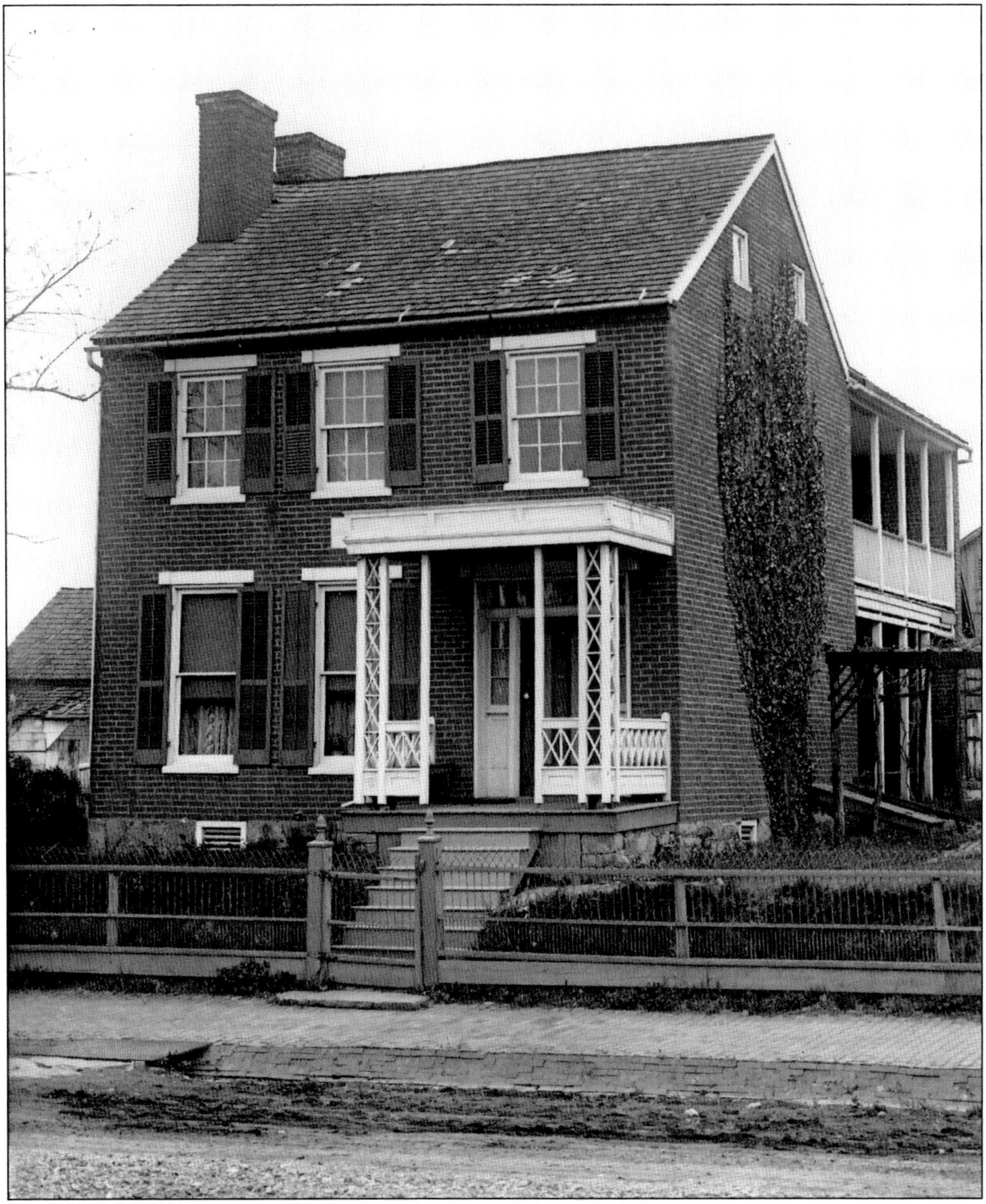

The old parsonage of the Reformed church on West Baltimore Street was built in 1848. A three-bay structure with side passage and double, interior gable-end chimneys, the house displays late Federal or Greek Revival influences, as seen in the small front porch. In this photograph taken by Ed Zepp, minor alterations have been made to update the house, such as an enlarged window on the first story, louvered shutters, and an elaborate metal fence. (An earlier photograph of the house may be seen on page 67.) The structure was torn down in the early 20th century. (Courtesy of Michael and Susan Reifsnider.)

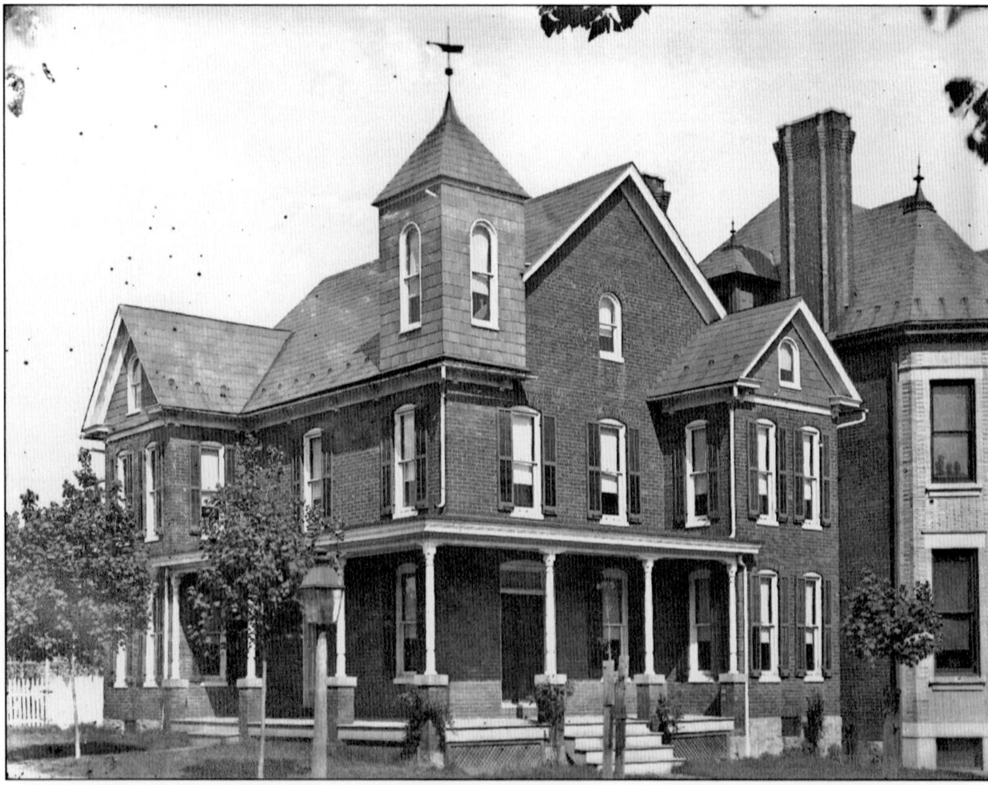

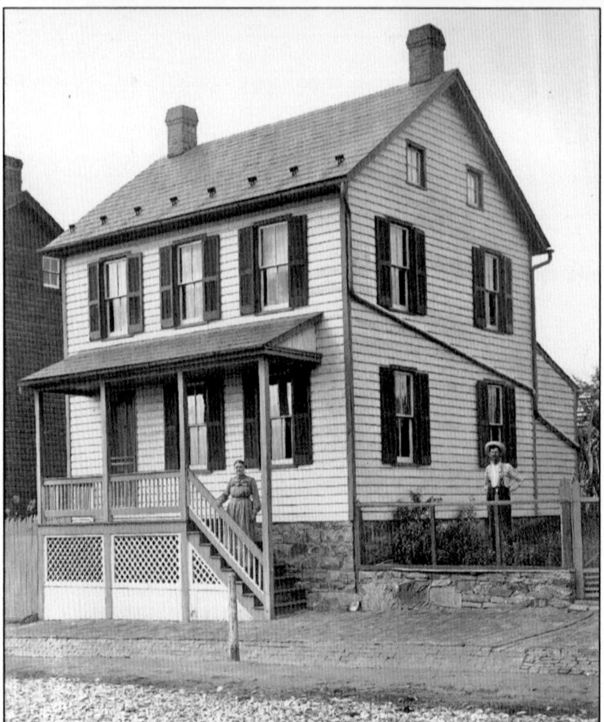

Located on the corner of East Baltimore and Middle Streets, this handsome brick house was built in the late 1800s. A small, slate covered tower crowned with a weather vane juts out from the corner of the house. (Courtesy of Michael and Susan Reifsnider.)

The owners of this neat and tidy frame house on West Baltimore Street proudly pose for a photograph. (Courtesy of Michael and Susan Reifsnider.)

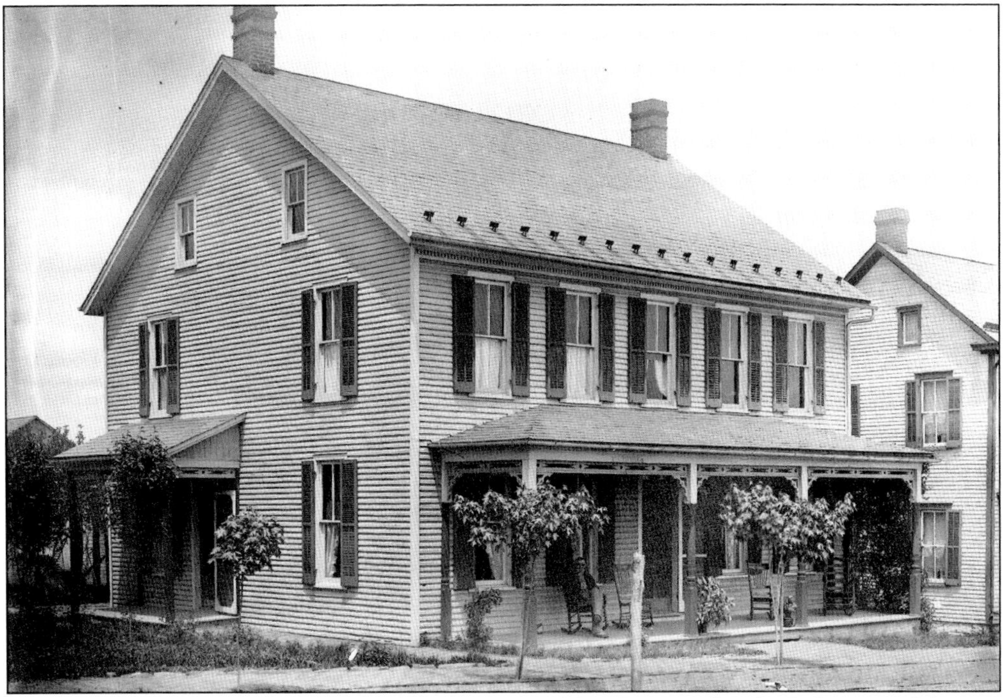

This house on Middle Street illustrates how the regional farmhouse style, which dominated the area from the late 1700s to the early 1900s, was updated to suit new tastes. Here, hourglass-patterned spandrels and brackets embellish the porch, while double hung sash window with two panes over a single pane bring this house up to date. (Courtesy of Michael and Susan Reifsnider.)

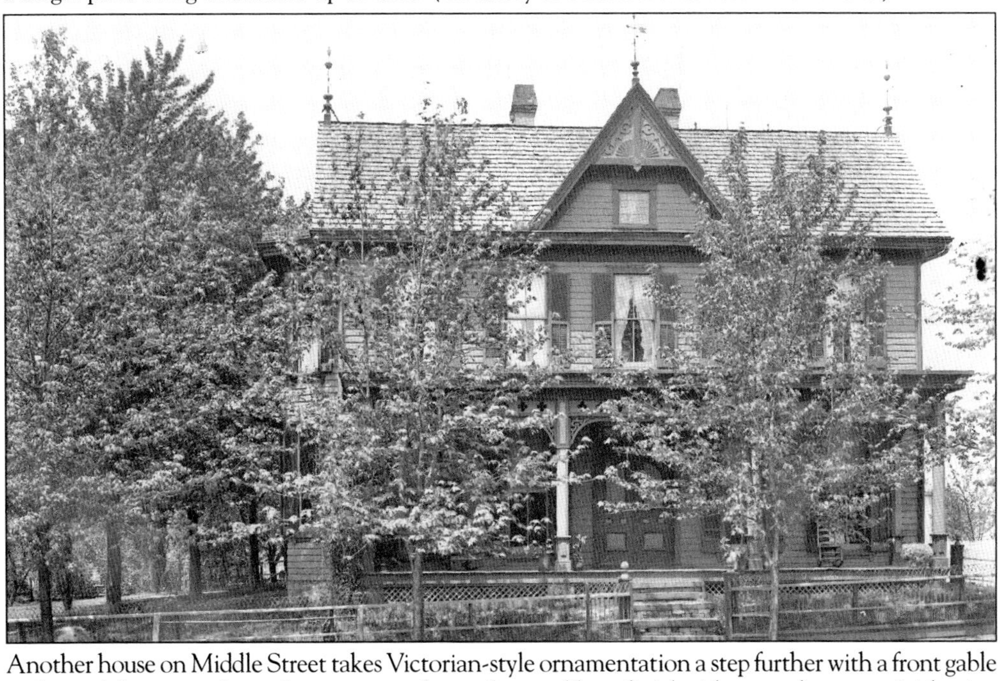

Another house on Middle Street takes Victorian-style ornamentation a step further with a front gable with an elaborate sunburst decoration and a roof topped by a finial with a weather vane. Lightning rods occupy opposite ends of the roof ridge. (Courtesy of Michael and Susan Reifsnider.)

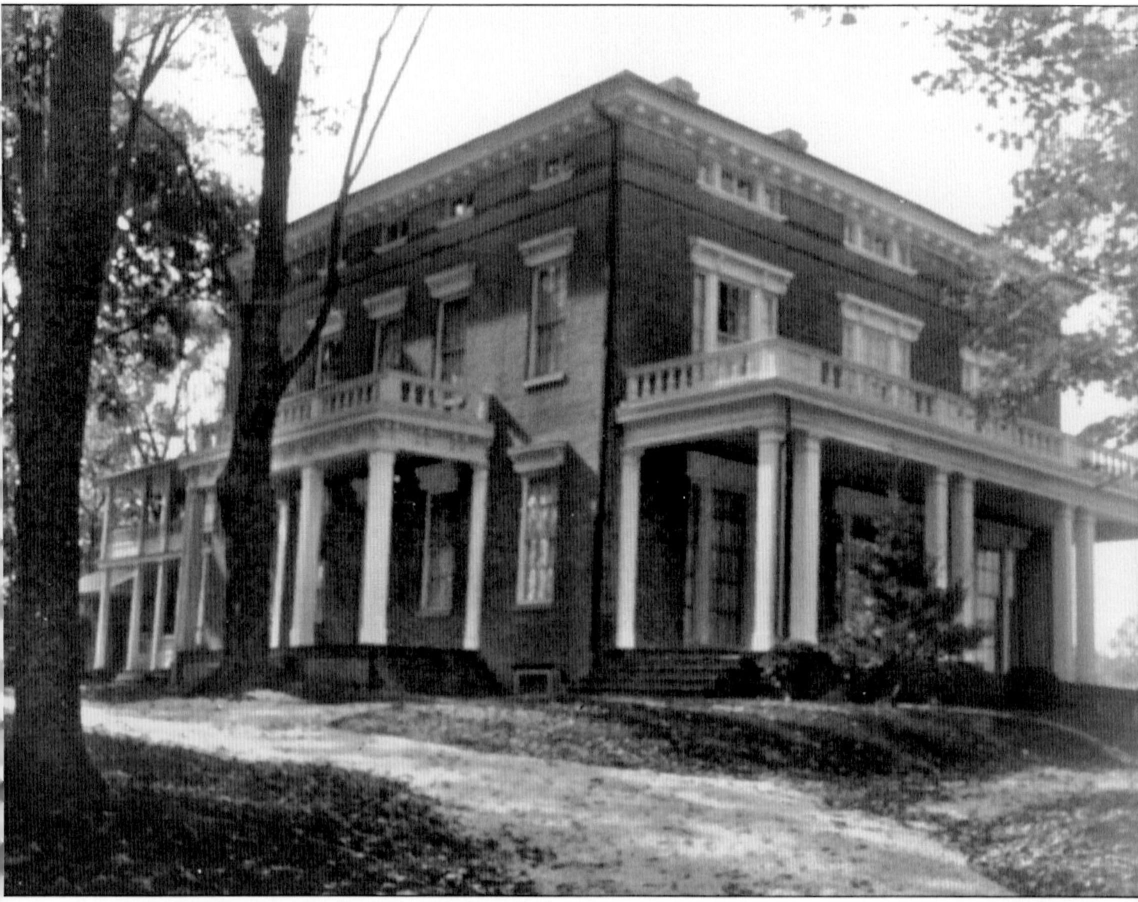

Col. Andrew Ege built Antrim in 1844 on land presented to him by his father-in-law, Maj. John McKaleb. Named after Colonel Ege's Irish birthplace—County Antrim—the plantation is a gem of Greek Revival architecture. The interior features ornate plaster ceiling medallions and a three-story elliptical staircase. Today, proprietors Richard and Dorothy Mollett have transformed Antrim into a nationally acclaimed country inn and restaurant. (Courtesy of the Historical Society of Carroll County.)

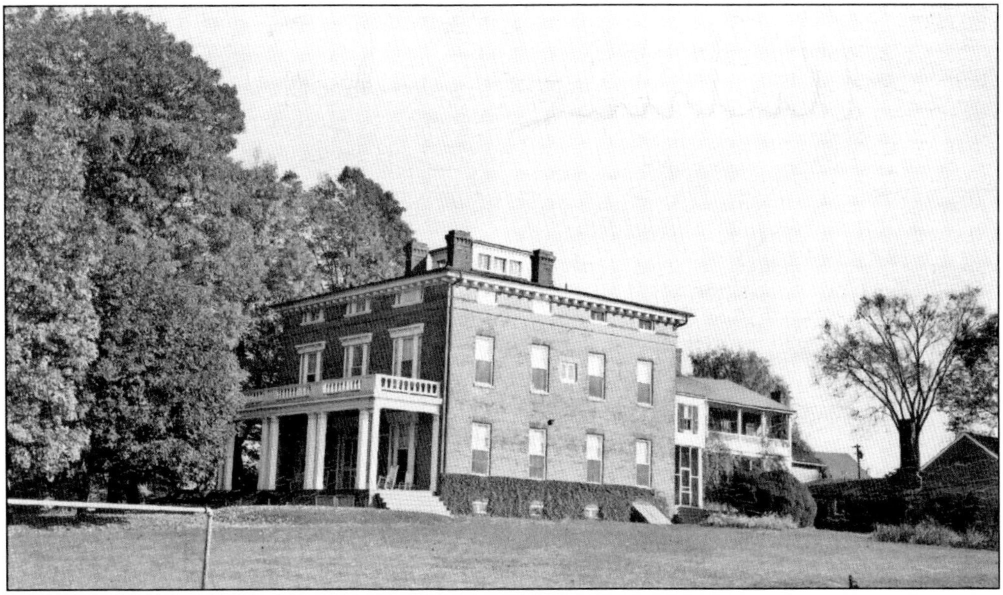

George Washington Clabaugh purchased Antrim in 1873. His son, Harry Morris Clabaugh, was elected attorney general of Maryland (1895–1898) and was appointed chief justice of the Supreme Court by President Roosevelt in 1903. Antrim remained in the possession of the Clabaugh family for nearly 100 years. (Courtesy of the Historical Society of Carroll County.)

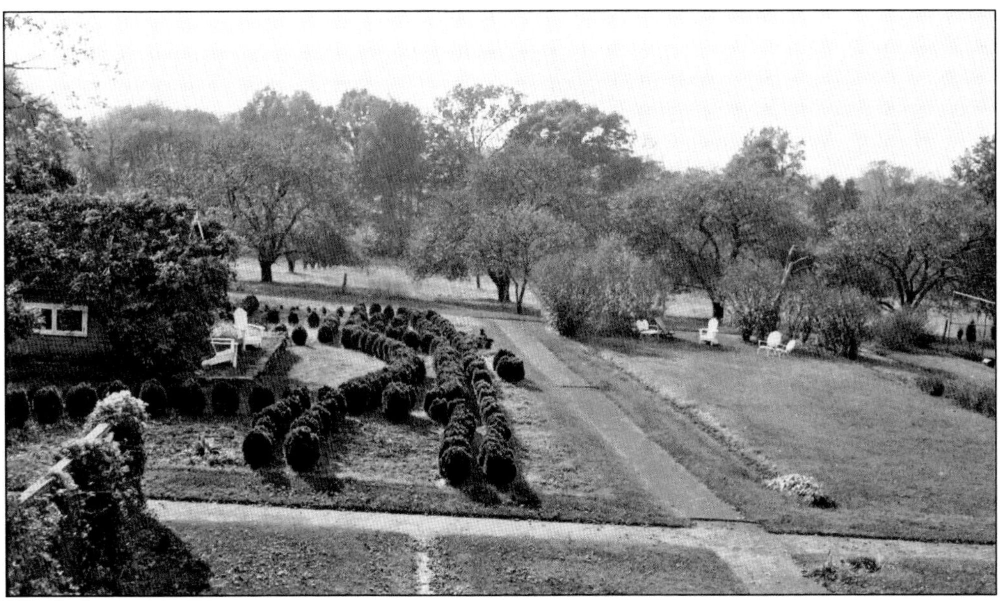

This snapshot from the 1940s shows carefully clipped boxwoods and white Adirondack chairs surrounding the icehouse in Antrim's garden. (Courtesy of the Historical Society of Carroll County.)

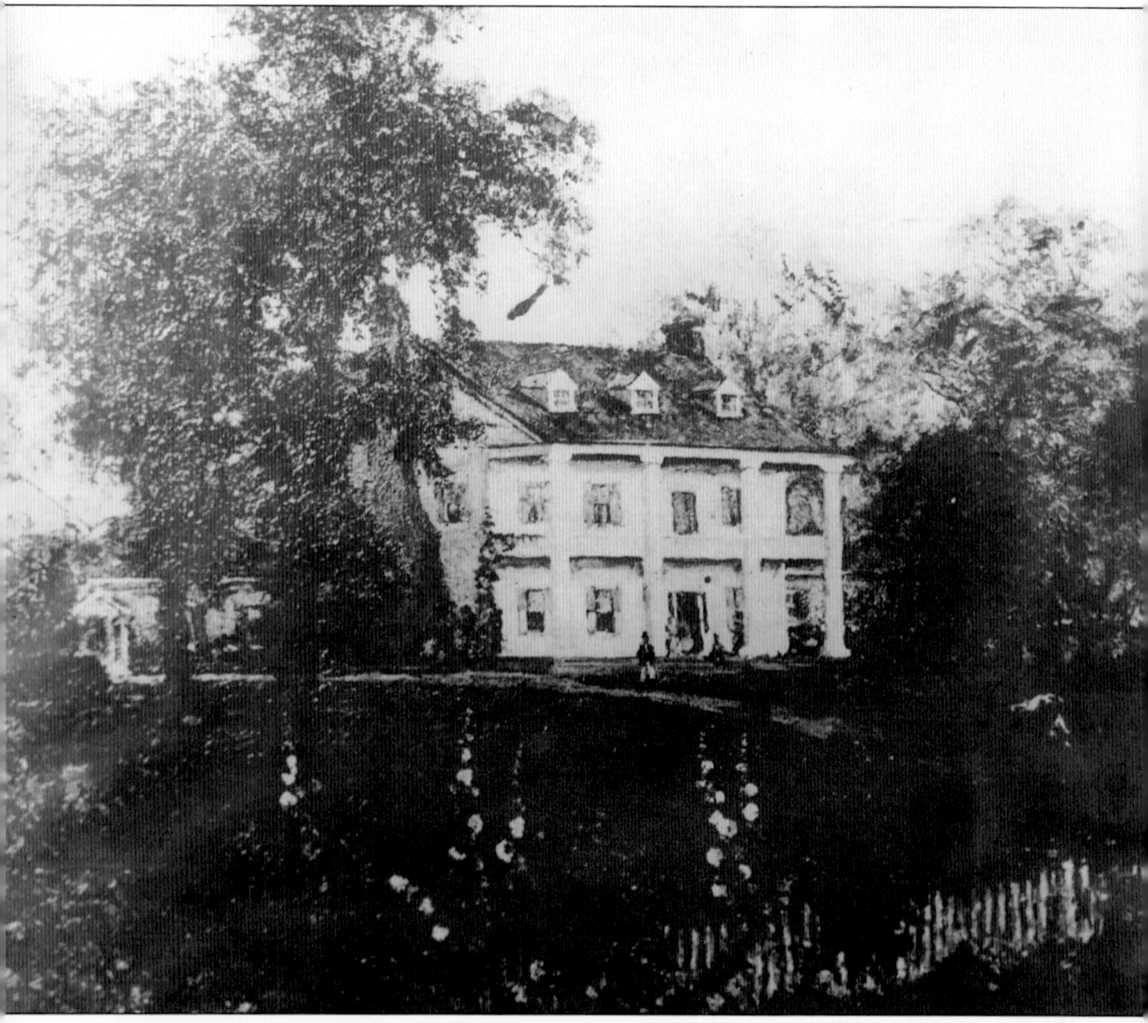

A painting by the grandson of Francis Scott Key depicts the original house at Terra Rubra—birthplace of the author of "The Star Spangled Banner." Built in the 1770s for John Ross Key, the original plantation house was a two-and-a-half story structure with a portico supported by four large columns. It was here, on August 1, 1779, that Francis Scott Key was born. The estate was sold after Key's death and deteriorated until a storm in the late 1850s furthered its destruction. Shortly thereafter, it was torn down and a new house built in its place. (Courtesy of the Historical Society of Carroll County.)

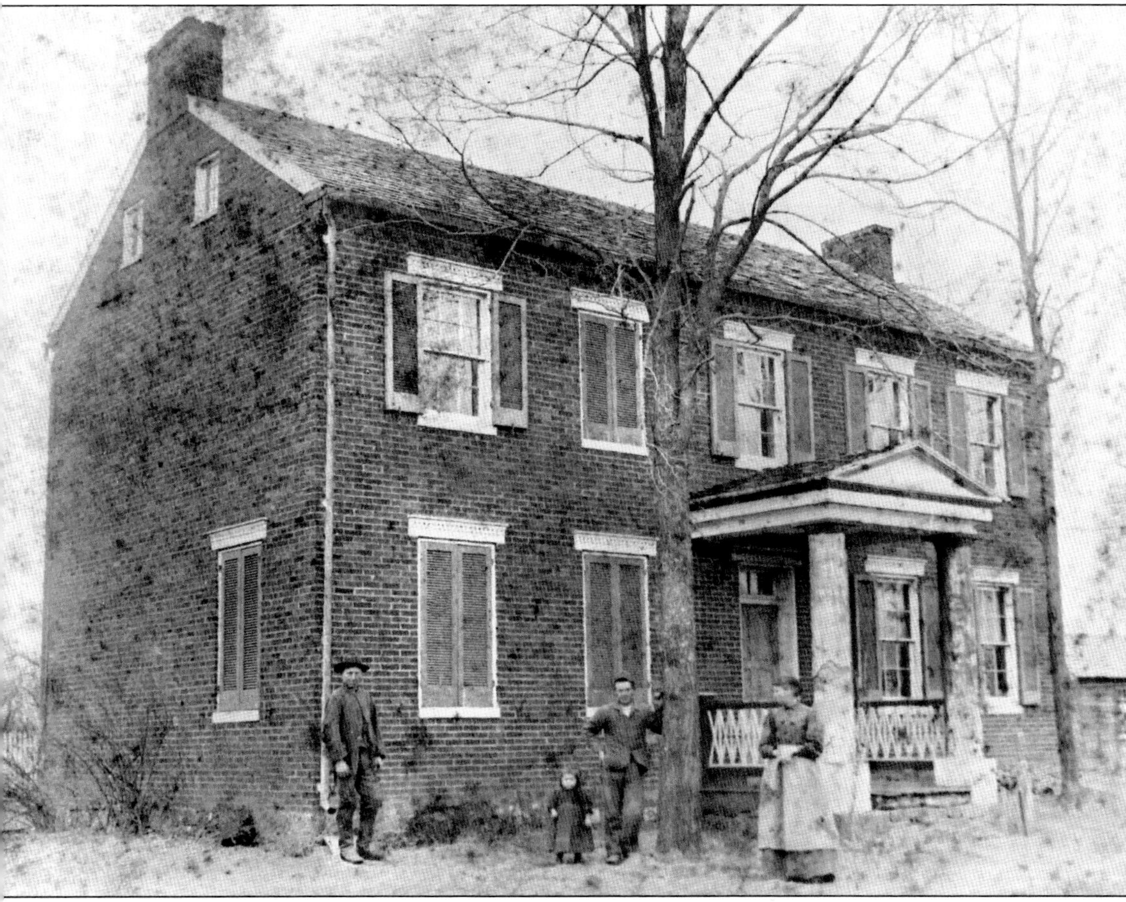

Terra Rubra is pictured as it appeared in the 1890s. Peter Baumgardner purchased the farm in 1893 and shortly thereafter posed for this photograph with his young family and farmhand. The following are pictured from left to right: Harry Freet, Elsie or Lillie Baumgardner, Peter Baumgardner, and his wife Annie. The present brick farmhouse at Terra Rubra is believed to be part of the original house's fieldstone foundation. (Courtesy of the Historical Society of Carroll County.)

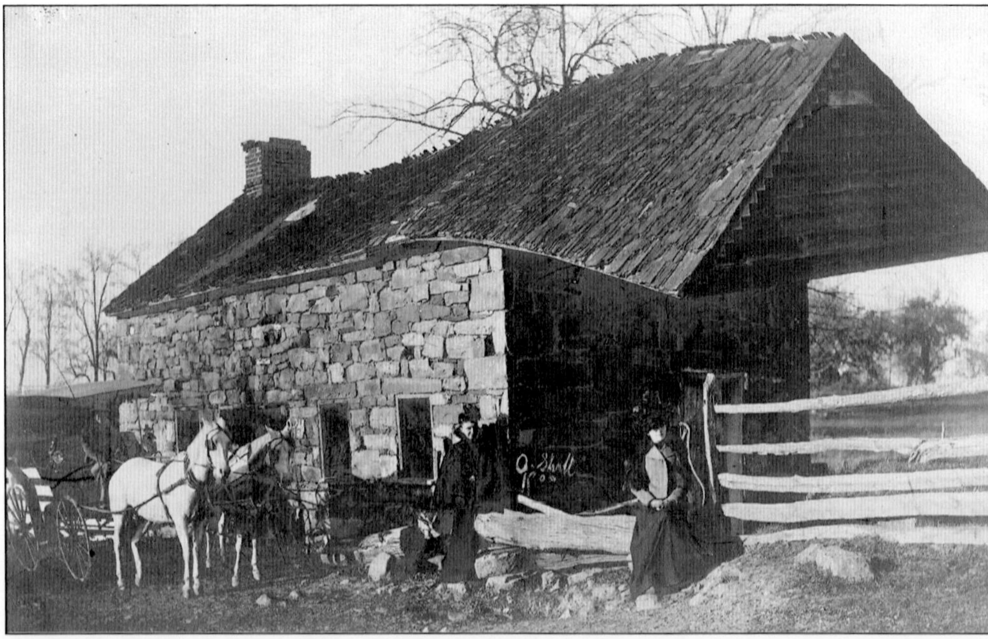

The home of the author of "The Star Spangled Banner" was a popular tourist attraction in the late 19th century. These two ladies are dressed in their best clothes for this visit to Terra Rubra around 1900. The sagging roof of the old springhouse, a last survivor of the original estate, must have captivated them or the photographer. (Courtesy of the Historical Society of Carroll County.)

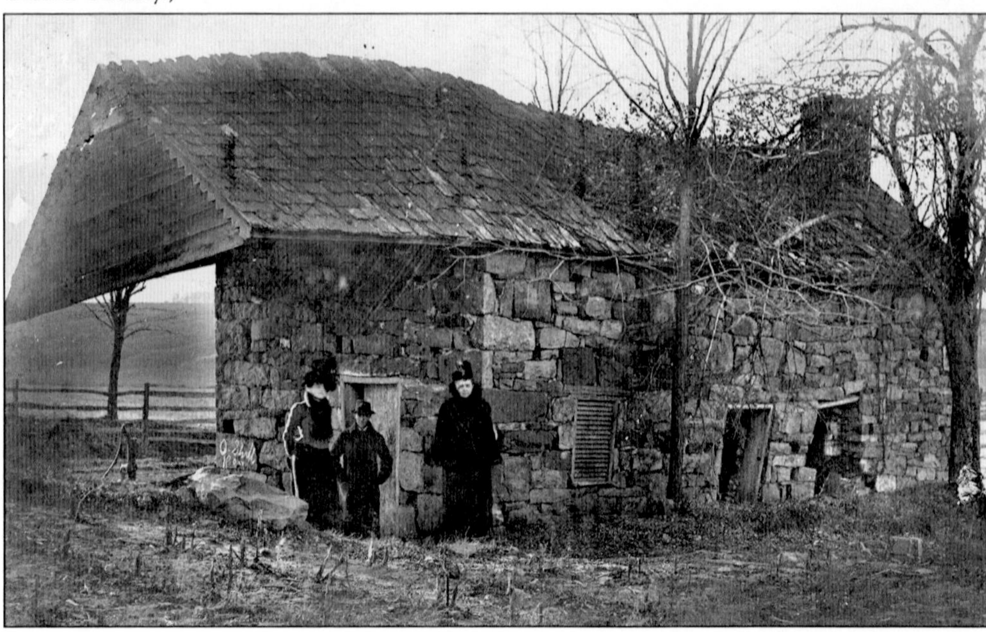

A groundbreaking ceremony for the Francis Scott Key Memorial was held at Terra Rubra on September 15, 1914. Among those in attendance was a grandson of Key's. Unveiled on June 12, 1915, the monument was a gift from the Patriotic Order Sons of America and the pupils of the public schools. (Courtesy of the Historical Society of Carroll County.)

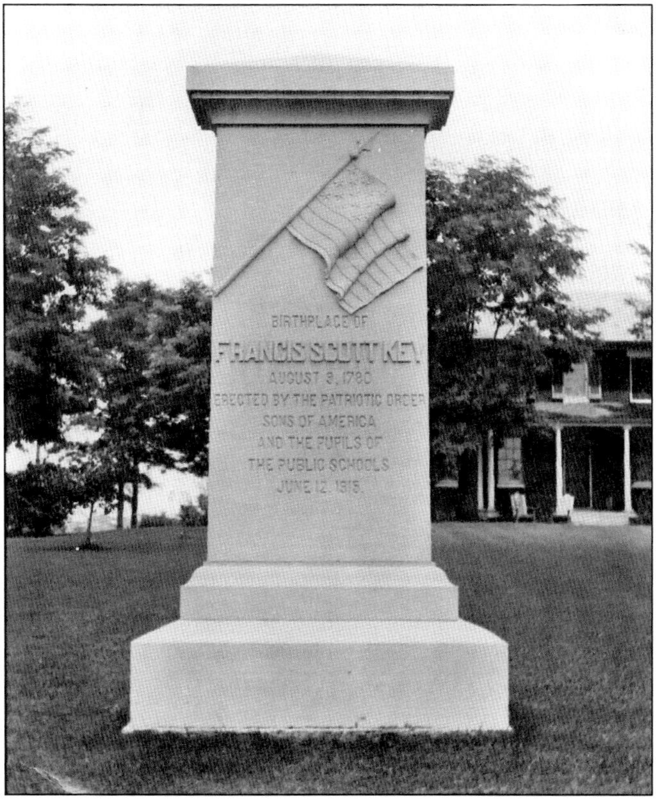

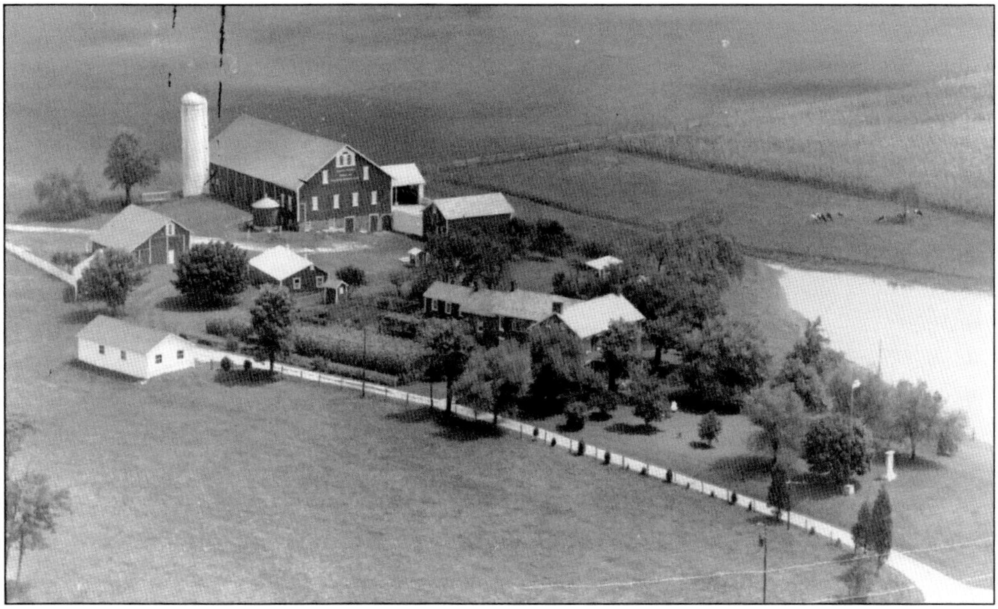

This is an aerial view of Terra Rubra from the 1950s. (Courtesy of the Historical Society of Carroll County.)

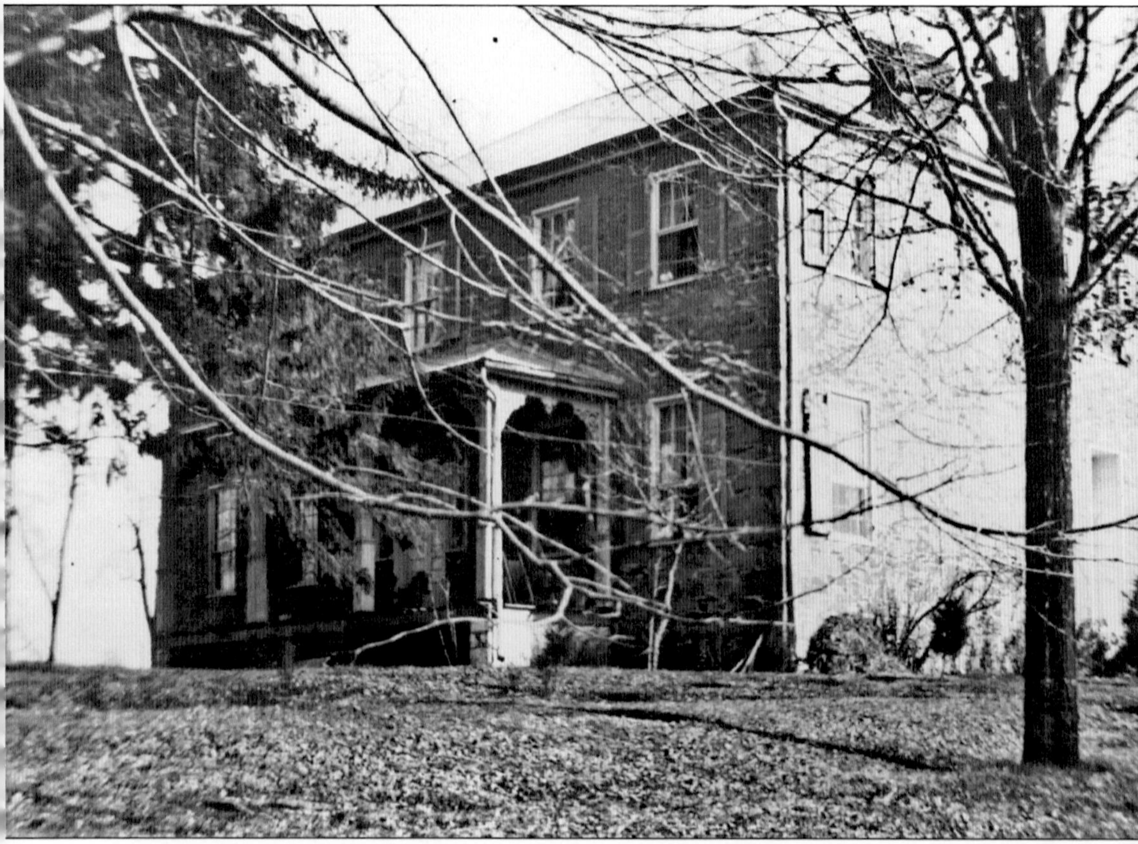

John Scott and his wife, Elizabeth Key Bruce, a cousin of Francis Scott Key, built this house situated atop a hill along the banks of Pipe Creek around 1812. Constructed of massive stones cut from the nearby creek bed, the house reputedly cost $10,000 to build. The names of the Scott children that were carved into the parlor window many years ago can still be seen. (Courtesy of the Historical Society of Carroll County.)

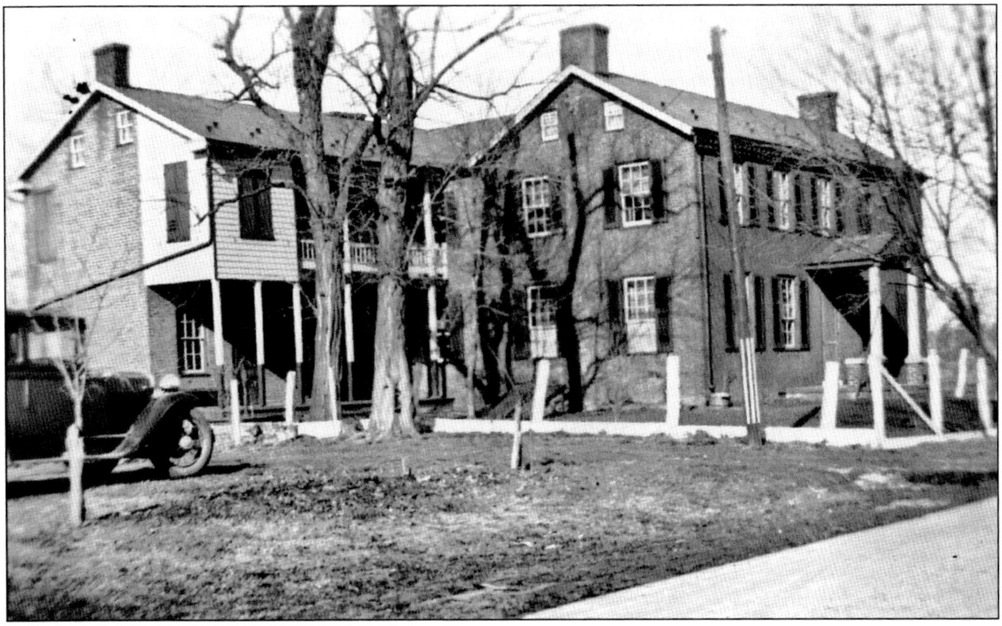

Galt's Fancy, just outside of town, was owned by the prominent Galt family from 1764 until 1956, when it was purchased by Mr. and Mrs. Malcolm Tebbs, esq. The present brick farmhouse with federal influence was built in the early 19th century. (Courtesy of the Historical Society of Carroll County.)

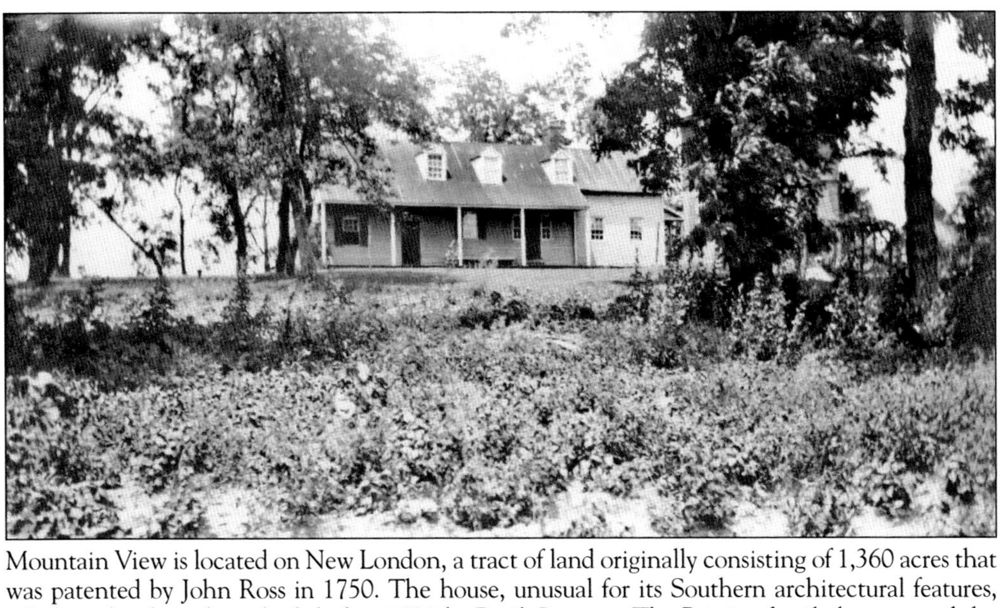

Mountain View is located on New London, a tract of land originally consisting of 1,360 acres that was patented by John Ross in 1750. The house, unusual for its Southern architectural features, is believed to have been built before 1800 by Basil Crapster. The Brining family later owned the house and 250 adjoining acres. (Courtesy of the Historical Society of Carroll County.)

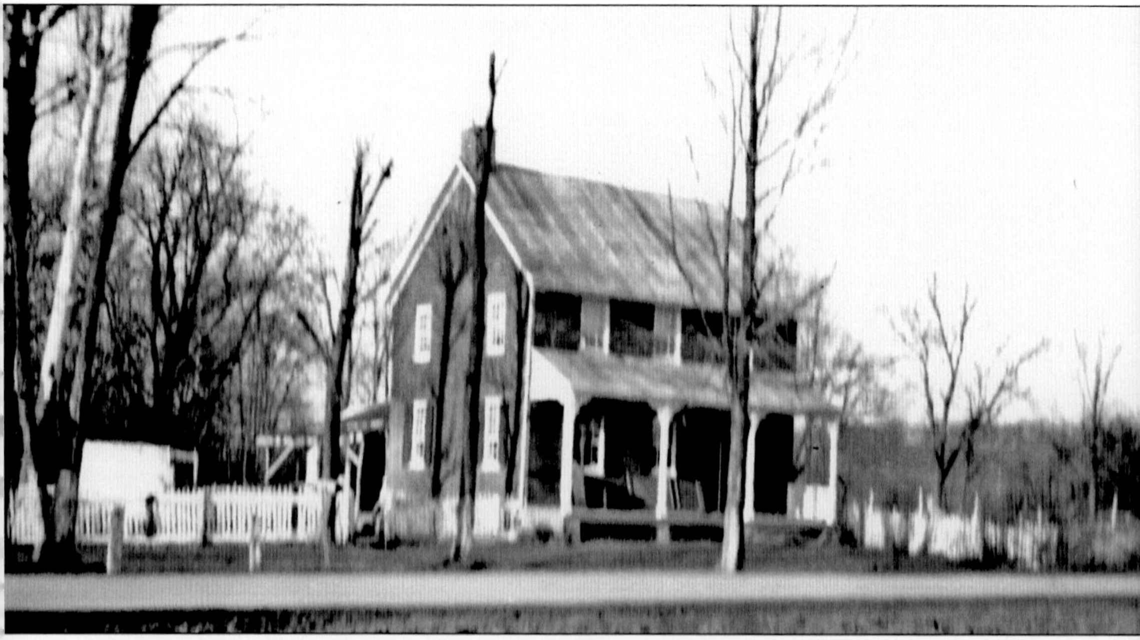

During the Gettysburg Campaign, the farm of Benjamin Shunk hosted Maj. Gen. George Meade. He arrived early on the morning of June 29, 1863, and established his field headquarters there, developing his Pipe Creek Line Plan. (Courtesy of the Historical Society of Carroll County.)

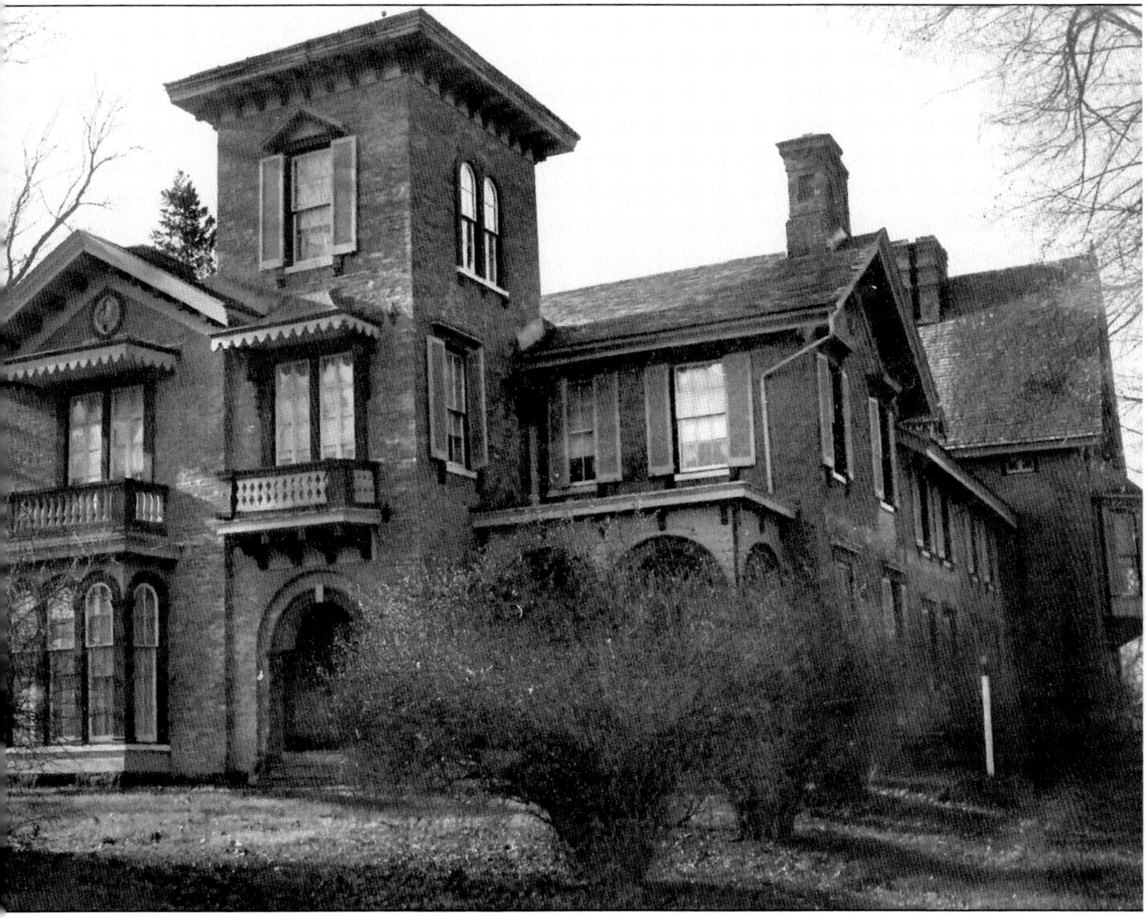

Trevanion, meaning "the meeting of streams" in Welsh, was also a family name of W.W. Dallas, who owned the property in the mid-1800s. Dallas was described as being "suave as a Chesterfield, brave as a lion, generous as a prince," and was known for his gregarious spirit. A friend of Mr. Dallas later recounted, "Mr. Dallas had stocked the streams with fish for the amusement of his angler guests and had preserved partridges through the winter and turned them out in the spring to fill the covers for his hunting friends, and already Trevanion hospitality was far famed and his house was filled with guests from far and near." (Courtesy of the Historical Society of Carroll County.)

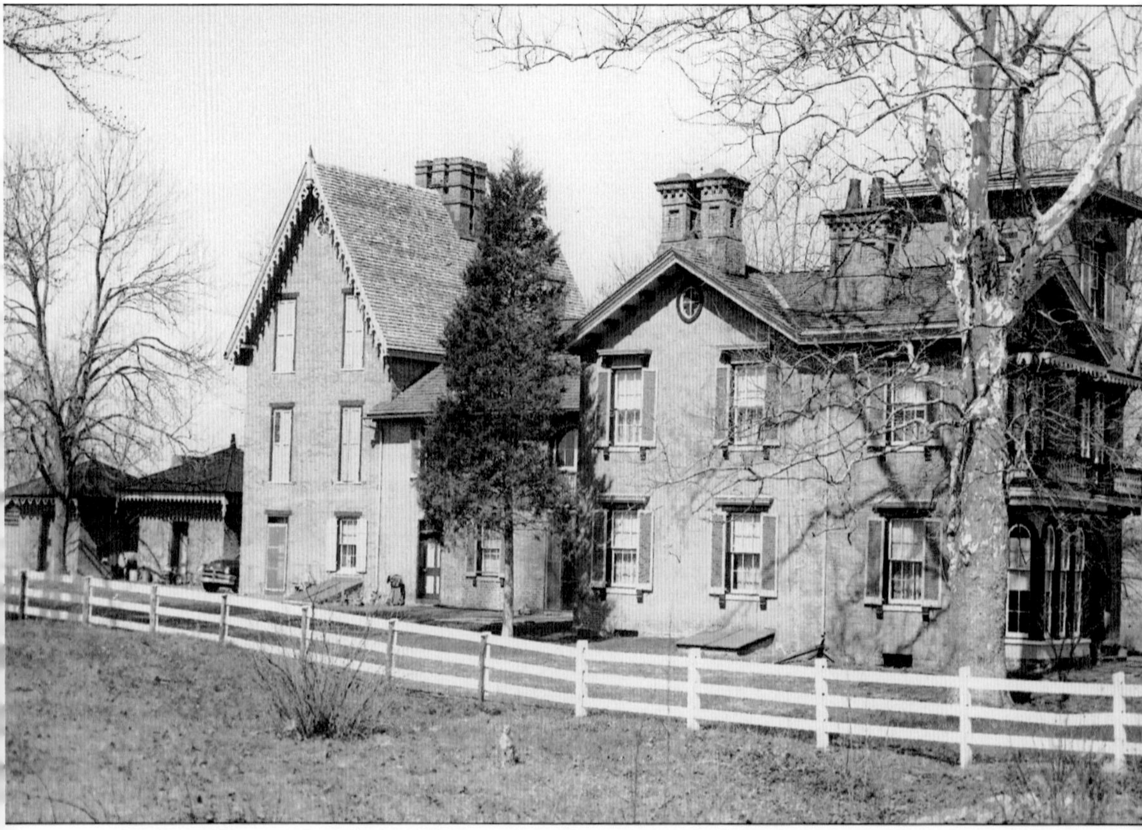

Built in 1817 as a simple farmhouse, Trevanion was transformed into an Italianate and Gothic-style mansion by William Wallace Dallas between 1855 and 1857. Yale-educated Dallas was from a family of prominent lawyers and judges that included a United States vice president. Dallas's varied travels exposed him to current architectural trends, which he employed at his own home. Trevanion was probably one of the first houses in the Carroll County area to apply the fashionable ideas included in nationally circulated builders' guides and pattern books, creating a thoroughly up-to-date structure in a rural area otherwise dominated by a cultural lag. (Courtesy of the Historical Society of Carroll County.)

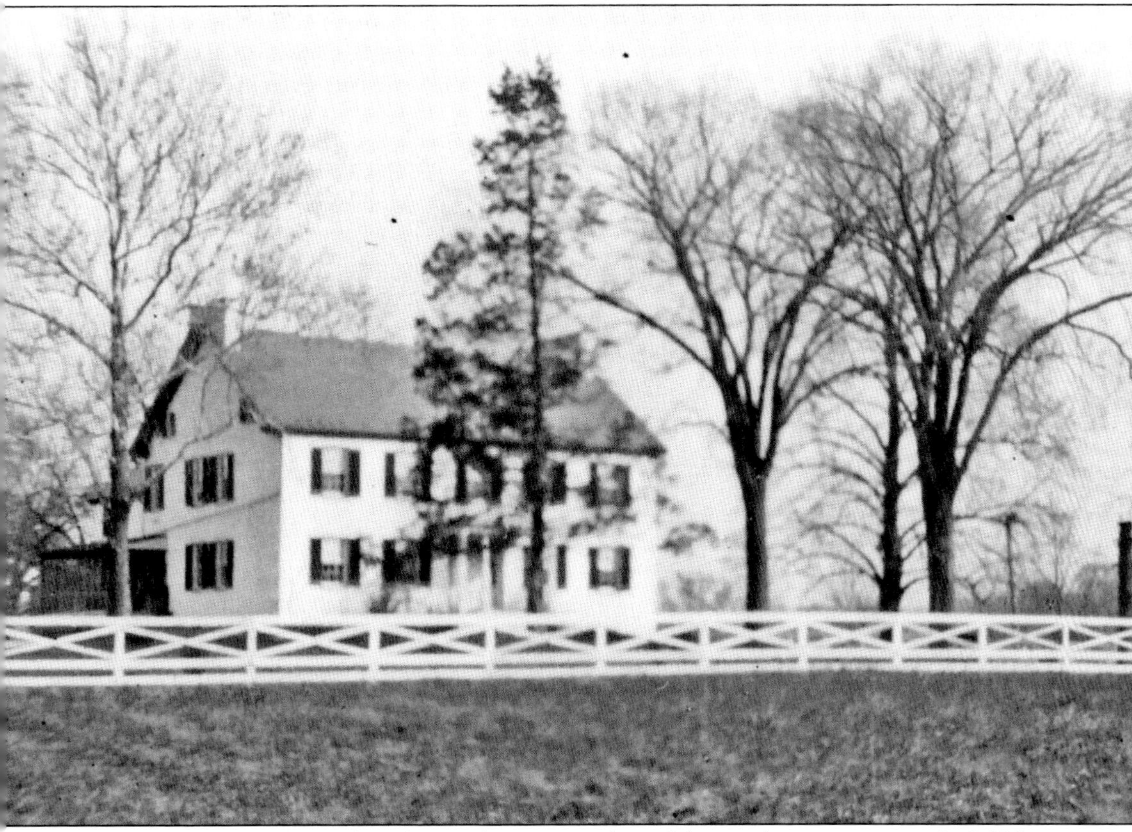

Built between 1832 and 1833 by Clotworthy Birnie, Thorndale was the centerpiece of a 3,000-acre tract of land known as Runnymede Enlarged. Birnie, originally from Belfast, Ireland, inherited the property from his uncle, Dr. Upton Scott of Annapolis. Between 1837 and 1872, Birnie's daughters operated a school—the Thorndale Seminary for Young Ladies—at their home. A prospectus from the school carries the following information: "The course of instruction comprises the usual branches of an English education with needlework. The pupils have the advantage of daily association with a family, and are under their constant care and supervision. Particular attention is given to religious instruction." The property was sold out of the family in 1907. (Courtesy of the Historical Society of Carroll County.)

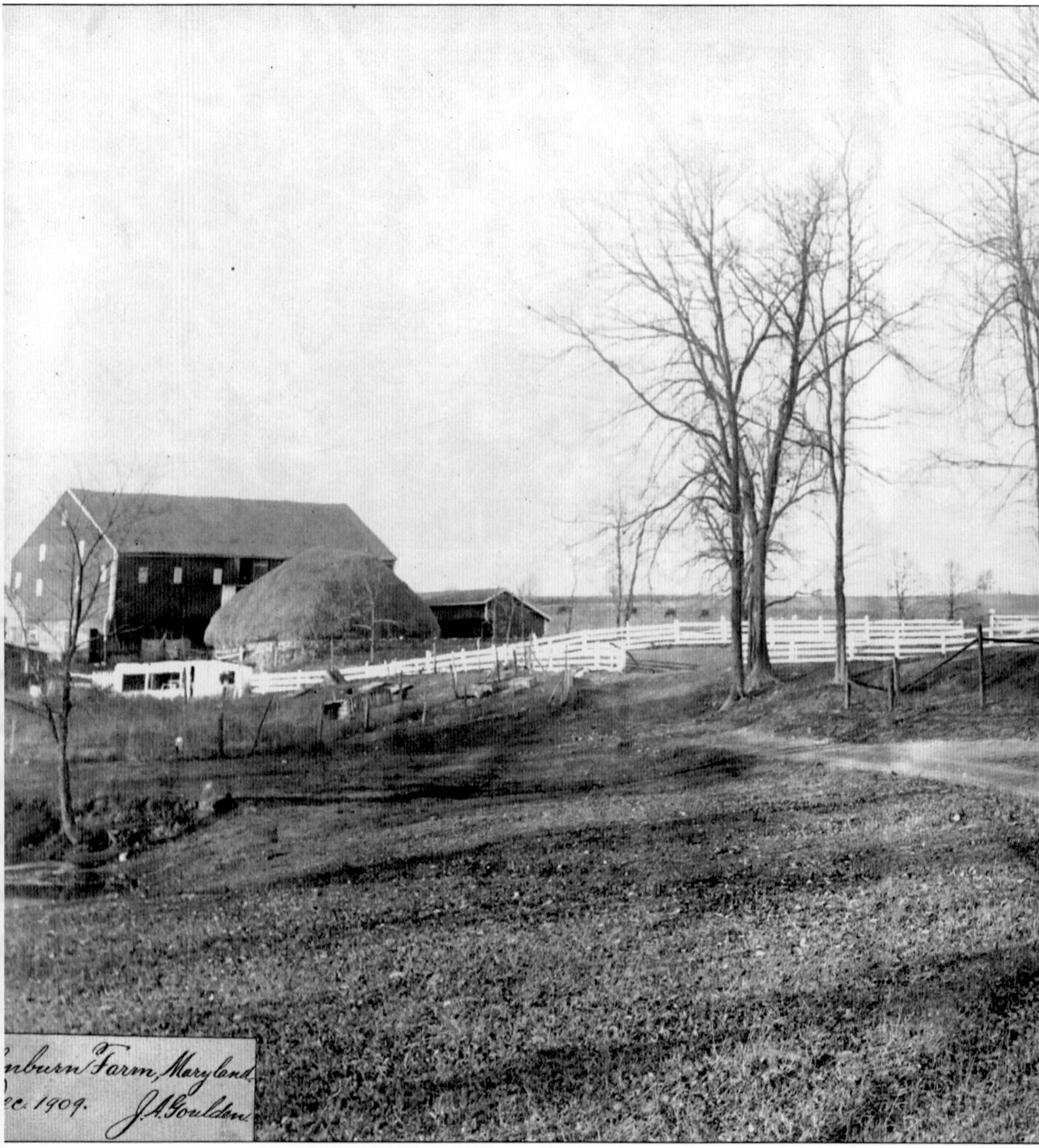

Glenburn was built in 1840 by Rogers Birnie. He operated a boys' boarding school at his home from 1847 to 1877, while his sisters operated a girls' school at nearby Thorndale. In the late 1800s,

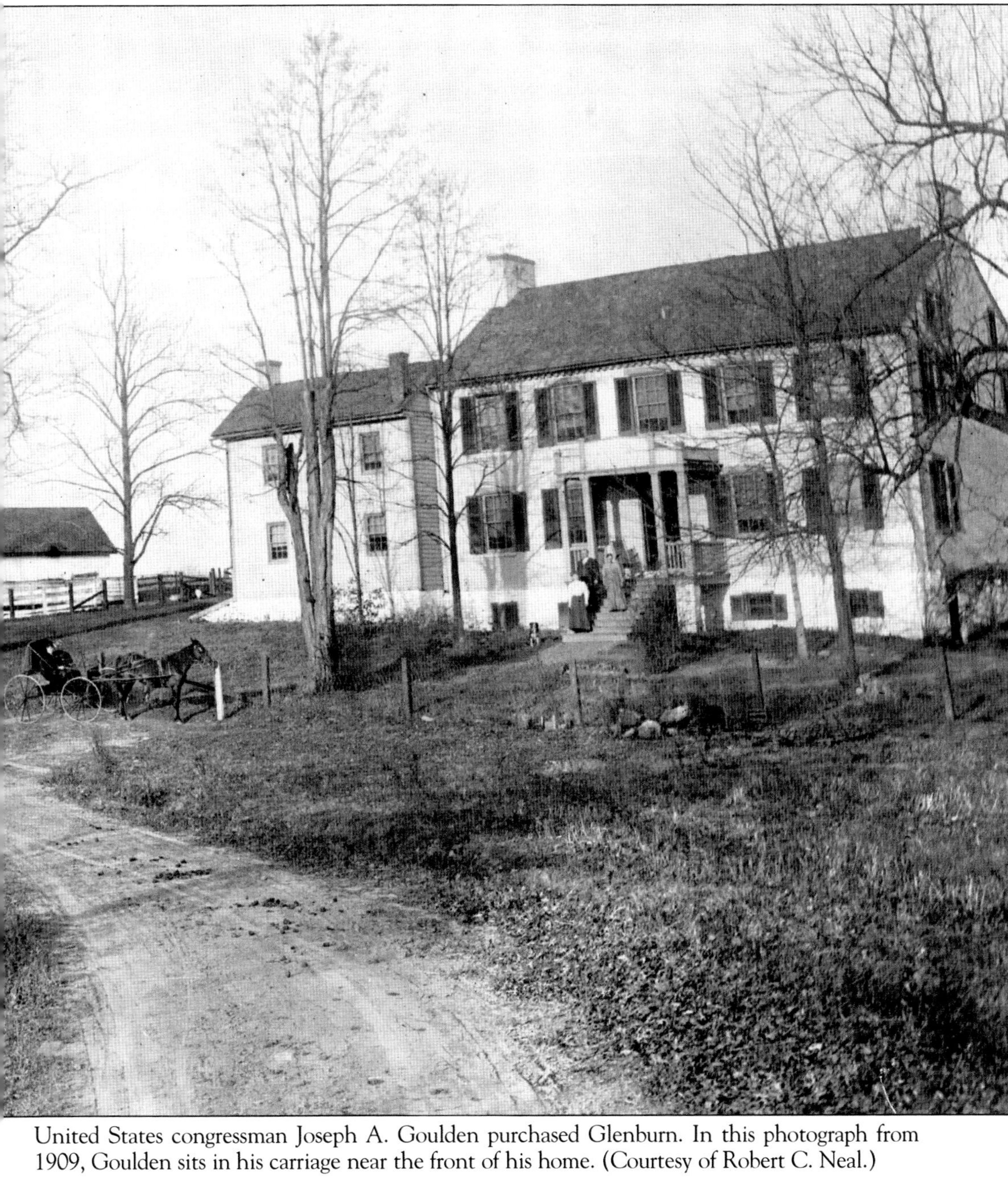

United States congressman Joseph A. Goulden purchased Glenburn. In this photograph from 1909, Goulden sits in his carriage near the front of his home. (Courtesy of Robert C. Neal.)

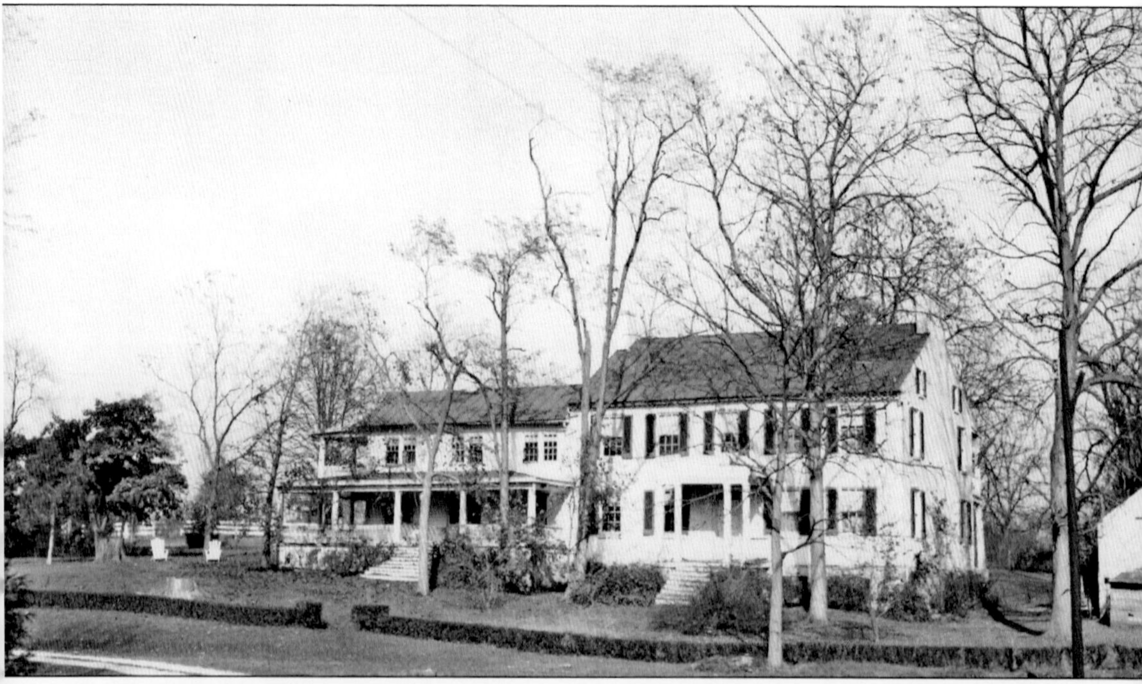

Situated along the banks of Bear Branch, Glenburn was purchased in 1937 by Chester and Gippie Neal of Kentucky. Currently owned by their son, Glenburn has the distinction of being Carroll County's first bed and breakfast, opened in 1983. (Courtesy of the Historical Society of Carroll County.)

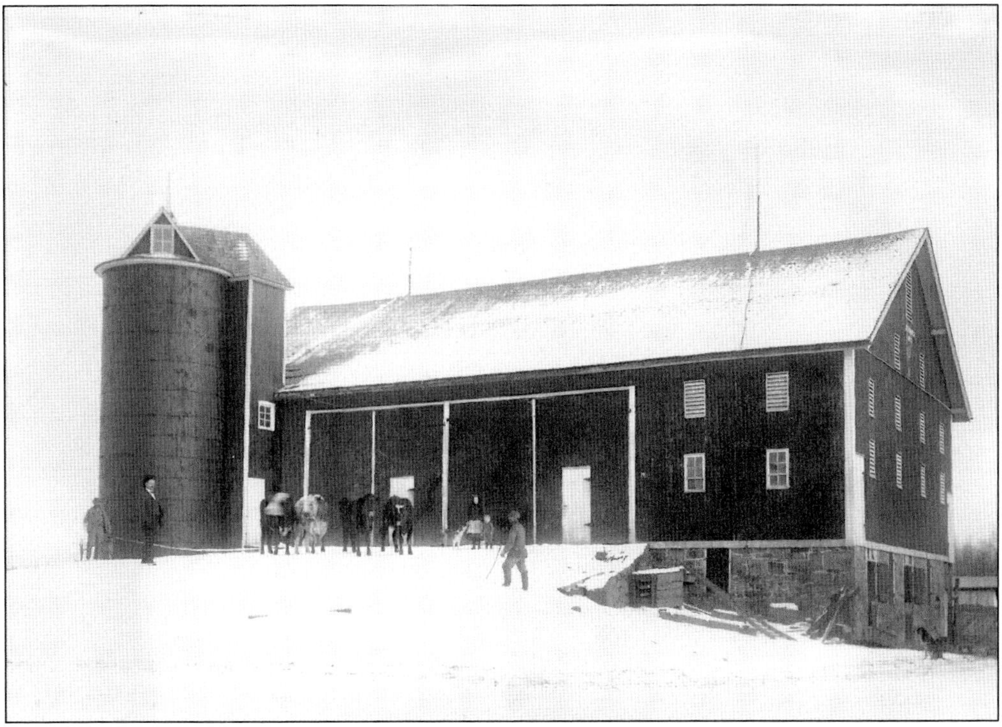

The barn of J. Haines, built about 1870, is covered with a dusting of snow in this early 20th century photograph. (Courtesy of Michael and Susan Reifsnider.)

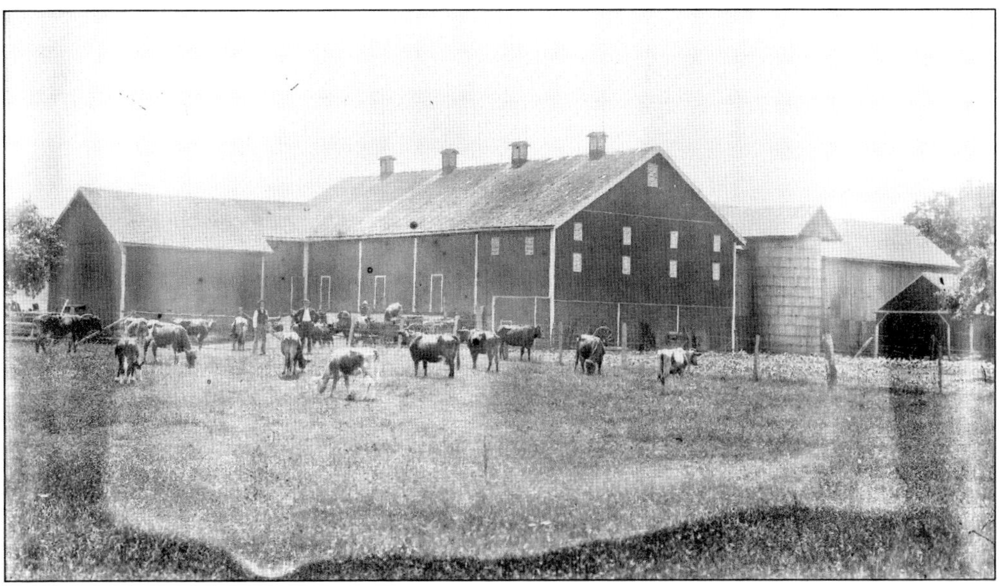

Cattle graze in the pasture near the barn on the farm of E.E. Reindollar. The farm was later purchased by the Sauble family and housed their famous inn. (Courtesy of Michael and Susan Reifsnider.)

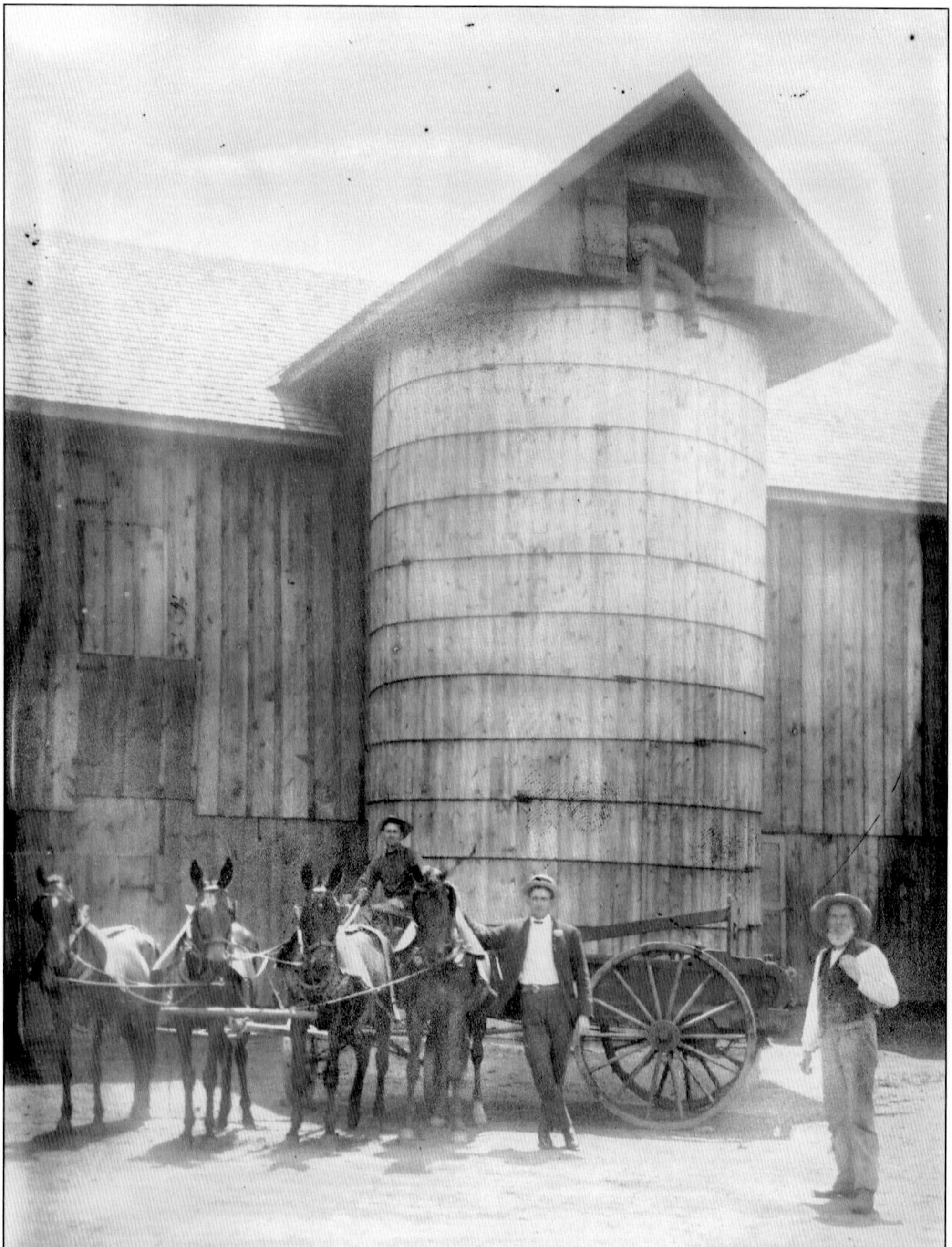

Three gentlemen with horse and wagon pose for a photograph in front of the wooden silo at the Reindollar farm in the early 1900s. Note the brave young man perched atop the silo dangling his feet. (Courtesy of Michael and Susan Reifsnider.)

Four

HOUSES OF WORSHIP

When landowners Edward Diggs and Raphael Taney began laying out the town, they set aside certain lots dedicated to religious purposes. Taney, a Catholic, devoted Lot 87 to the construction of a Lutheran church and Lot 88 for a church of his own faith. The many Germans, who migrated from Pennsylvania, established Lutheran and Reformed churches. In Taneytown, as in other communities, these two congregations shared the same building for a time. The Roman Catholic faith arrived by way of Jesuits from Conewago, Pennsylvania. The Scotch-Irish settlers brought Presbyterianism and established their church at Piney Creek.

Clearly, religion has played an important role in the lives of the people of Taneytown since its founding. Even today, Taneytown contains several flourishing churches that minister to the spiritual needs of their congregations.

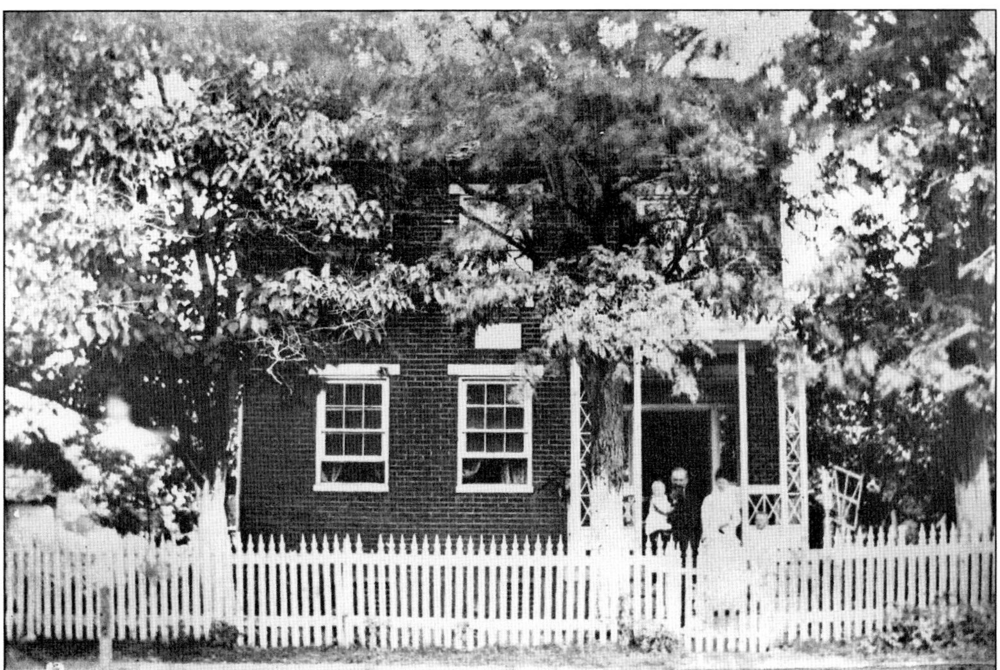

In the 1880s, Rev. P. Allison Long and his wife Araminta posed for a photograph at the old parsonage of the Reformed church. (Courtesy of the Historical Society of Carroll County.)

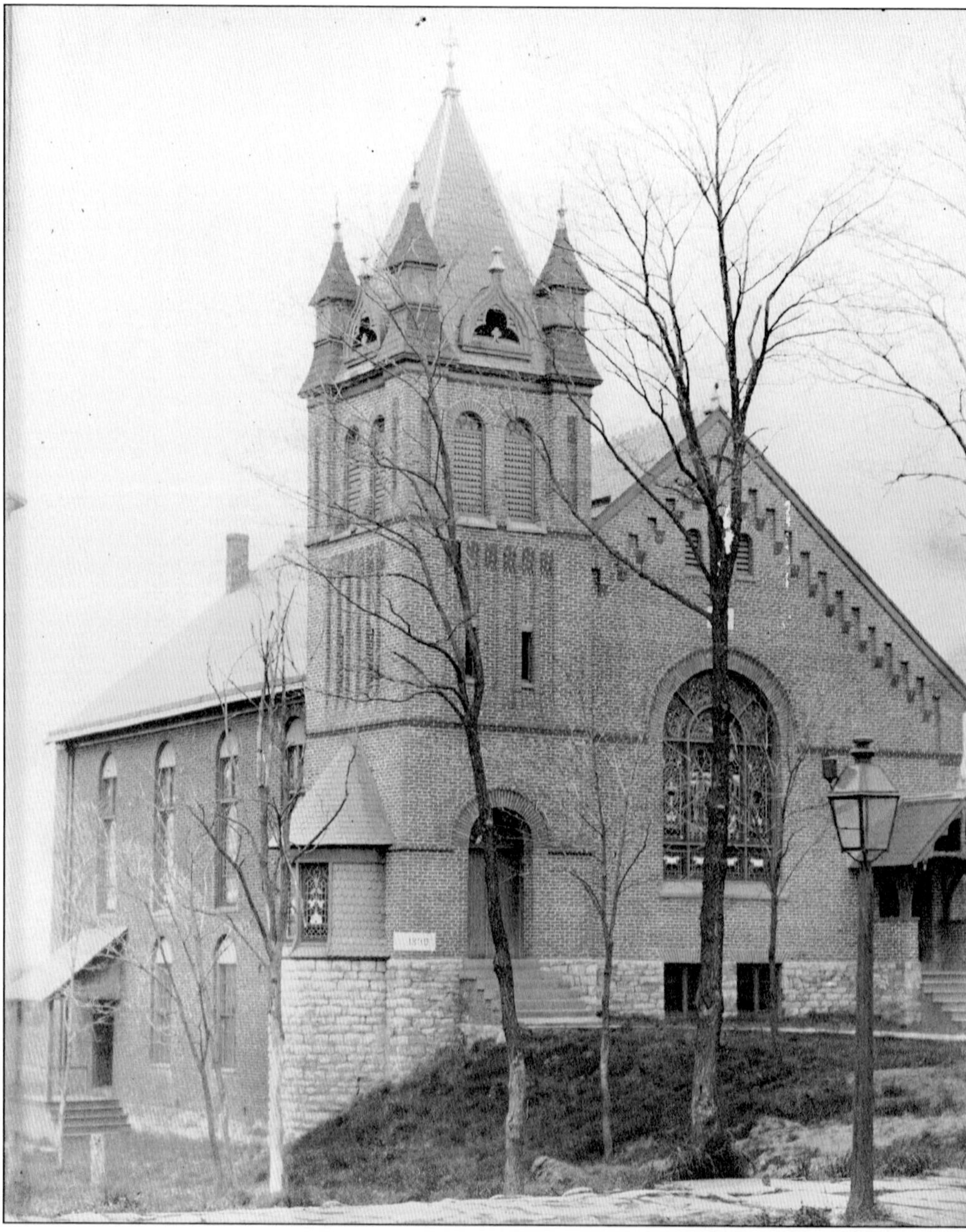

Grace United Church of Christ traces its origins back to the mid-1700s, when Rev. Michael Schlatter, an itinerant Reformed pastor, is believed to have organized the first congregation in Taneytown. The original church building, referred to as the "Old Yellow Church," was constructed in the 1760s and was located in what is now the Reformed cemetery. The present church was erected between 1820 and 1822, at a cost of $3,500. The church was renovated in 1890; this Victorian makeover produced its distinctive bell tower. (Courtesy of the Historical Society of Carroll County.)

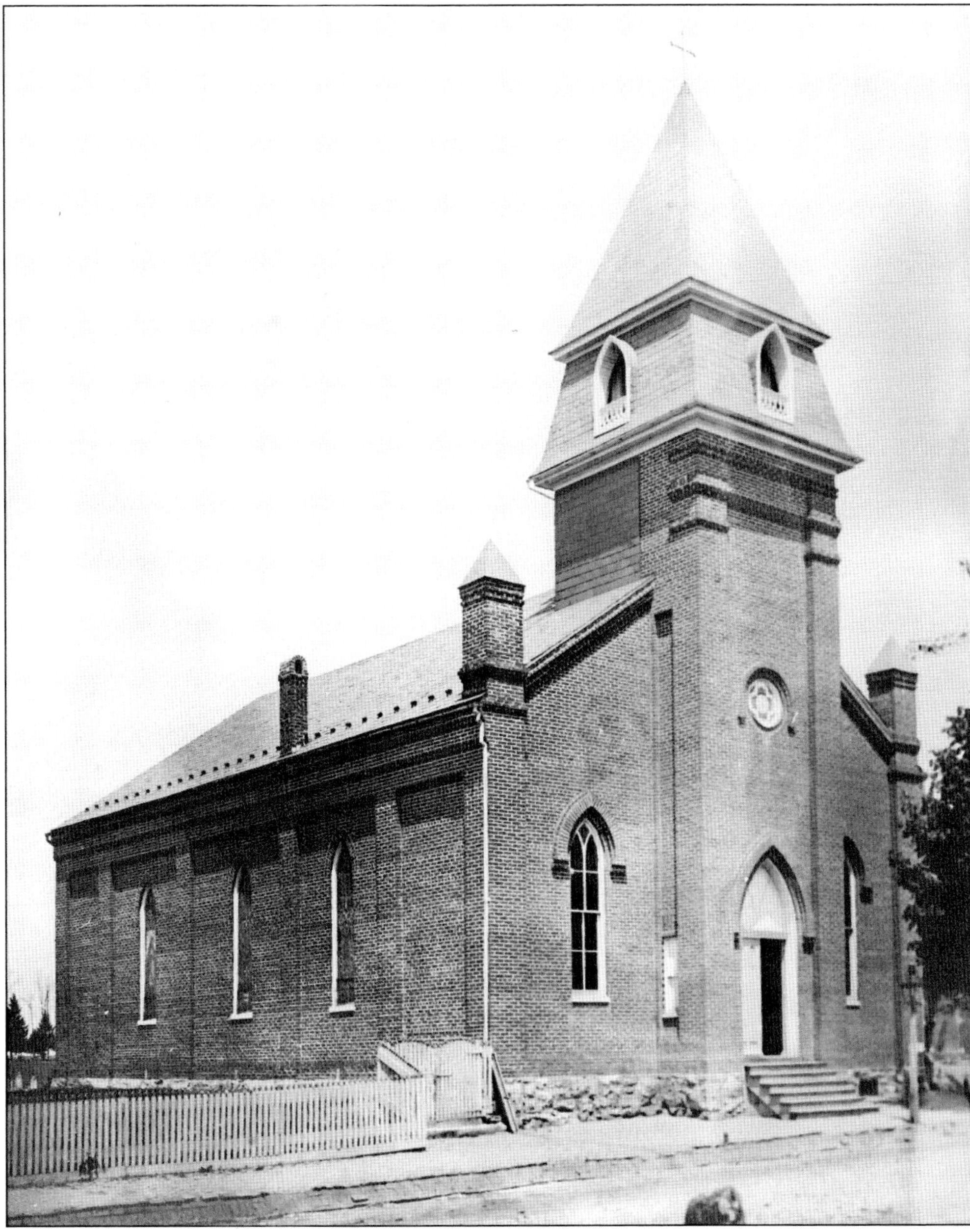

St. Joseph's Roman Catholic Church on Frederick Street was founded in 1797; however mass had been celebrated in private homes for some years prior. Mr. Brooks built the original church at his own expense using locally made bricks. The present church was constructed in 1876. Among the church's records can be found the entry recording the 1806 marriage of future Supreme Court chief justice Roger Brook Taney to Ann Key, sister of Francis Scott Key of nearby Terra Rubra. (Courtesy of the Historical Society of Carroll County.)

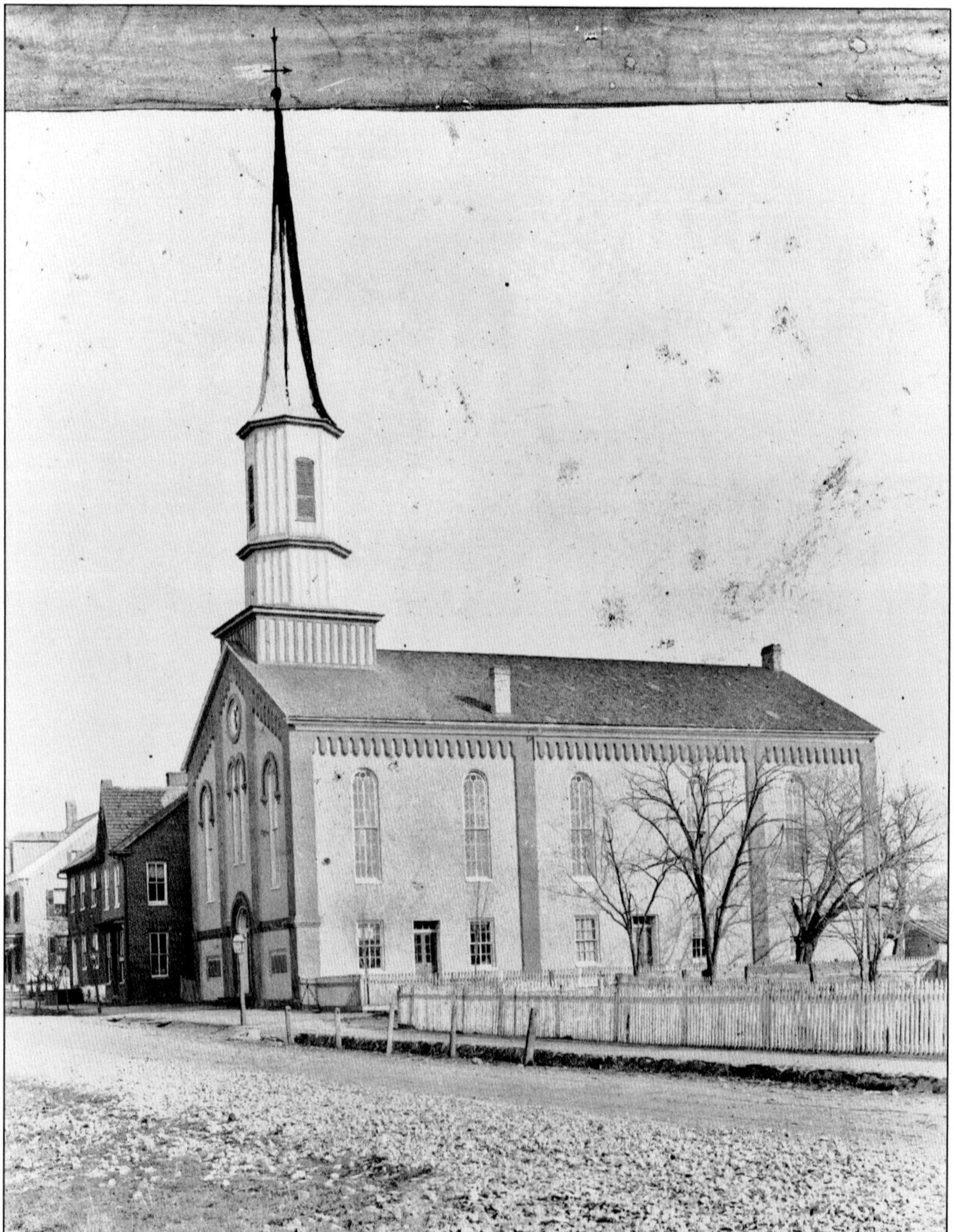

The congregation of Trinity Evangelical Lutheran Church is believed to have been organized about 1750. After sharing a building with the Reformed congregation, the Lutherans erected their own church between 1811 and 1813. The church was renovated three times in the 19th century. This photograph shows the church as it appeared from 1871 to 1896. Local legend has it that union troops used the tower to observe troop movements prior to the battle of Gettysburg. (Courtesy of the Historical Society of Carroll County.)

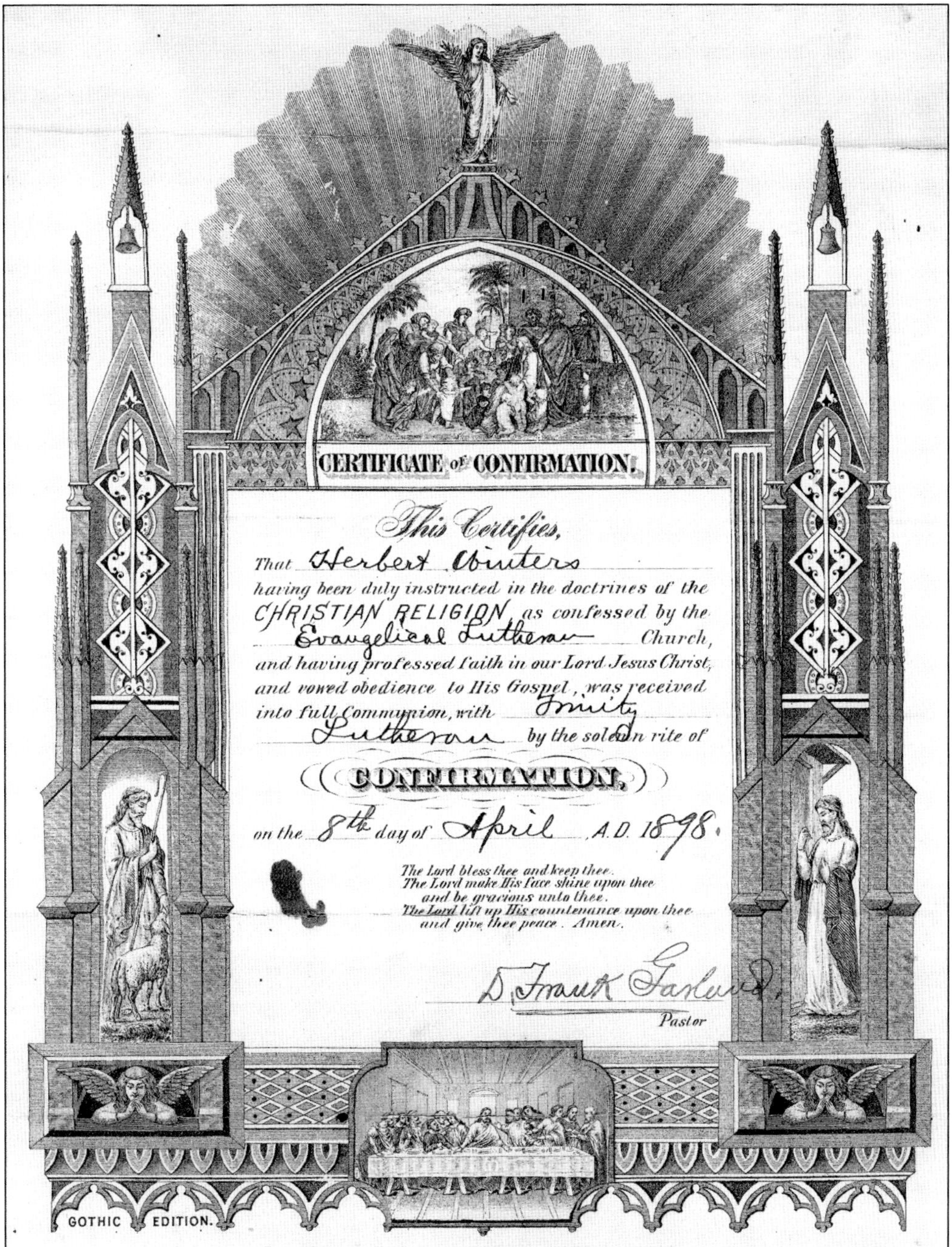
CERTIFICATE OF CONFIRMATION.

This Certifies,

That Herbert Winters

having been duly instructed in the doctrines of the CHRISTIAN RELIGION, as confessed by the Evangelical Lutheran Church, and having professed faith in our Lord Jesus Christ, and vowed obedience to His Gospel, was received into full Communion, with Trinity Lutheran by the solemn rite of

CONFIRMATION,

on the 8th day of April A.D. 1898.

The Lord bless thee and keep thee.
The Lord make His face shine upon thee and be gracious unto thee.
The Lord lift up His countenance upon thee and give thee peace. Amen.

D. Frank Garland
Pastor

GOTHIC EDITION.

Published by J. E. Stohlmann, No. 458 Pearl Str. New York.

Shown above is a confirmation certificate from Trinity Evangelical Lutheran Church from 1898. (Courtesy of the Historical Society of Carroll County.)

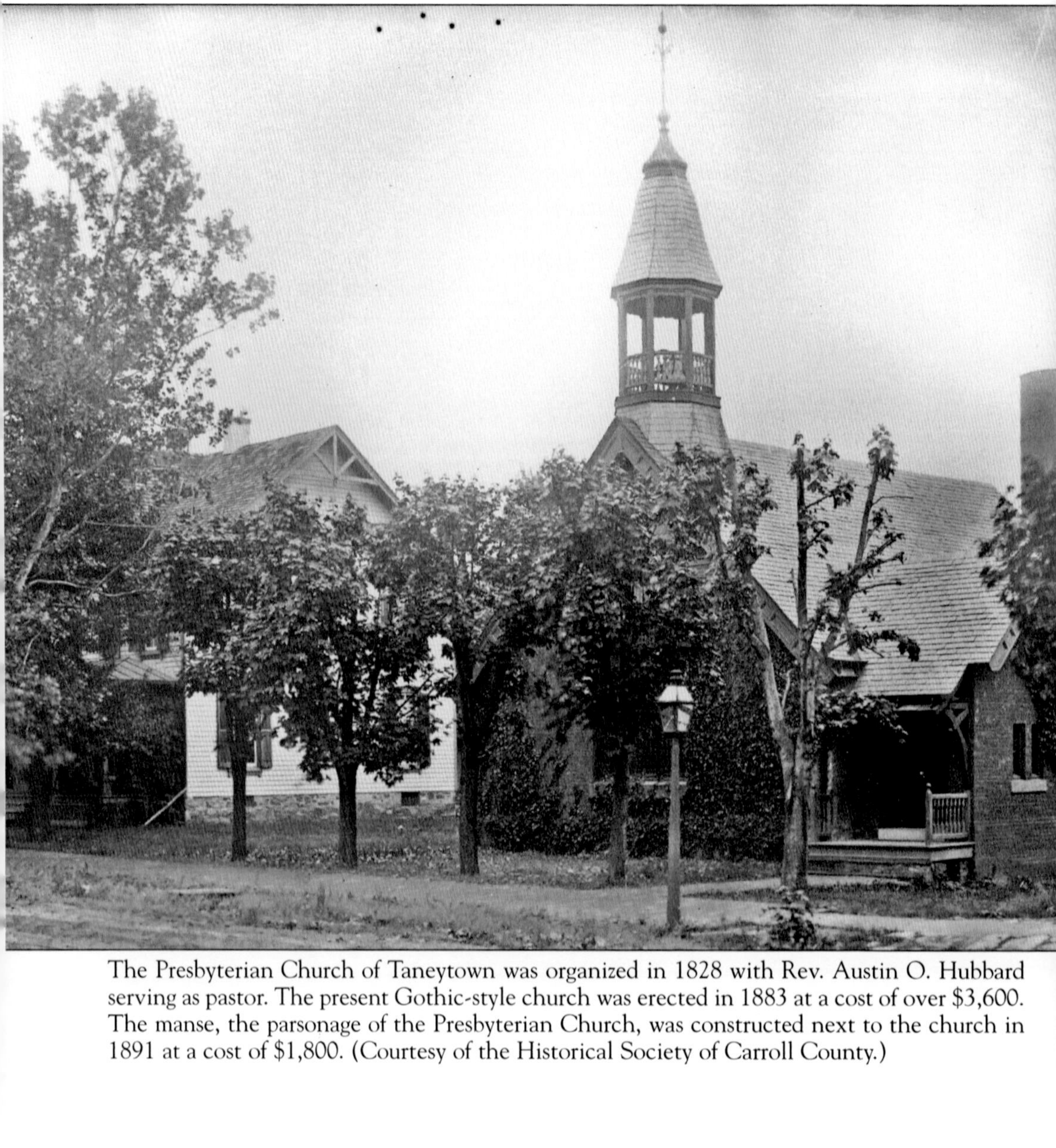

The Presbyterian Church of Taneytown was organized in 1828 with Rev. Austin O. Hubbard serving as pastor. The present Gothic-style church was erected in 1883 at a cost of over $3,600. The manse, the parsonage of the Presbyterian Church, was constructed next to the church in 1891 at a cost of $1,800. (Courtesy of the Historical Society of Carroll County.)

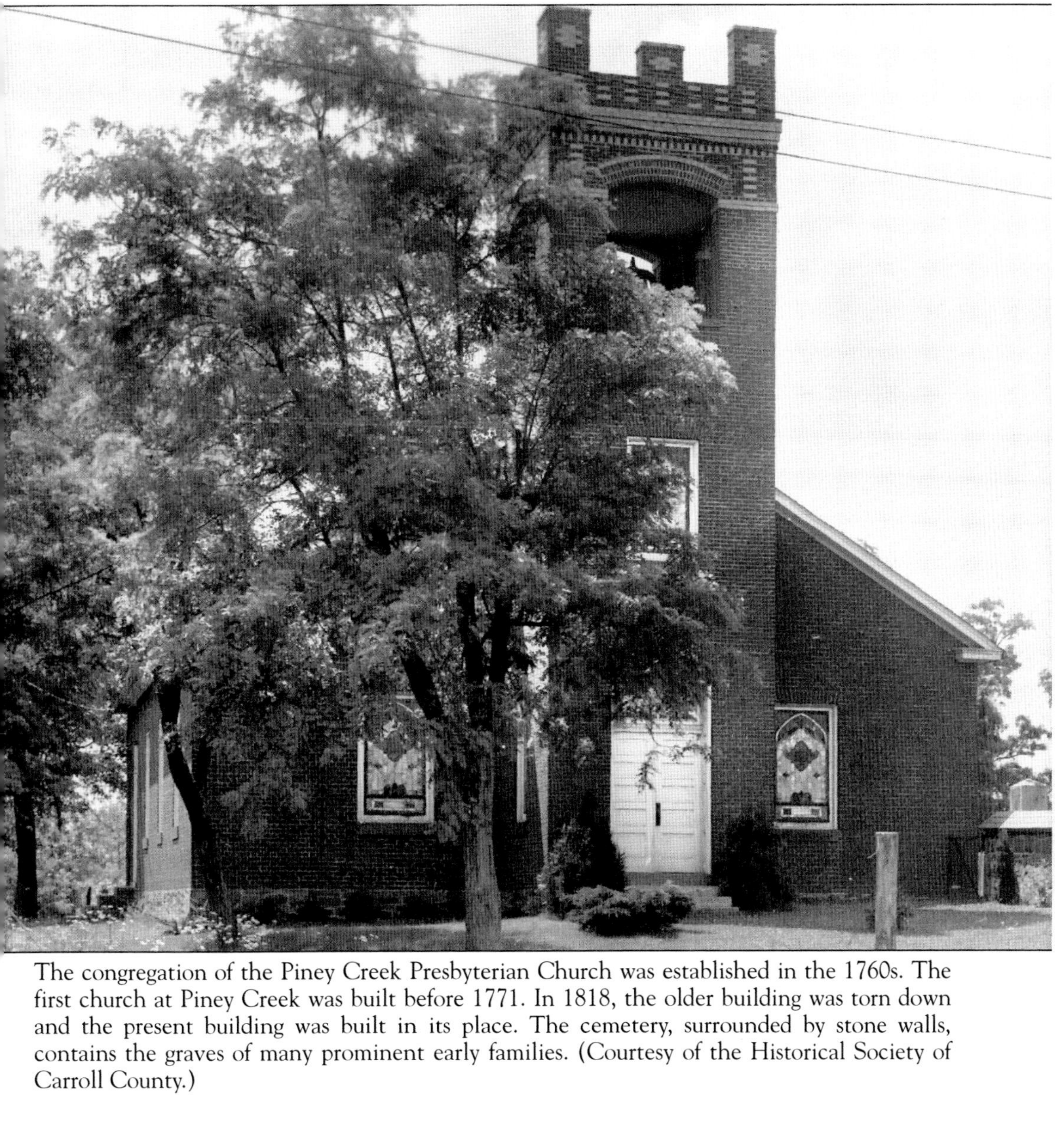

The congregation of the Piney Creek Presbyterian Church was established in the 1760s. The first church at Piney Creek was built before 1771. In 1818, the older building was torn down and the present building was built in its place. The cemetery, surrounded by stone walls, contains the graves of many prominent early families. (Courtesy of the Historical Society of Carroll County.)

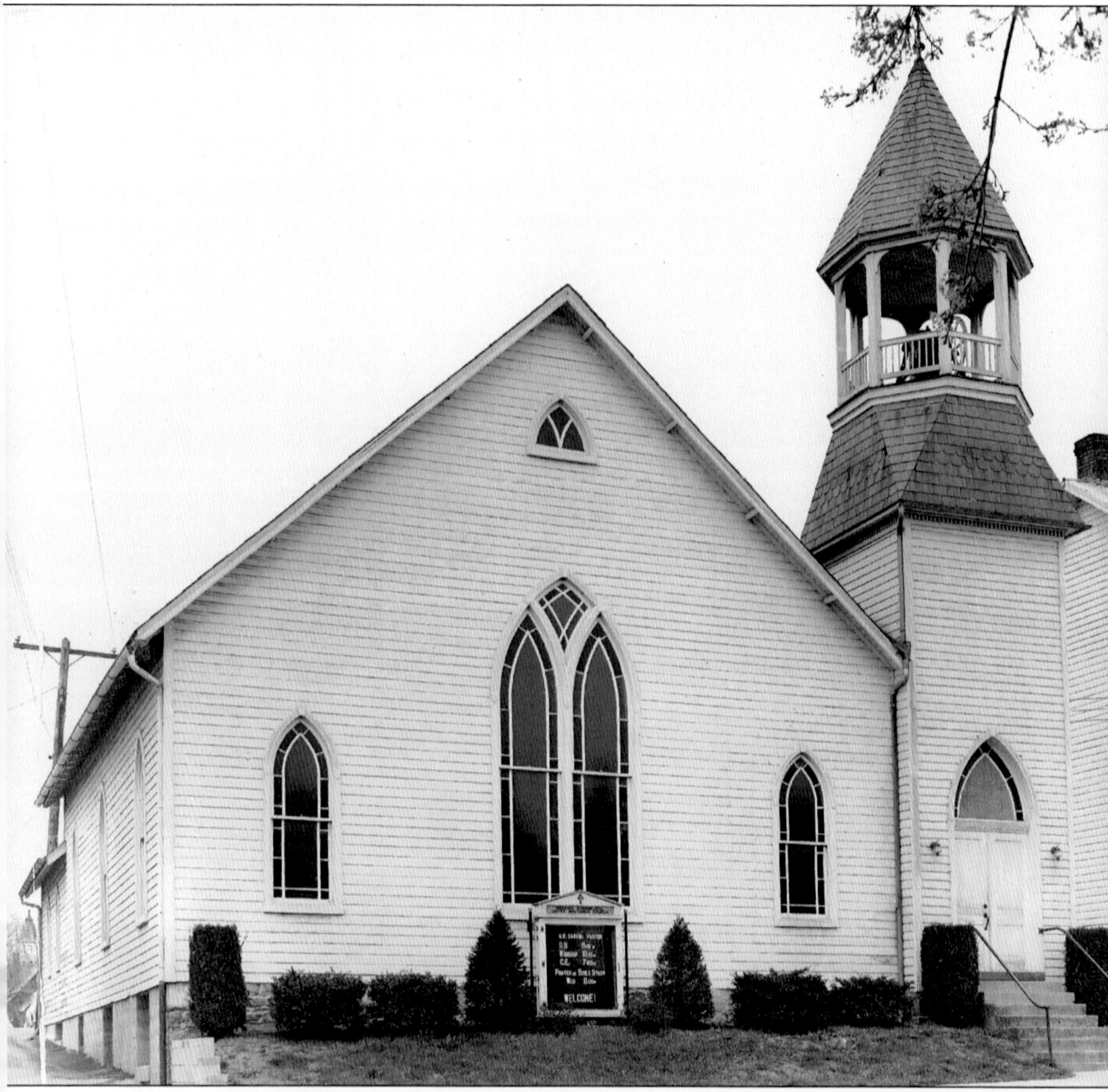

Messiah United Methodist Church was begun in the mid-1800s as the Mount Pleasant United Brethren Church. The church, which was located on Old Westminster Road, was constructed between 1851 and 1852. However, the congregation relocated to Taneytown and constructed the present church in 1894 at a cost of $2,200. (Courtesy of the Clem family.)

Five

THE TOWNSFOLK

What would a town be without its citizens? Simply a bunch of buildings and streets. The people are the lifeblood of every community, and Taneytown is no exception. For the past two-and-a-half centuries, many real people have lived here, experiencing aspects of life just as we do today. From the well-known and wealthy to the everyday working man, they have all had a hand in shaping the history and identity of Taneytown.

The individuals featured in the following chapter range from decorated war heroes to bouncing babies. They represent merely a slice of the many interesting, diverse, and memorable personalities who have called this place home.

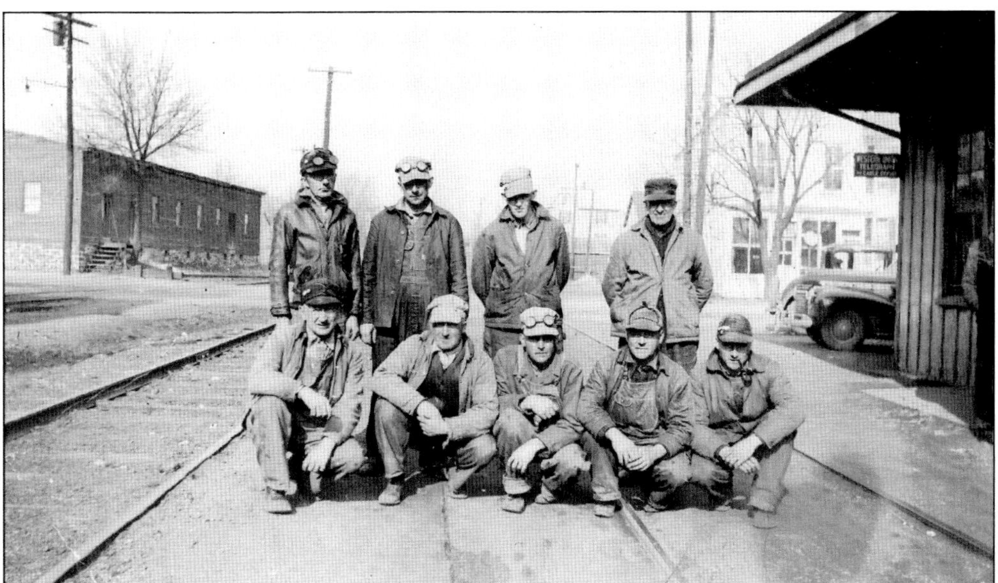

"The Railroad Gang" poses for a picture near the station in the 1930s. (Courtesy of the Clem family.)

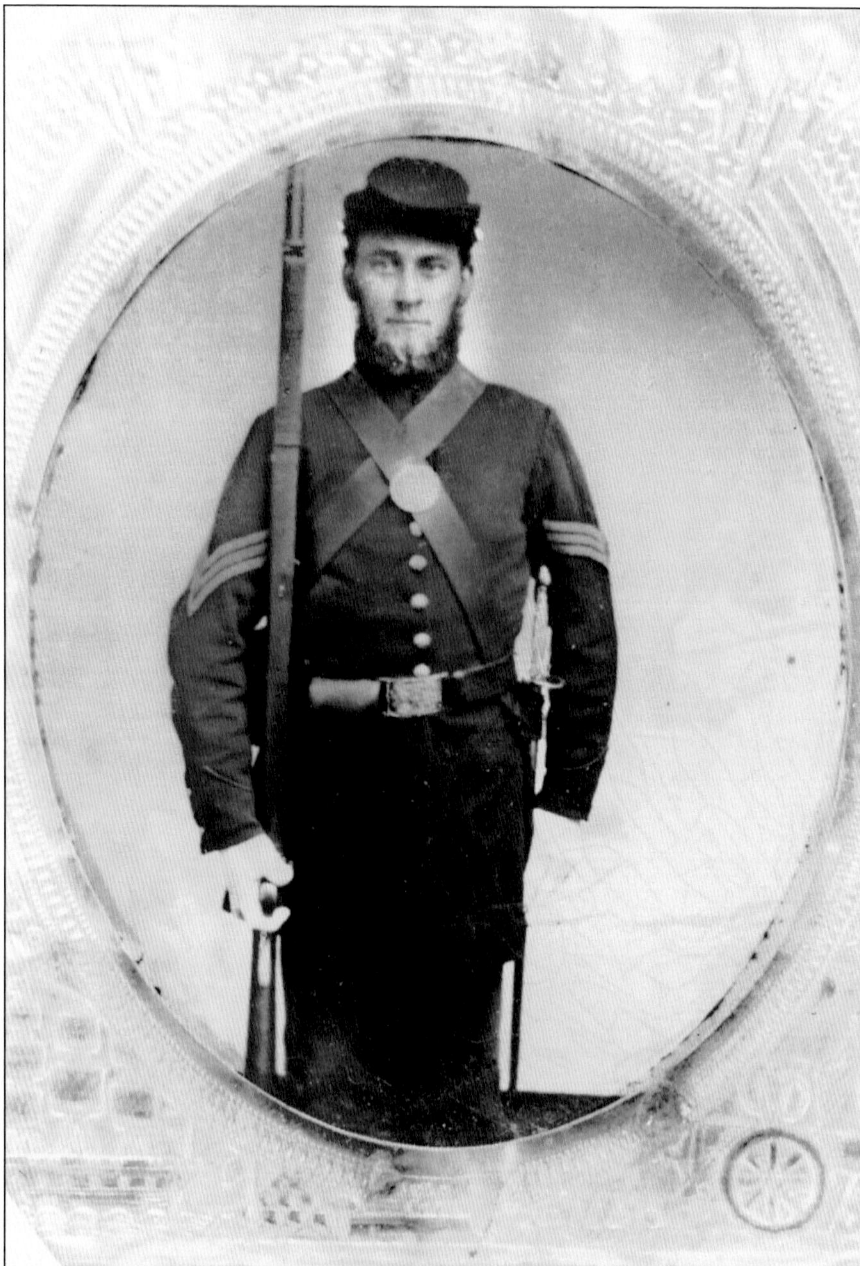

Sgt. John E. Buffington was born near Taneytown in 1841. With the outbreak of the Civil War, he enlisted to fight for the Union with Company C, Sixth Regiment, Maryland Volunteer Infantry. At the battle of Petersburg, Virginia, Buffington bravely pushed forward in the face of the enemy to become the first enlisted man of the Third Division to mount the parapet of the enemy's lines on April 2, 1865. For his gallantry, Buffington was awarded a cash prize by General Grant and the Congressional Medal of Honor for bravery in battle. However, because of his modesty, Sergeant Buffington never applied for the medal. It was not until 1908 that he finally received his long overdue award in a gala ceremony at the Taneytown Opera House. (Courtesy of Barry Garner.)

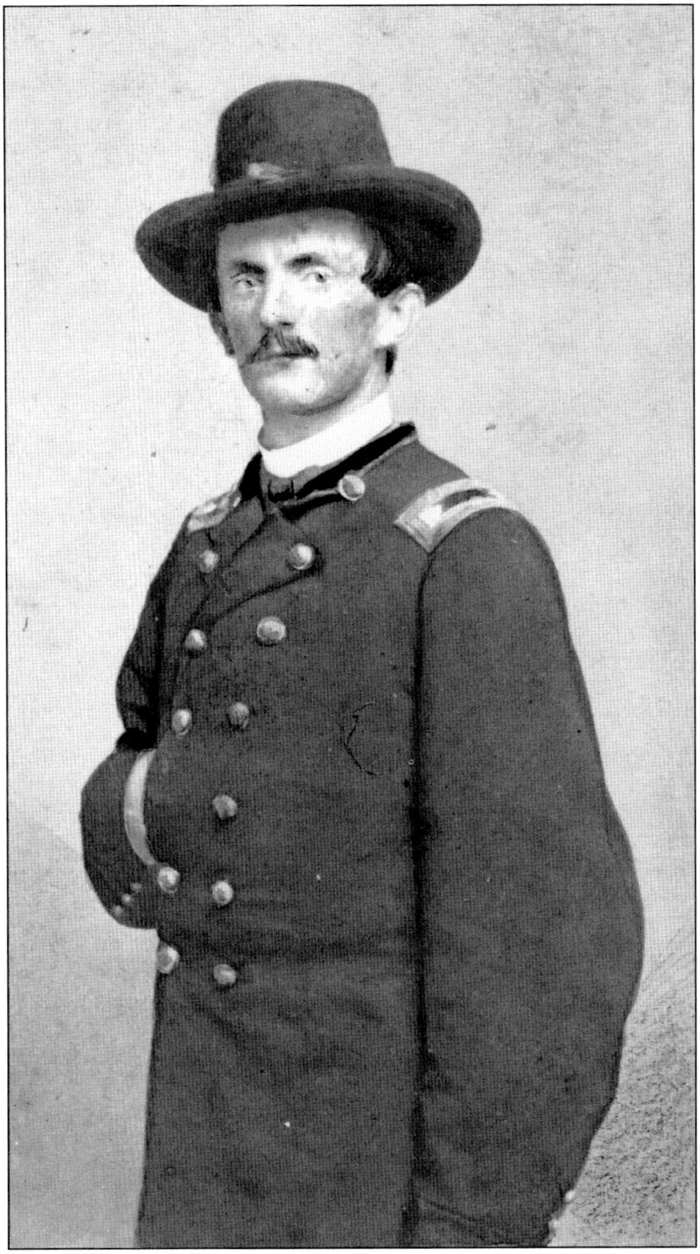

A native of Taneytown, William A. McKellip recruited and formed Company A, Sixth Regiment Infantry, Maryland Volunteers in 1862. He was commissioned a lieutenant and advanced quickly to captain, major, and finally lieutenant colonel of the Sixth Regiment. In 1862, the regiment that Colonel McKellip was temporarily commanding was in desperate need of arms. He went directly to Washington and obtained an interview with President Lincoln. The result was a note written on the back of the President's personal card: "Secretary of War: Please give bearer, Major McKellip, of the 6th Maryland Regiment, the best arms possible and oblige. A. LINCOLN." Colonel McKellip kept the card for many years afterward. In 1902, President Theodore Roosevelt appointed him consul to Madgeburg, Germany. He died at his post in 1904. (Courtesy of the Historical Society of Carroll County.)

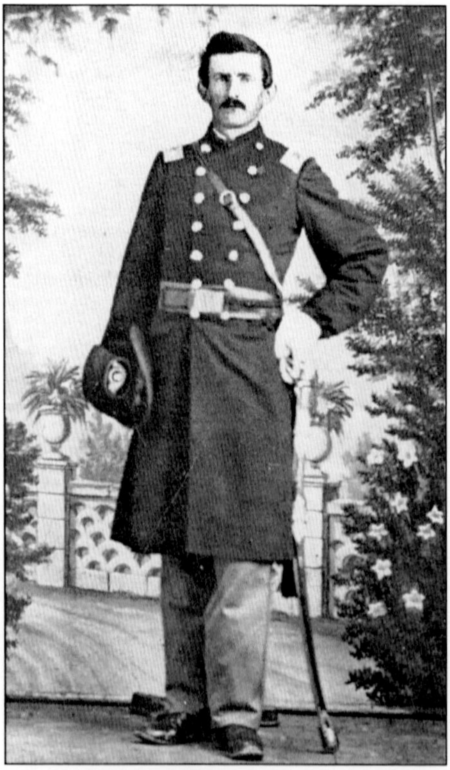

Shown here is a carte de visite of Colonel McKellip from the Civil War era. (Courtesy of the Historical Society of Carroll County.)

This ambrotype of the Sixth Regiment, Maryland Volunteer Infantry was probably taken at the Regiment's Virginia headquarters, c. 1863. Colonel McKellip stands in the central doorway. (Courtesy of the Historical Society of Carroll County.)

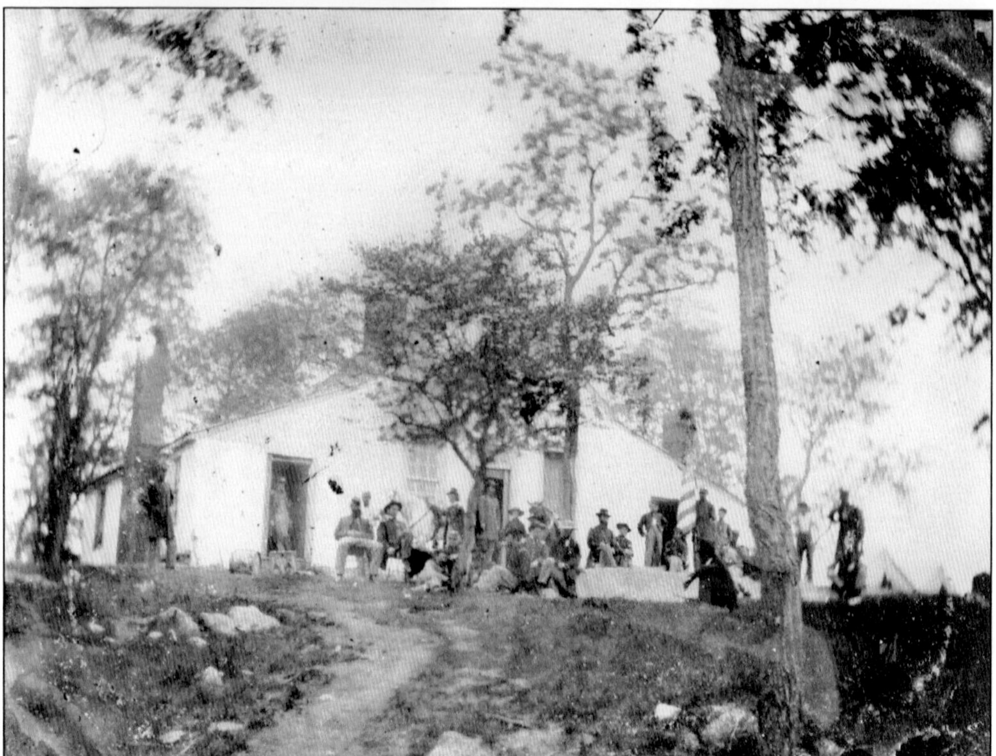

This is a cabinet card of William A. McKellip, c. 1880. (Courtesy of the Historical Society of Carroll County.)

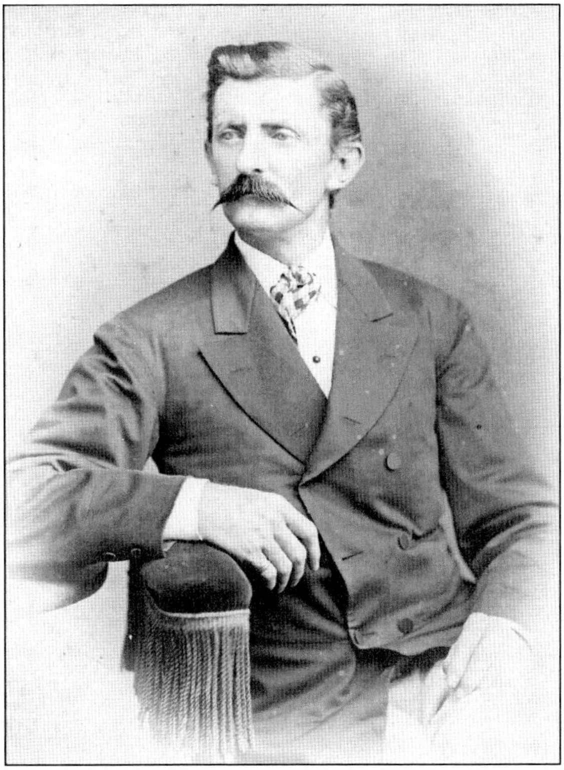

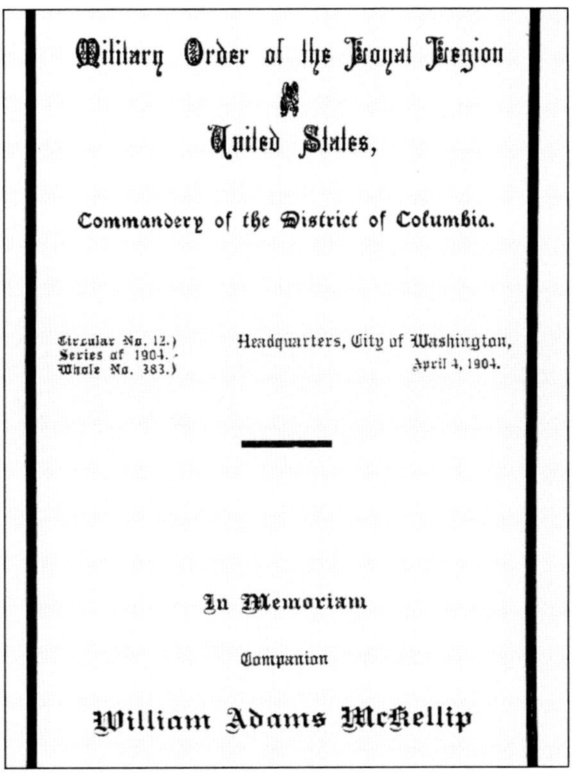

Military Order of the Loyal Legion of the United States,

Commandery of the District of Columbia.

Circular No. 12.)
Series of 1904.
Whole No. 383.)

Headquarters, City of Washington,
April 4, 1904.

In Memoriam

Companion

William Adams McKellip

At left is the funeral circular of Colonel McKellip from 1904. (Courtesy of the Historical Society of Carroll County.)

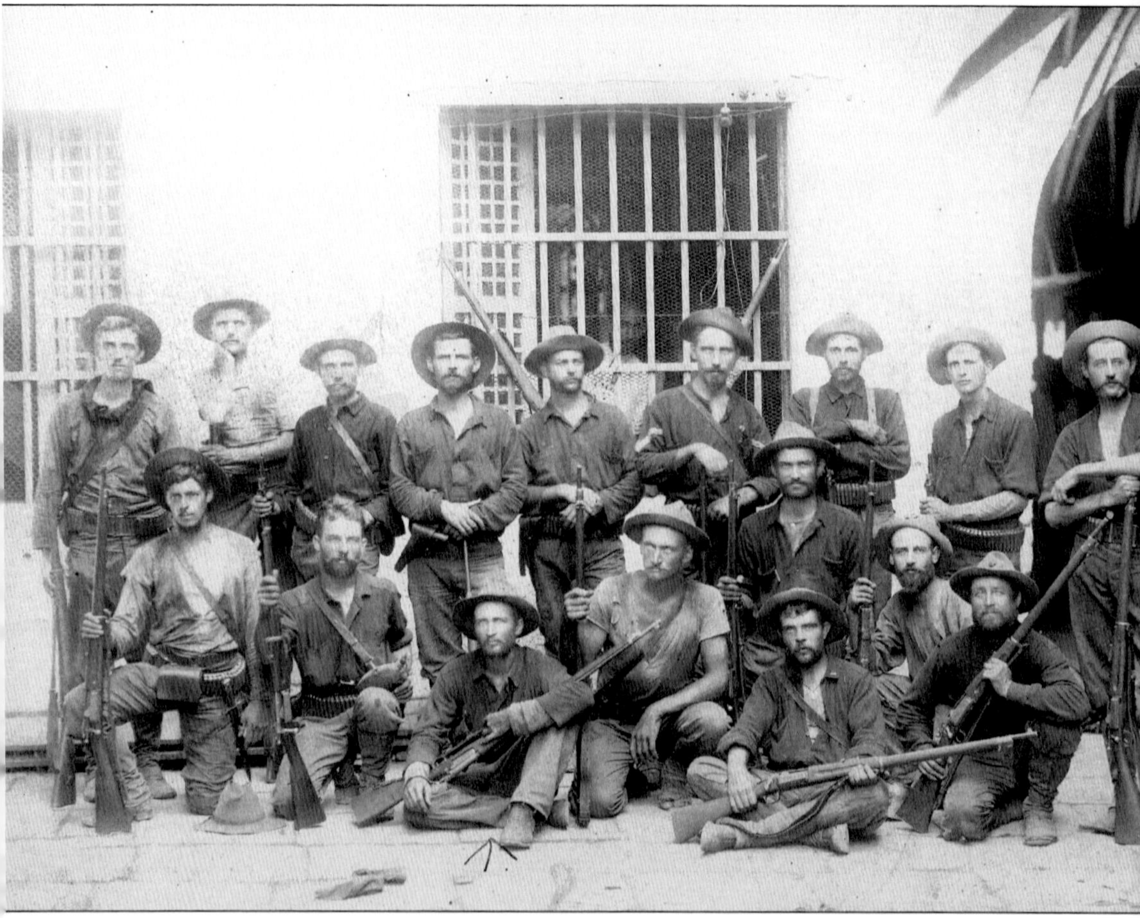

Sterling Archibald Galt (seated third from left), a Taneytown native, was a hero of the Spanish-American War. On November 9, 1899, while in the Philippine Islands, Galt swam across the Pampanga River with a rope held between his teeth. Upon reaching the far shore, he tied the rope to a tree. Galt then guided his fellow soldiers and officers across the river to safety while under crossfire from the enemy. He received the Congressional Medal of Honor on April 30, 1902, for "Distinguished Bravery and Conspicuous Gallantry in Action against Insurgents." (Courtesy of the Historical Society of Carroll County.)

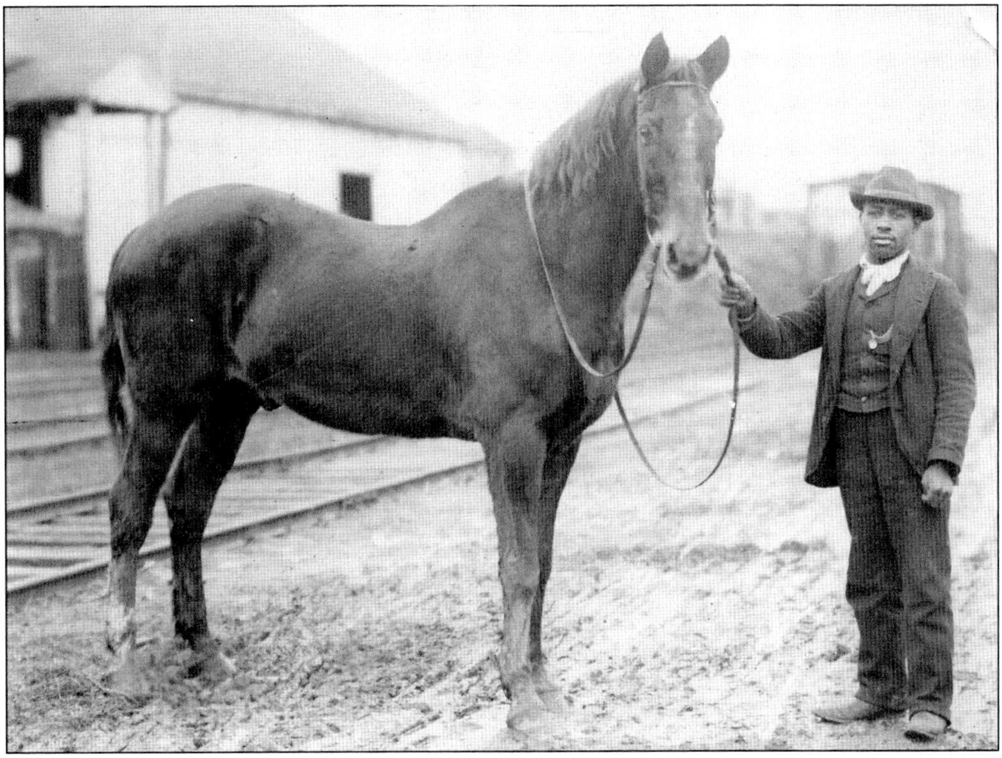

James Fennel Hill tends to Dr. Clotworthy Birnie's horse, Pat, *c.* 1915. (Courtesy of Ginny Henderson.)

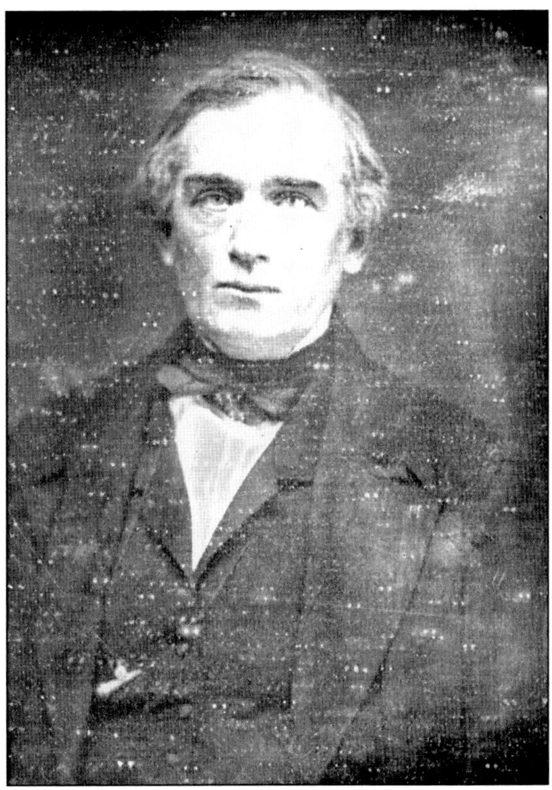

Judge John Thomas of Taneytown dedicated the Carroll County Court House in Westminster in 1838. This daguerreotype of the judge dates from the mid-19th century. (Courtesy of the Historical Society of Carroll County.)

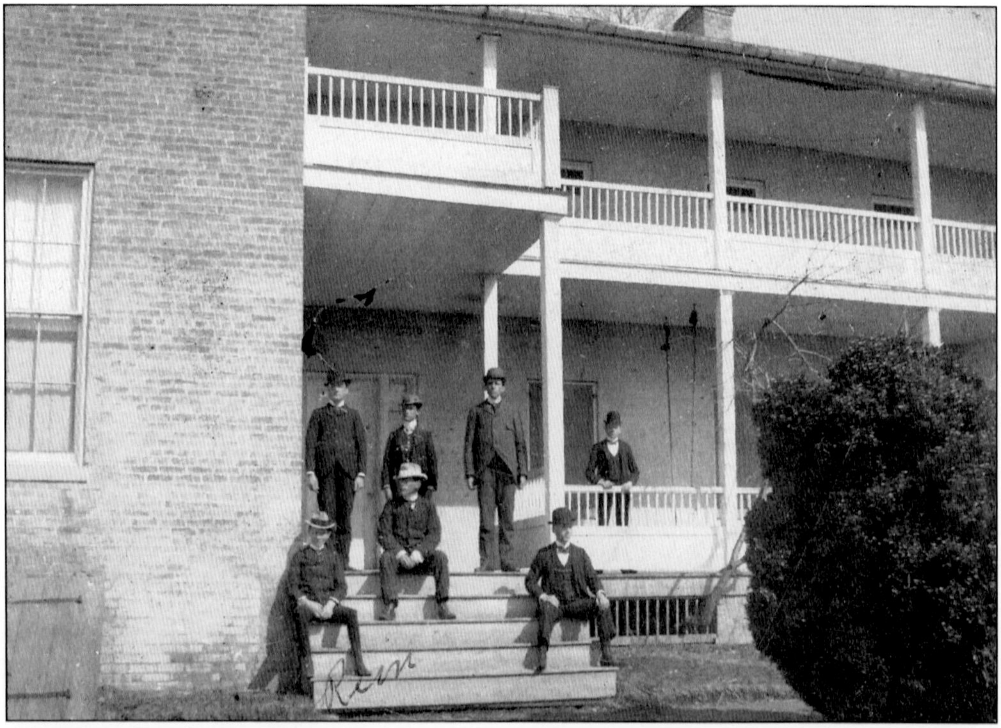

A group of smartly dressed gentlemen pose for a picture on the west-side porch of Antrim, *c.* 1900. Rein Motter is seated at left. (Courtesy of George and Anna Motter.)

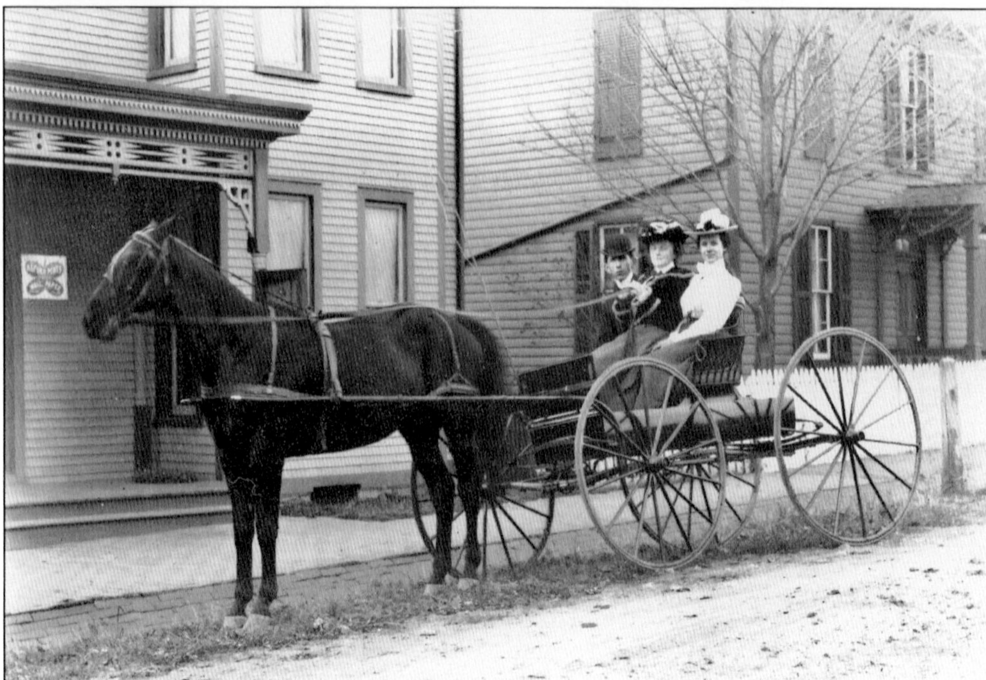

The Eline family sits in their carriage on George Street in the early 1900s. (Courtesy of Michael and Susan Reifsnider.)

James "Jimmy" Baumgardner stands on the steps of his restaurant at the Central Hotel in the 1940s. (Courtesy of Jean Brown.)

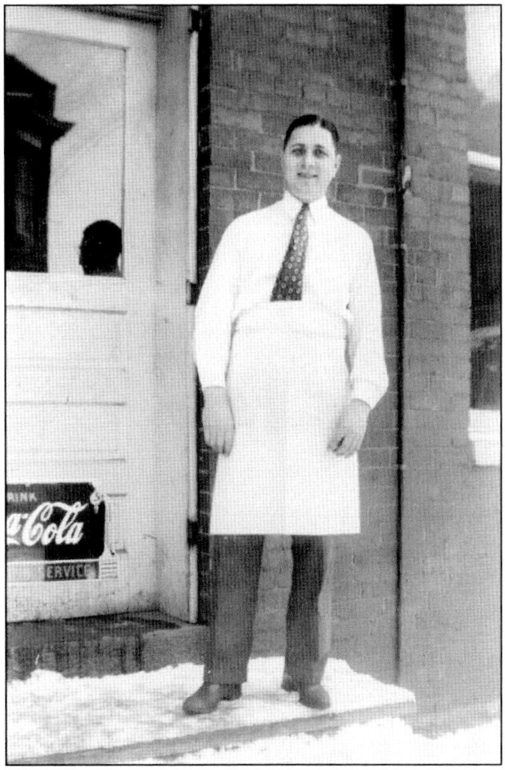

Joseph "Joe" Hill shovels coal at the Nusbaum Canning Company in 1946. (Courtesy of Joe Hill.)

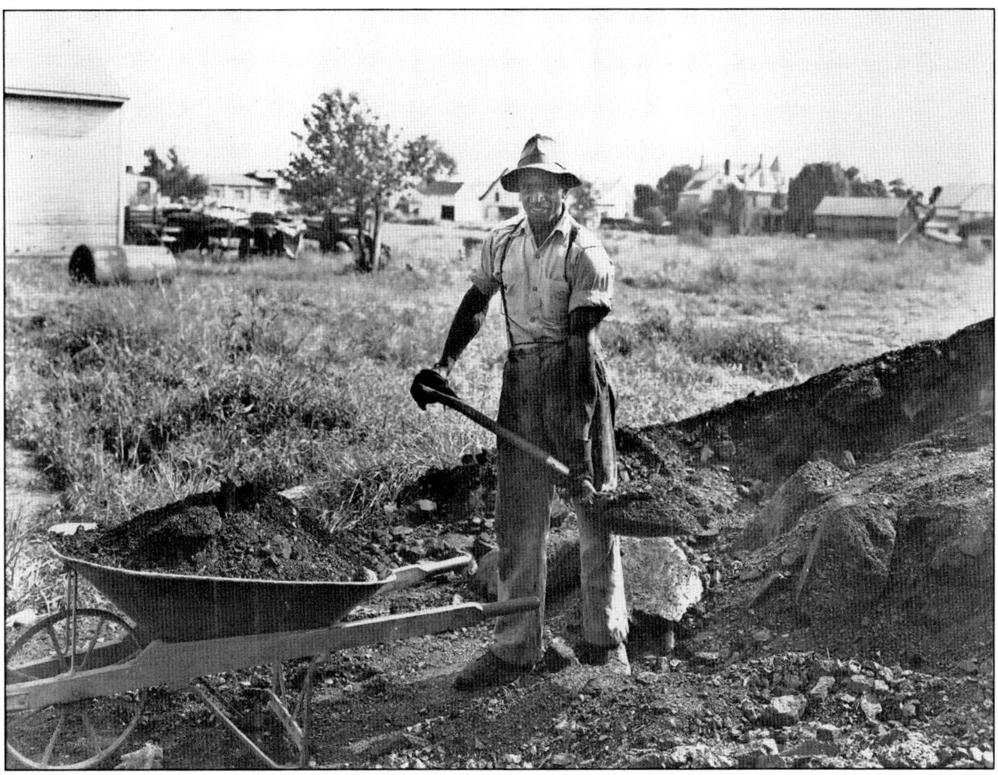

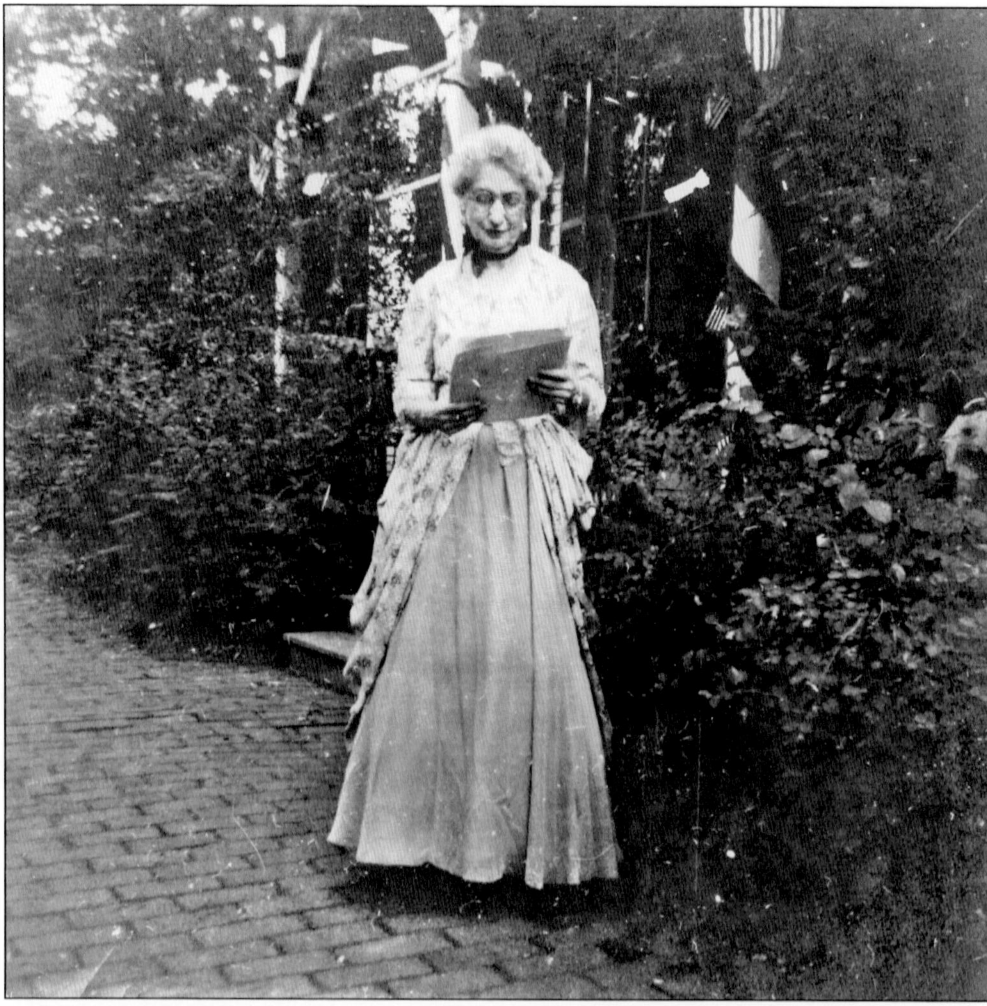

Amelia and Elizabeth Annan, descendants of the Birnie family, were actively involved in Taneytown's bicentennial celebration in 1954. They served as chairmen of the historical committee and also hosted a fashion show in their garden. Elizabeth Annan, pictured here in 1954, authored an official history of Taneytown. (Courtesy of the Historical Society of Carroll County.)

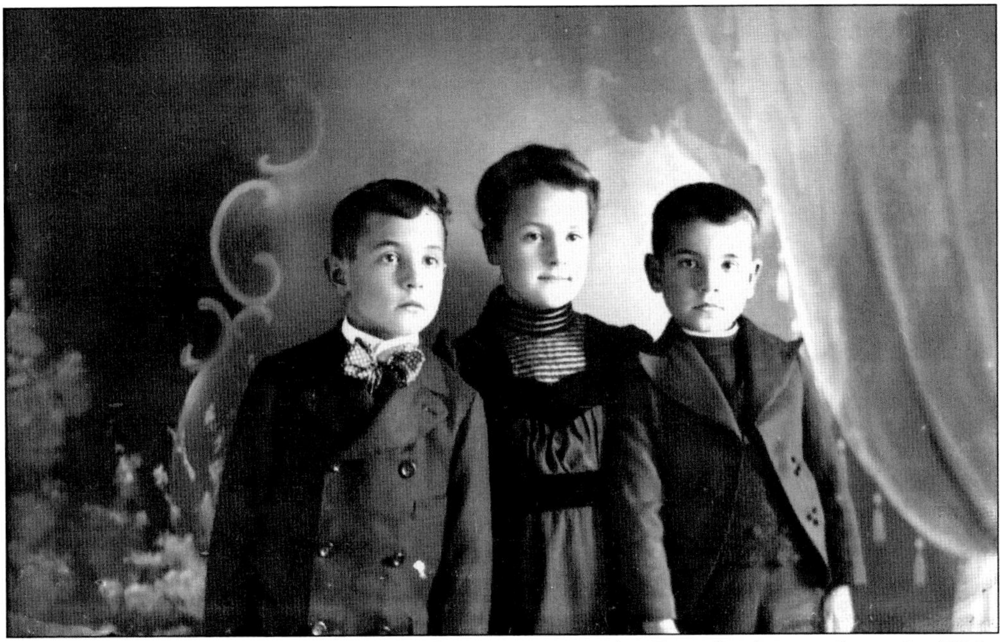

Harry, Grace, and Lester Witherow sit for a portrait at the Zepp Studios in the early 1900s. (Courtesy of Michael and Susan Reifsnider.)

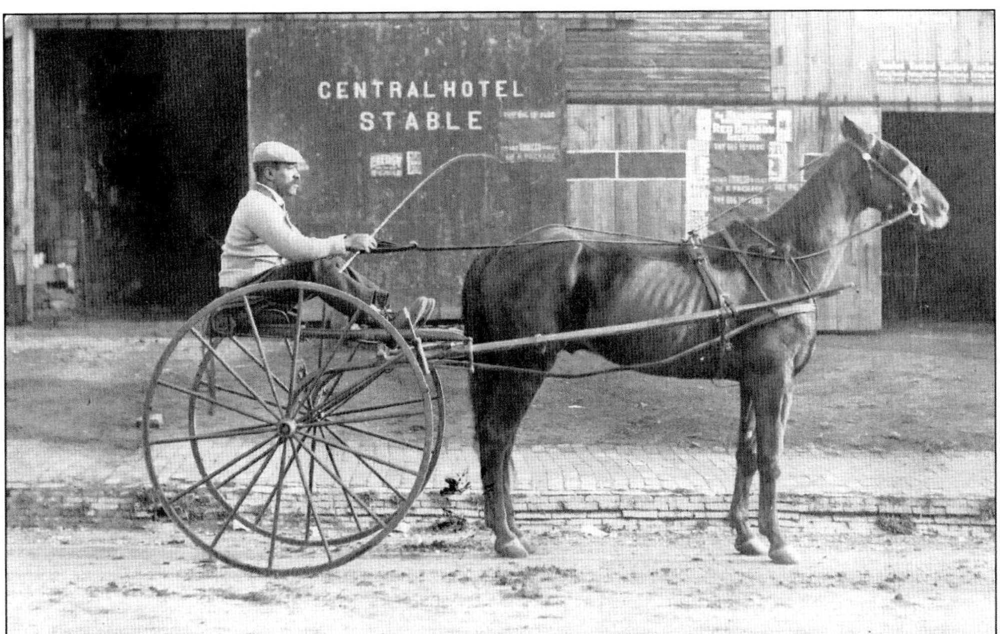

Burrier Hill drives a sulky in front of the Central Hotel Stable in 1909. (Courtesy of Joe Hill.)

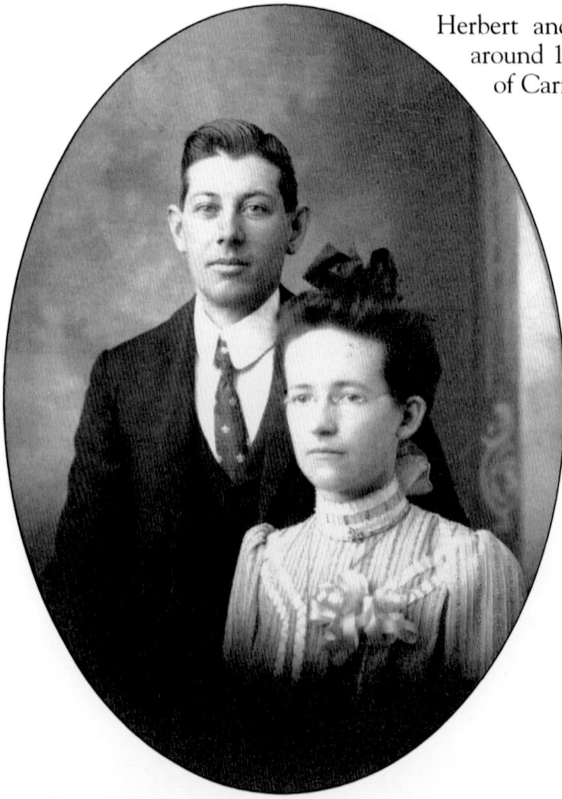

Herbert and Minnie Shriner Winter are pictured around 1905. (Courtesy of the Historical Society of Carroll County.)

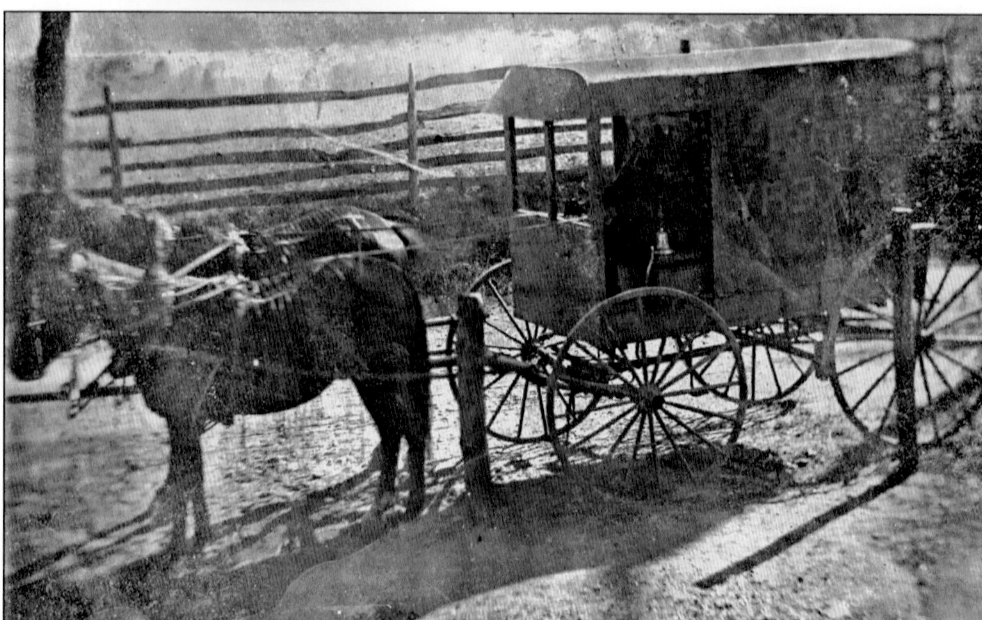

Herbert Winter worked as a traveling salesman for the Model Steam Bakery in Taneytown. He is pictured in this tintype in his horse-drawn bakery cart, *c.* 1920. (Courtesy of the Historical Society of Carroll County.)

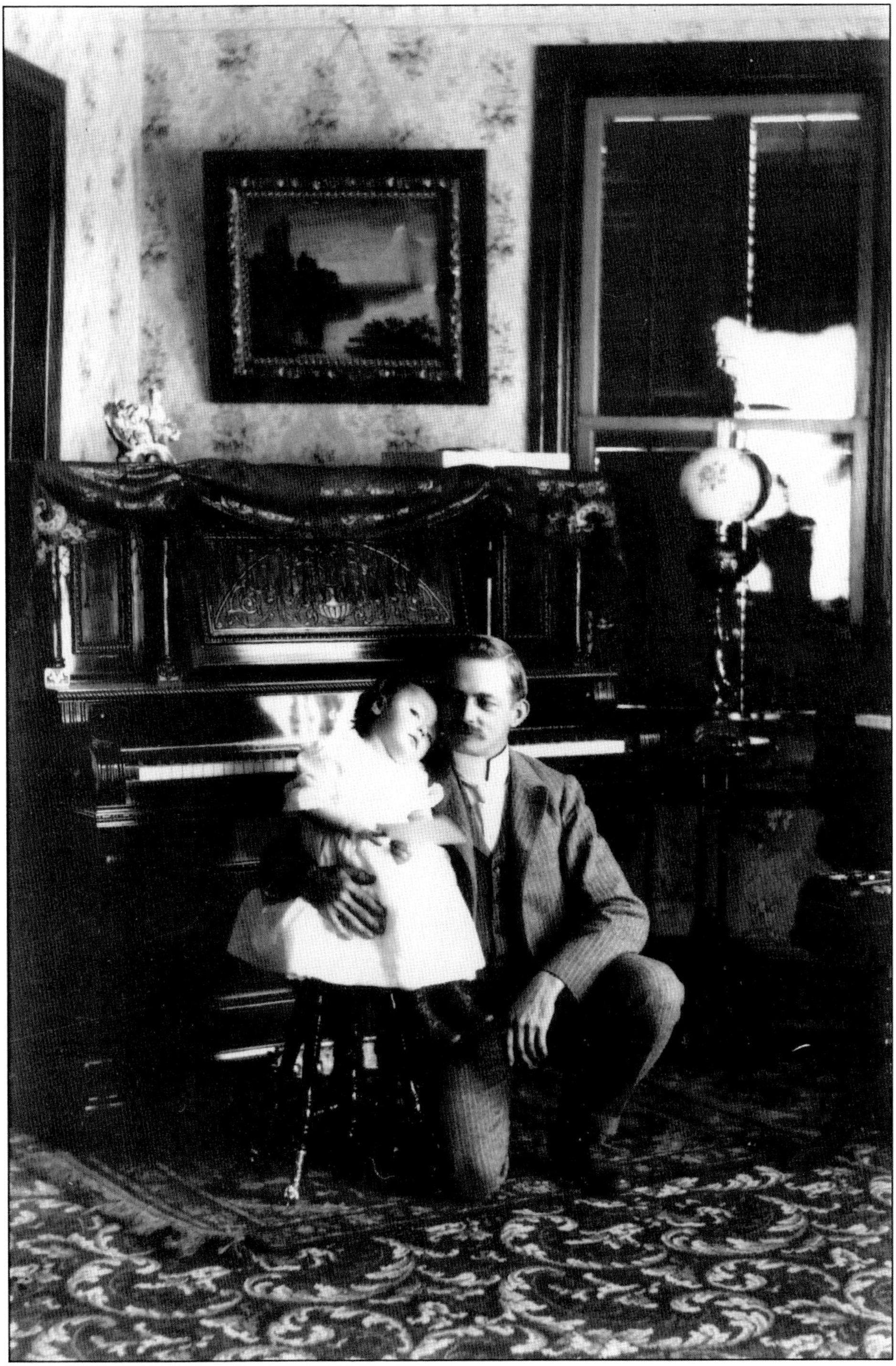

Photographer Edward P. Zepp sat for this touching portrait with one of his children in the parlor of his Taneytown home. Zepp is fondly remembered by many, not just for his beautiful photographs of Taneytown and its inhabitants, but also for his great musical talents. (Courtesy of Michael and Susan Reifsnider.)

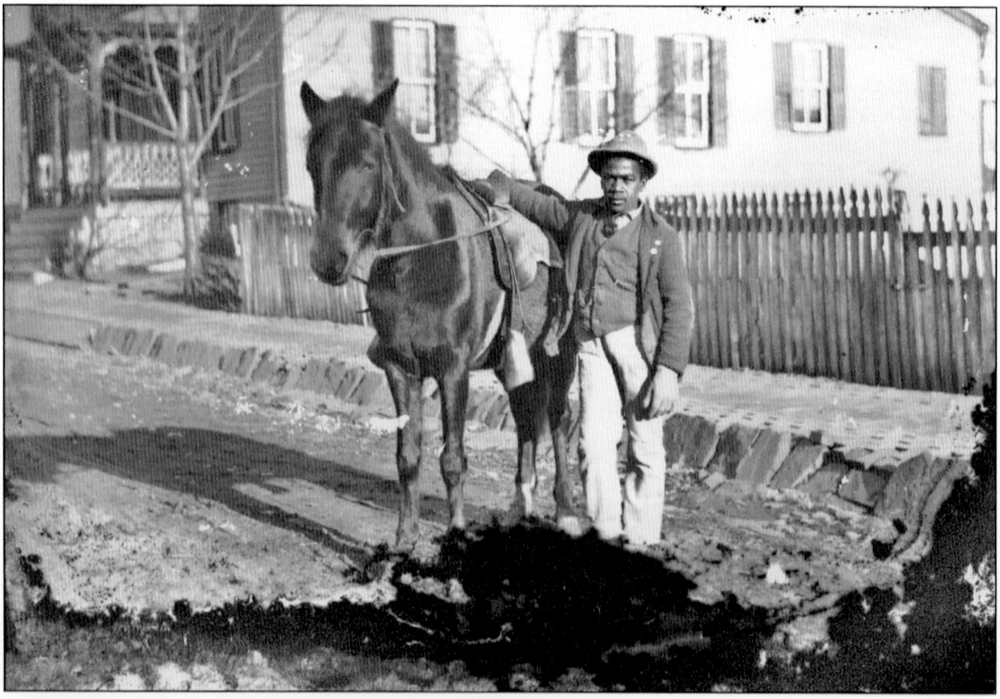

An unidentified African-American man poses with his horse for photographer Ed Zepp, c. 1905. (Courtesy of Michael and Susan Reifsnider.)

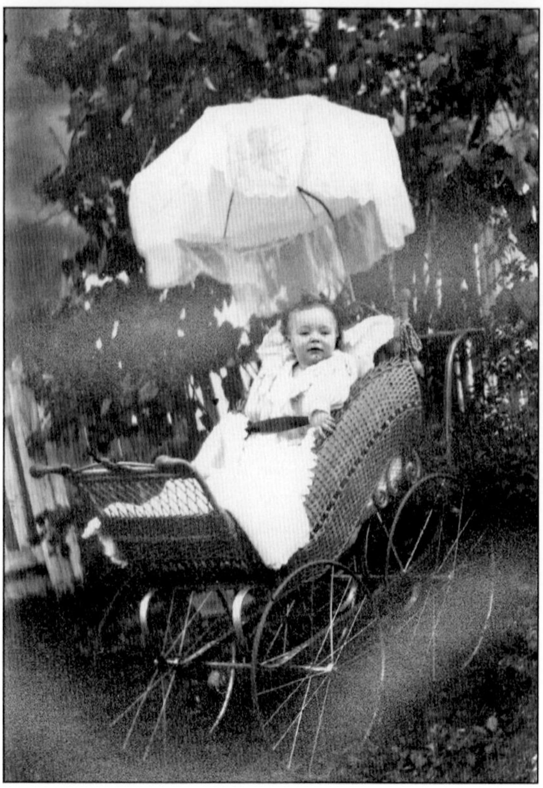

A beautiful Taneytown baby is seated in an elaborate Victorian baby carriage with parasol, c. 1900. (Courtesy of Michael and Susan Reifsnider.)

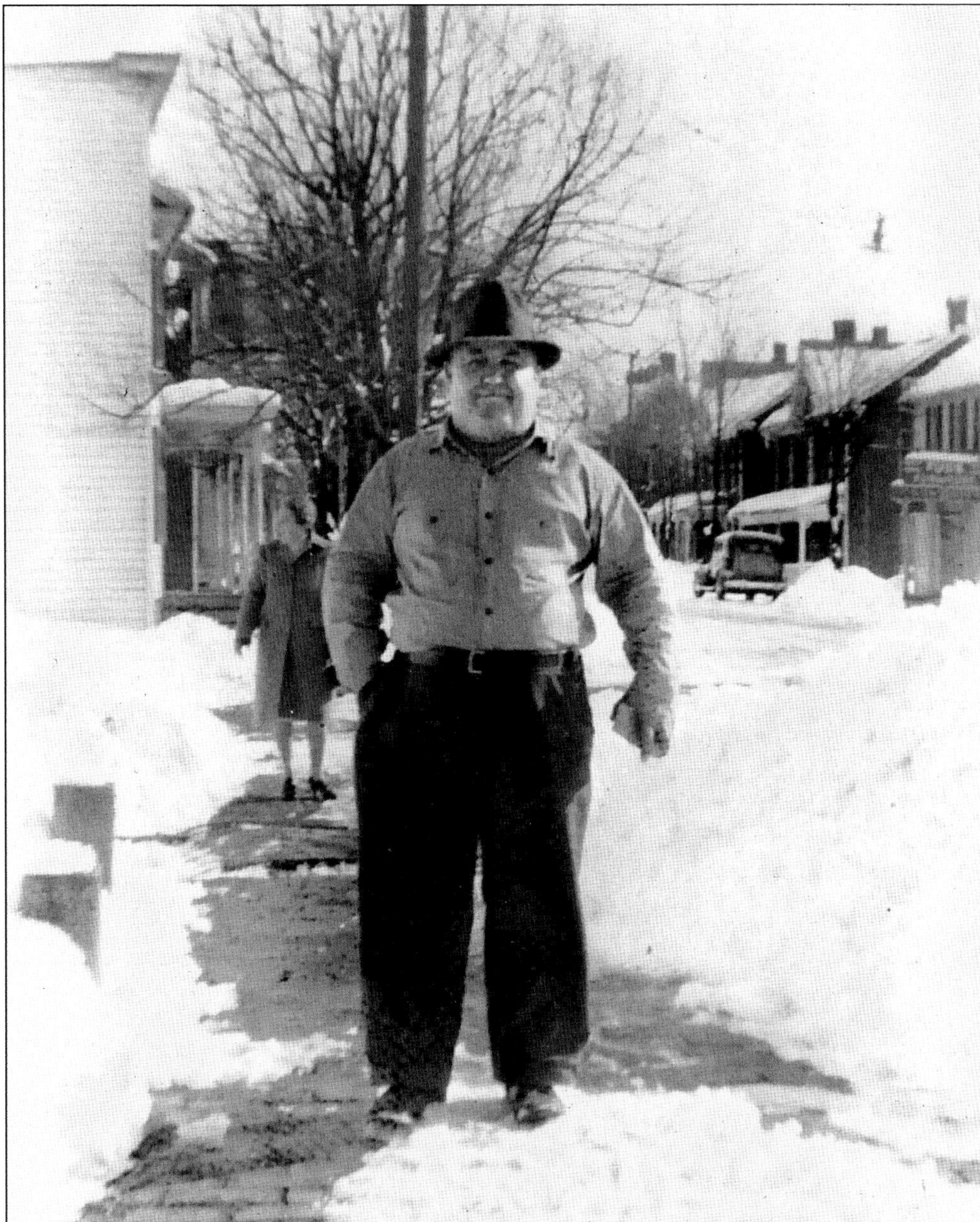

A young Jean McCleaf took this photograph of "Bumble Bee" on a cold winter's day in the 1940s. Bumble Bee, whose real name was Raymond Thuma, earned his nickname because of the buzzing sound he would make. He is fondly remembered by many in Taneytown for his elaborate paper cut outs and his penchant for travel. (Courtesy of Jean Brown.)

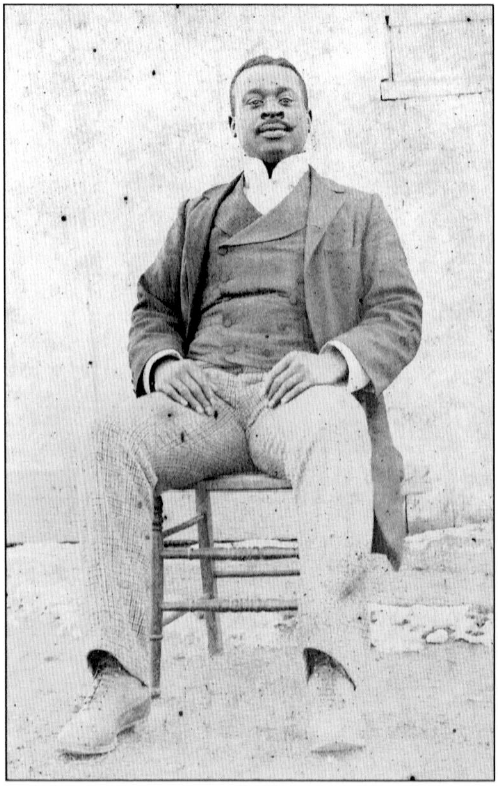

This is a photograph of Joseph Hill from the late 1800s. (Courtesy of Joe Hill.)

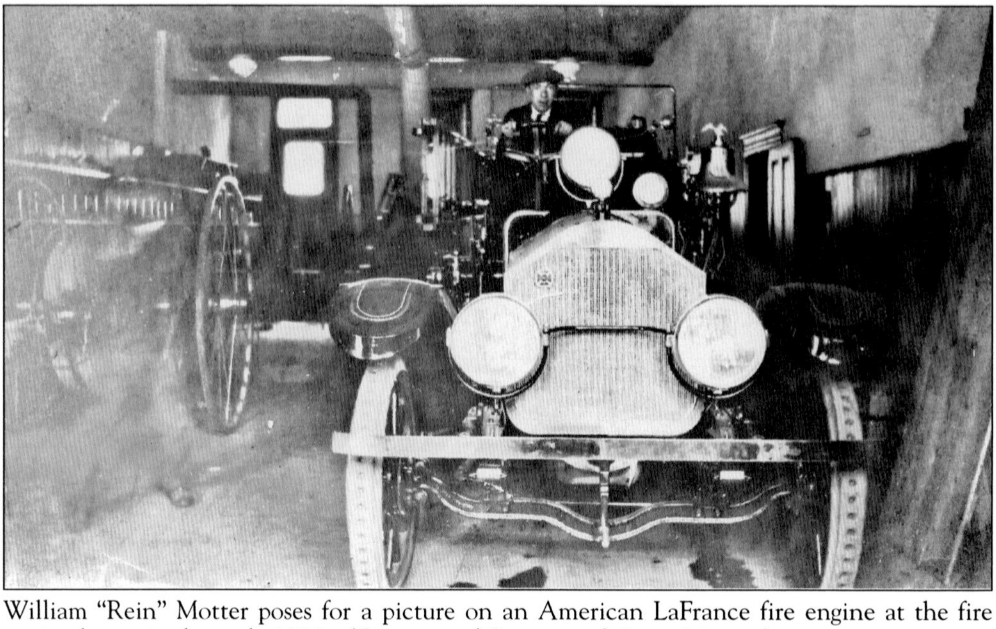

William "Rein" Motter poses for a picture on an American LaFrance fire engine at the fire engine house in the early 1900s. (Courtesy of George and Anna Motter.)

Laverne Zepp patiently sits in a high chair as his father, Ed Zepp, photographs him. (Courtesy of Michael and Susan Reifsnider.)

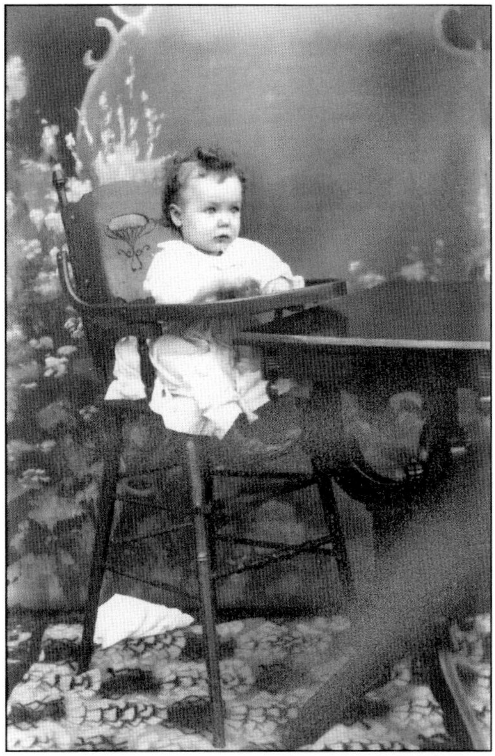

A bearded gentleman shows off his horse in front of the Eckenrode Building on Frederick Street. (Courtesy of Michael and Susan Reifsnider.)

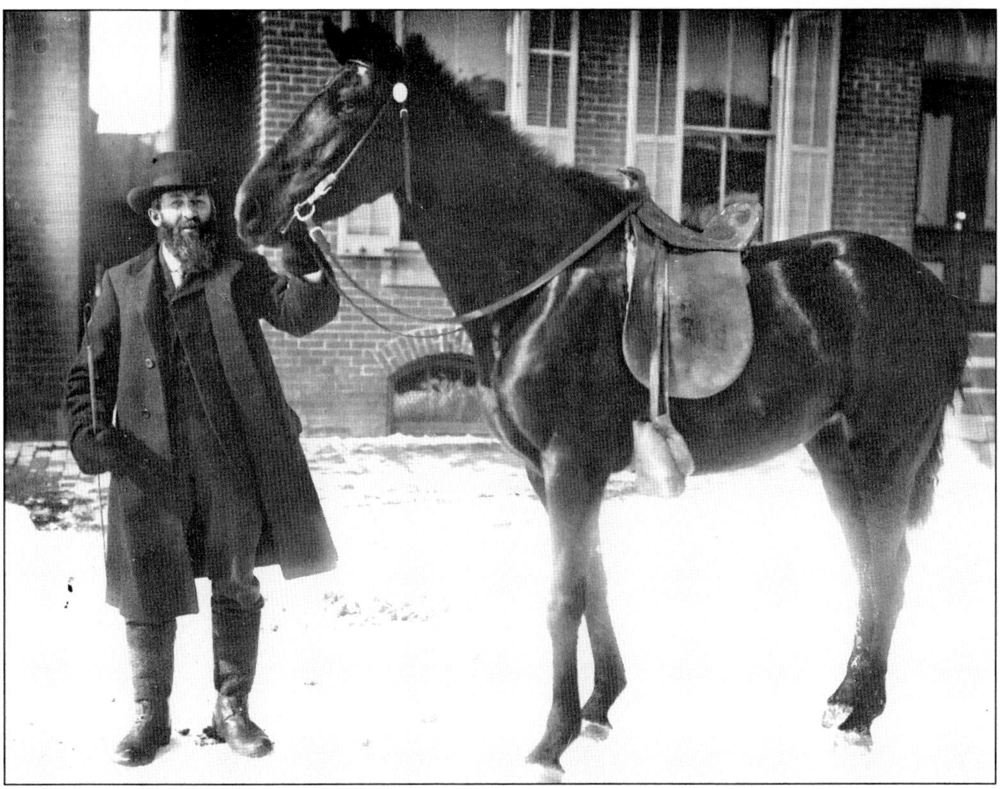

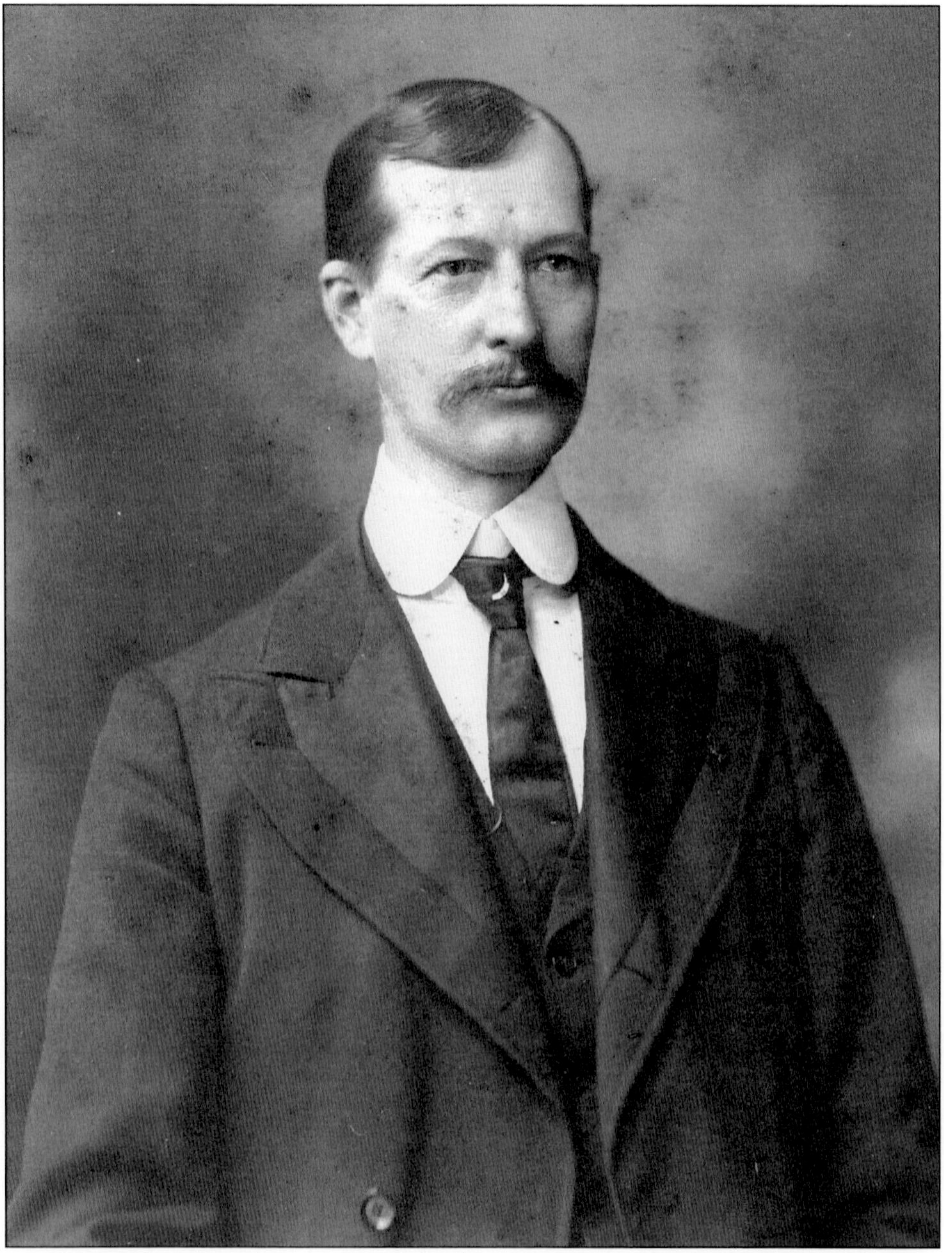

Robert S. McKinney was the son of Prof. Andrew McKinney, who founded Eagleton Institute on York Street in 1860. After graduation from his father's school in 1878, Robert matriculated in the Baltimore College of Pharmacy. In 1886, he returned to Taneytown to teach at Eagleton Institute for the next three years. In 1890, he established a successful drug store in town, which he continued to run for the rest of his life. McKinney served as town councilman, postmaster, and the first foreman of the Taneytown Volunteer Fire Co. No. 1. He was described with the following words by *The Democratic Advocate* in 1910, "Mr. McKinney was born in Taneytown and possesses the southern attributes of courtesy, frankness, and unalloyed civic pride with the unselfish interest that prompts him to lend his aid to every cause designed for the betterment of his profession, town, community or state." (Courtesy of Dean Reindollar.)

Shown here is Maggie McKinney, the wife of Robert S. McKinney, *c.* 1900. (Courtesy of Dean Reindollar.)

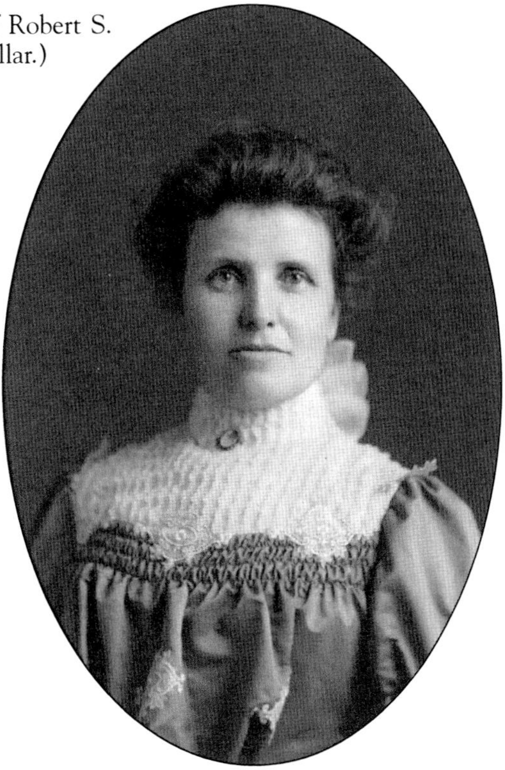

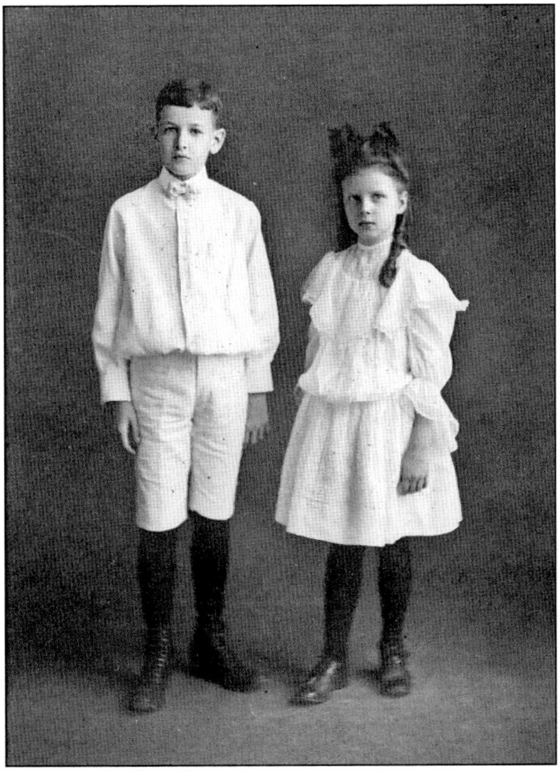

Andrew and Isabella McKinney were the children of Mr. and Mrs. Robert S. McKinney, *c.* 1900. (Courtesy of Dean Reindollar.)

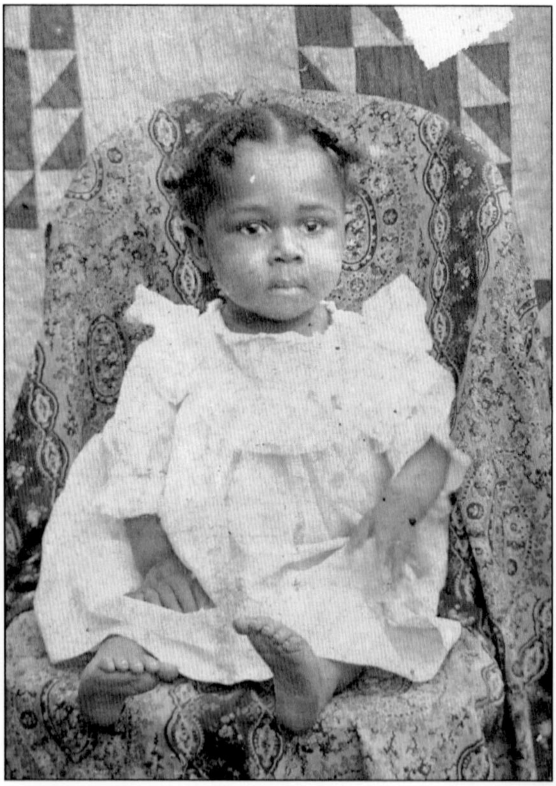

Theodore "Ted" Hill is pictured at seven months of age in 1902. Ted, descended from an old Taneytown family, grew up to become a well-known stone mason and carpenter in the Taneytown area. (Courtesy of Ginny Henderson.)

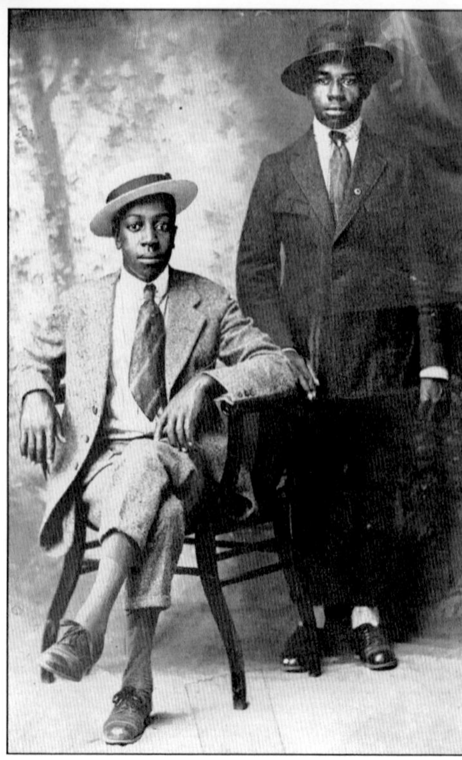

Anthony and Ted Hill are photographed at a Taneytown studio, c. 1920. (Courtesy of Ginny Hill.)

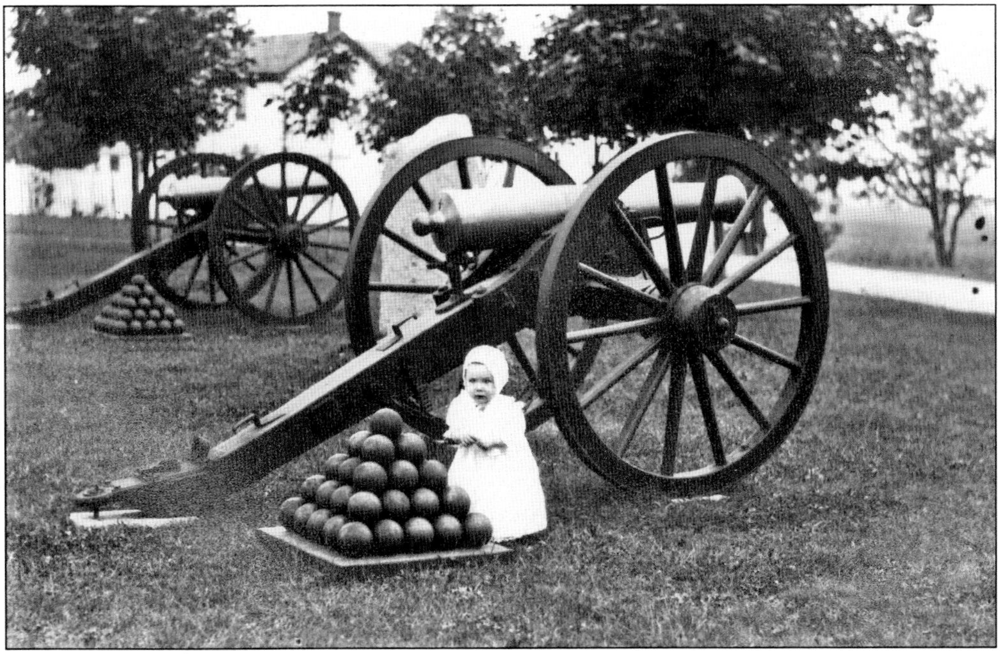

Laverne Zepp gazes curiously at some cannon balls in Gettysburg, Pennsylvania. (Courtesy of Michael and Susan Reifsnider.)

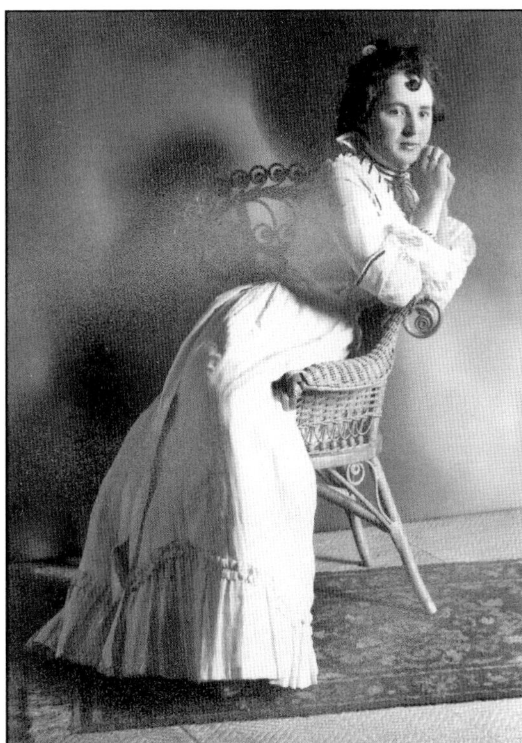

Eatha Baumgardner strikes a pose for this portrait taken about 1900. (Courtesy of Michael and Susan Reifsnider.)

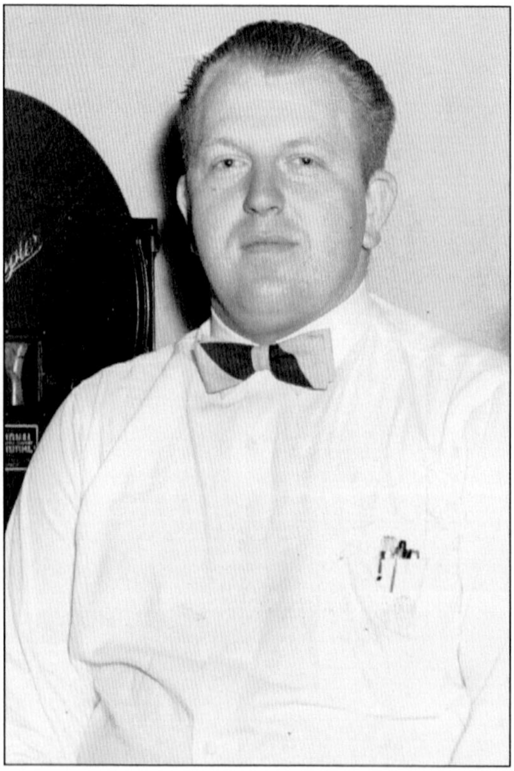

Kenneth Clem, a local photographer, was also the manager of the Taneytown Movie Theater and the Monocacy Drive-In. Clem, pictured here with the movie projector, took many of the photos featured in this book in the 1940s and 1950s. (Courtesy of the Clem family.)

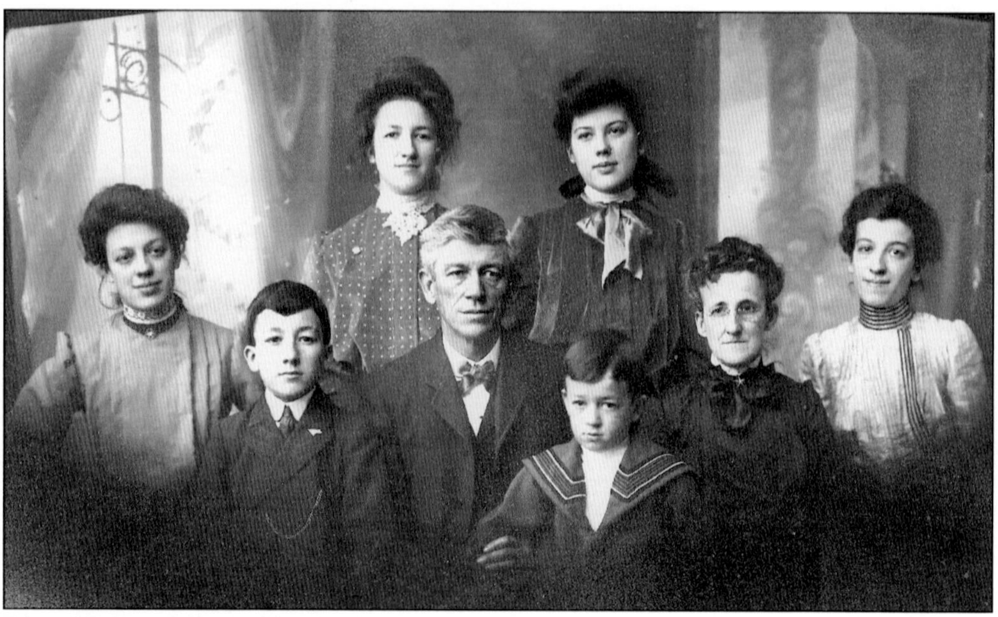

Edward E. Reindollar and his family sit for a portrait at the Zepp Studios. (Courtesy of Michael and Susan Reifsnider.)

Adelaide Hill holds grandson Joseph Hill on the front steps of her home, *c.* 1920. (Courtesy of Joe Hill.)

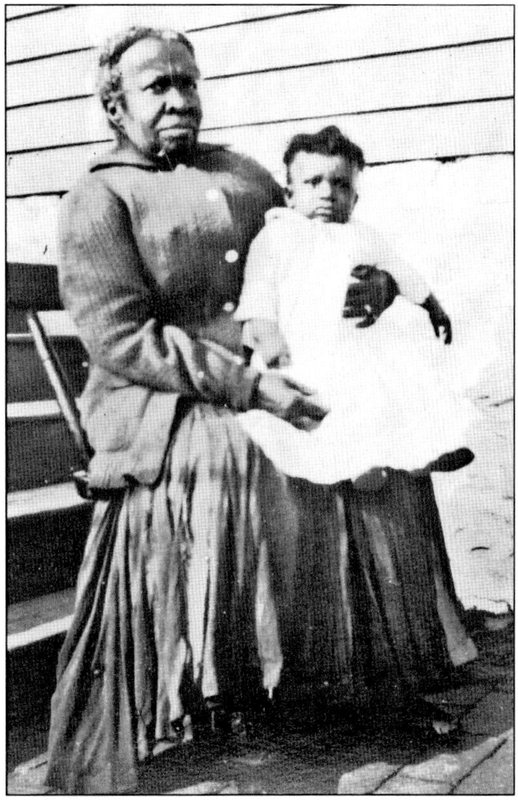

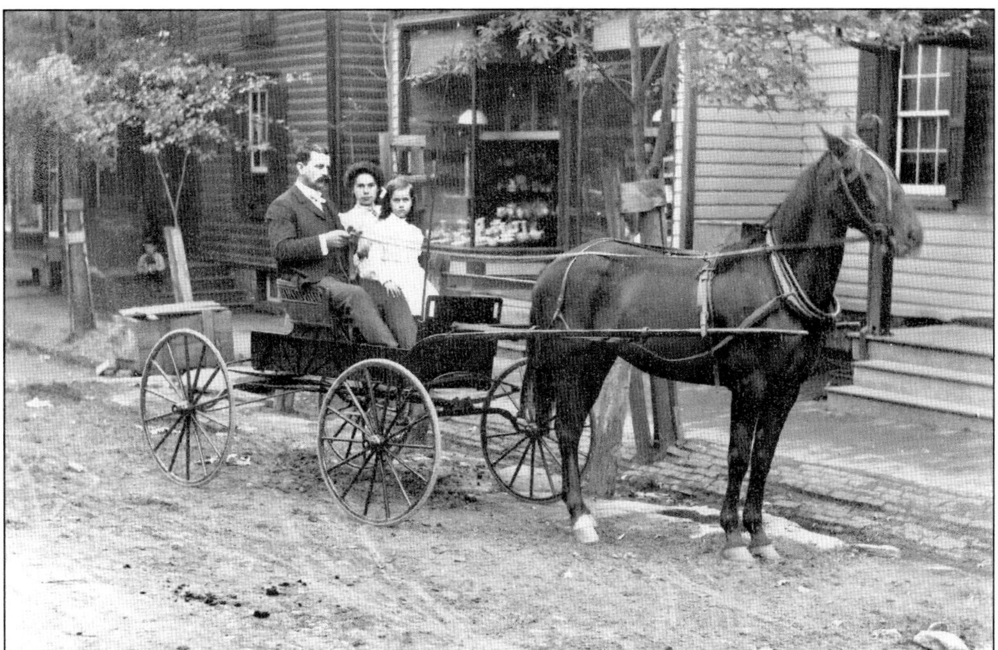

D. Garner and family prepare to leave in their carriage after a busy day of shopping. (Courtesy of Michael and Susan Reifsnider.)

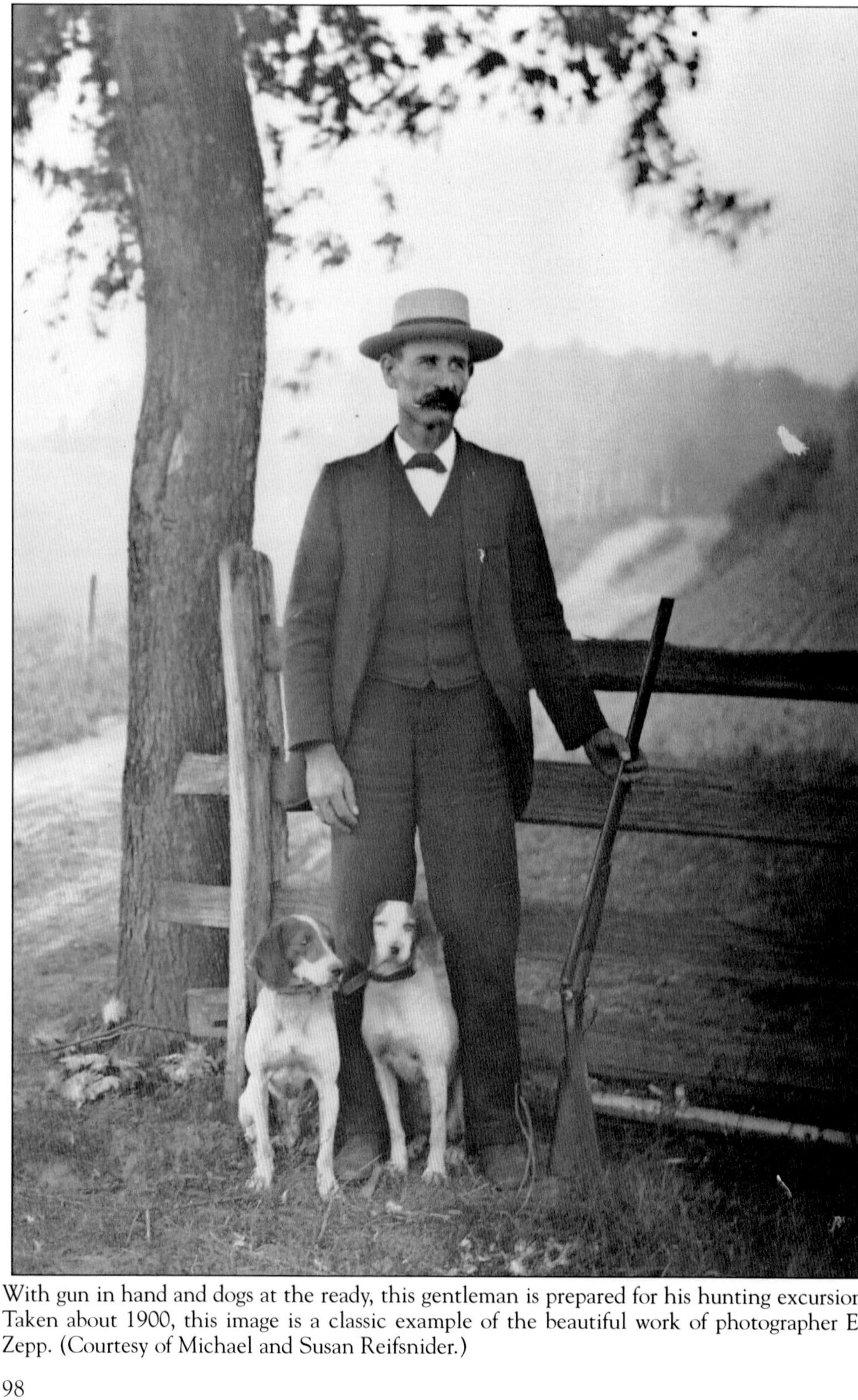

With gun in hand and dogs at the ready, this gentleman is prepared for his hunting excursion. Taken about 1900, this image is a classic example of the beautiful work of photographer Ed Zepp. (Courtesy of Michael and Susan Reifsnider.)

Six

READING, WRITING, AND ARITHMETIC

The three R's were taught in a variety of schools that operated in and around Taneytown in the 19th and early 20th centuries. From boarding schools to one-room country schoolhouses, the educational opportunities available to area children were diverse.

In the 1830s, the Lutheran Church operated a parochial school where children learned the alphabet through Bible quotations and did sums of arithmetic by computing numbers of years from the fall of Adam and Eve to the beginning of the Christian era. Later in the 19th century, the Catholic Church established its own parochial school taught by nuns. From 1837 to 1871, the Misses Birnie operated a girls' boarding school at their home, Thorndale. Their brother, Rogers Birnie, had a boys' school at his home, Glenburn. Many of his pupils attained prominence in later life. In 1843, a group of citizens organized the Taneytown Literary and Classical Institute; classes were held in a house on York Street. Also on York Street was Eagleton Institute, opened by Andrew McKinney in the 1860s. A school for African American children was located near Frederick Street—Edward Burke served as the first teacher. Public education in Maryland began in 1865. By 1870, Taneytown boasted a fine public school building located on York Street with nearly 100 pupils, while the one-room schoolhouses in the surrounding countryside afforded children in outlying areas the benefit of an education.

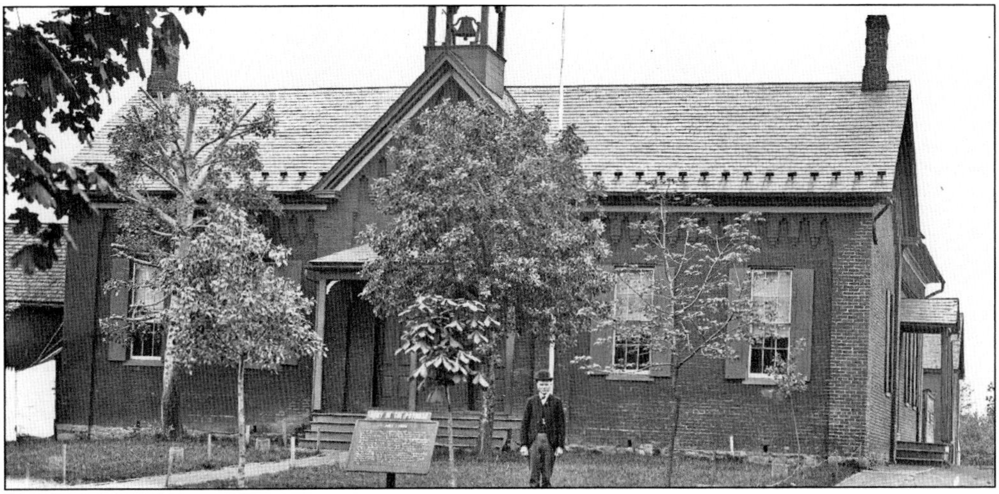

Principal Levi D. Reid stands in front of the Taneytown School on York Street. The schoolhouse was originally built in 1870 and was later remodeled. In 1925, the school on York Street was closed. (Courtesy of the Historical Society of Carroll County.)

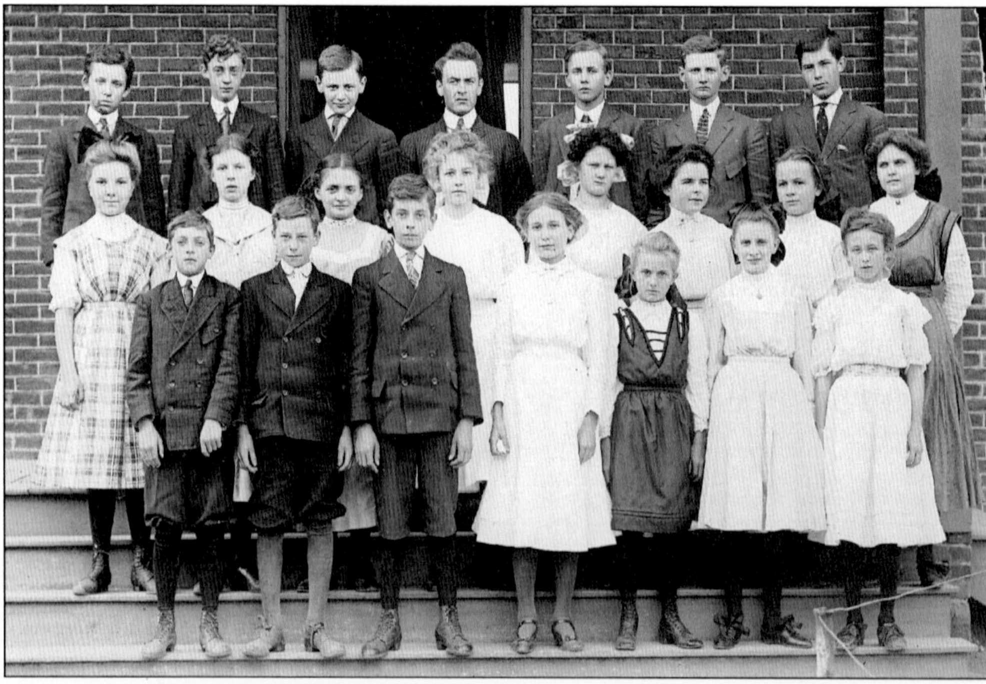

The pupils of Taneytown High School are pictured in 1909. (Courtesy of Dean Reindollar.)

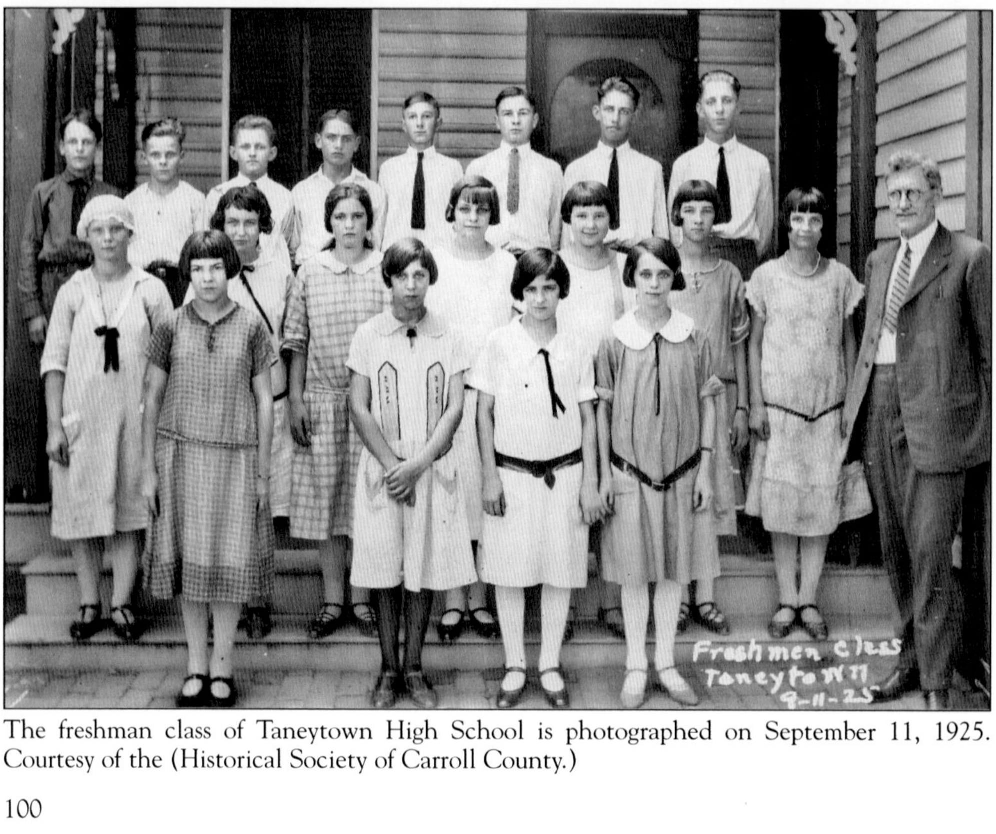

The freshman class of Taneytown High School is photographed on September 11, 1925. Courtesy of the (Historical Society of Carroll County.)

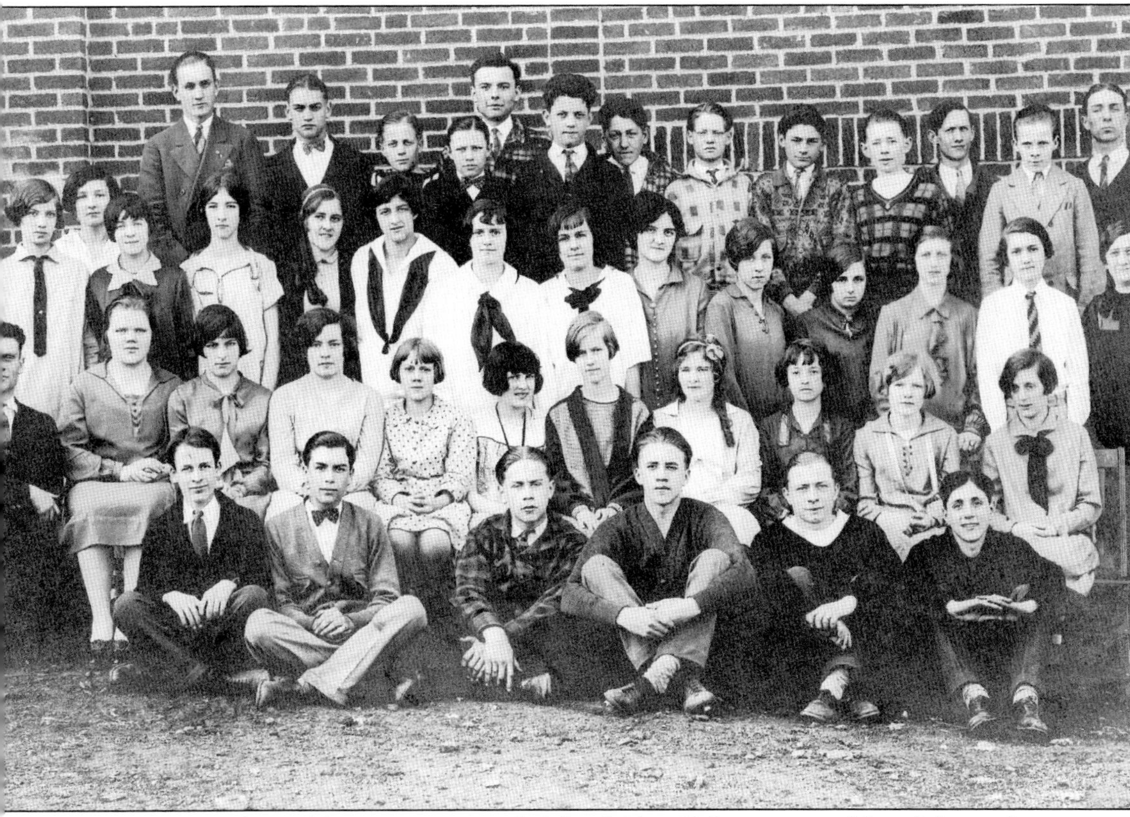

The following members of the Taneytown High School Glee Club are pictured from left to right in 1927: (first row) Daniel Teeter, Bernard Utz, Jack Bower, John Bricker, unidentified, and James Baumgardner; (second row) Ralph Ealy, Marion Hitchcock, Janet Burke, Margaret Crebs, Mary Isabel Elliot, Jane Long, Frances Utz Moyers, Dorothy Haugh, and Mary Alice Chenowith; (third row) Agatha Hahn, Pauline Stonesifer, Evelyn Zimmerman, Mary Hahn, Leah Katherine Reindollar, Ellanora Shoemaker, Margaret Hitchcock, Edith Graham, Annie Lutz, Elizabeth Lambert, Elizabeth Wilt, Mary Alice Chenowith, Virginia Ott, and Viola Broadwater; (fourth row) Robert Baumgardner, Elwood Crebs, John Chenowith, Robert Clingan, Alton Flickinger, Stanely Lutz, William Six, Franklin Baker, Morris Becker, Delmar Riffle, Ezra Stuller, Ralph Davidson, and Elton Kindleberger. (Courtesy of the Historical Society of Carroll County.)

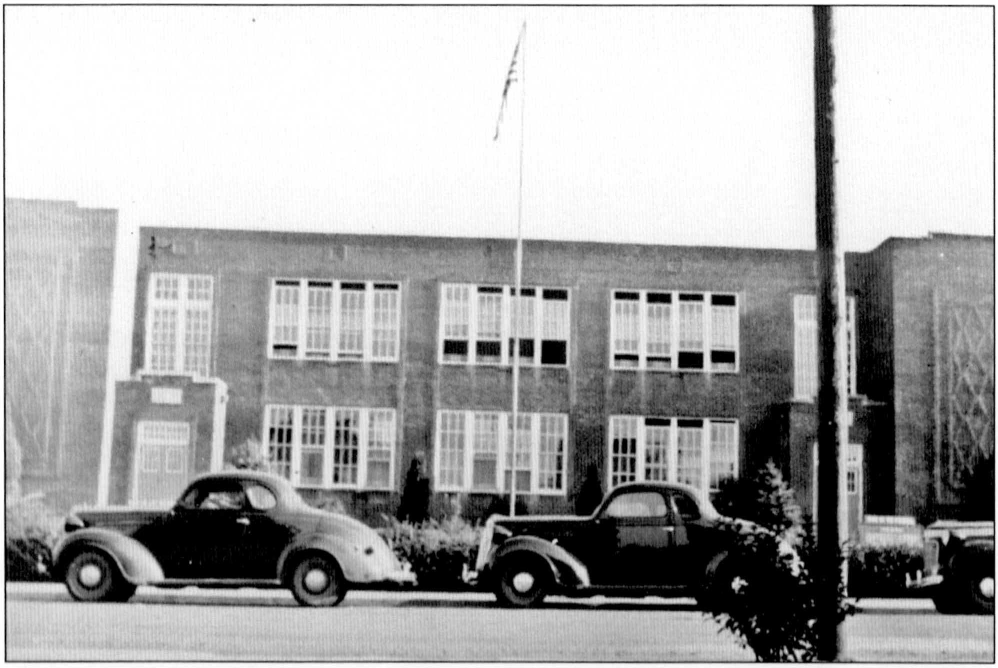

Taneytown High School was constructed between 1924 and 1926 at a cost of $35,000. Shown above is a photograph of the school as it appeared in 1936. The structure is now demolished. (Courtesy George and Anna Motter.)

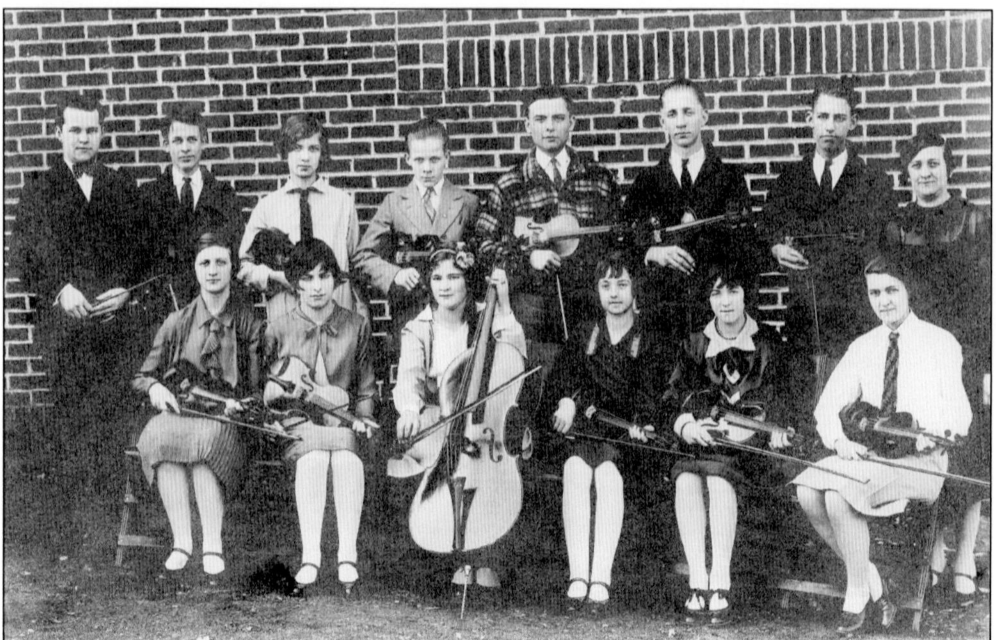

The Taneytown High School band is pictured in 1927. (Courtesy of the Historical Society of Carroll County.)

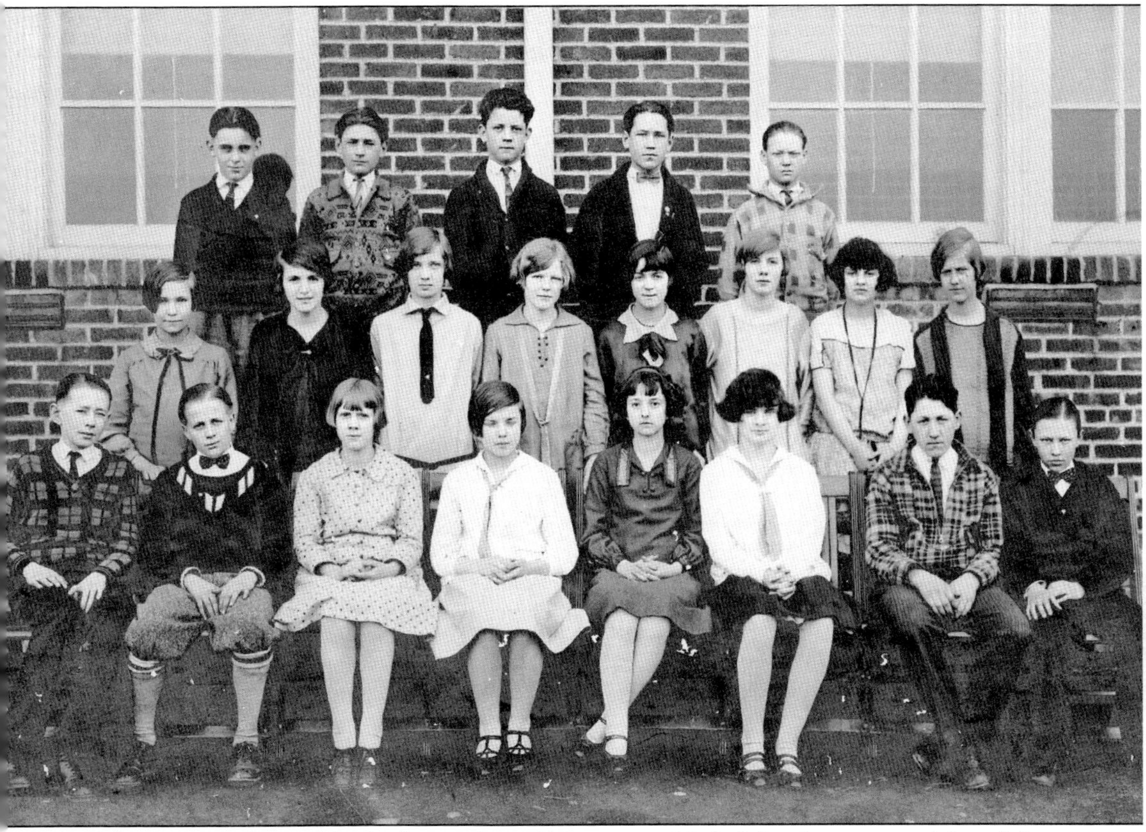

The following members of the freshman class of Taneytown High School are pictured from left to right in 1927: (front row) Delmar Riffle, John Chenowith, Dorothy Thompson, Ruthanna Flickinger, Dorothy Haugh, Ethel Clingan, William Six, and Robert Clingan; (middle row) Amelia Null, Mary Young, Agatha Hahn, Mildred Shriner, Evelyn Zimmerman, Romaine Valentine, Isabelle Elliot, and Jane Long; (back row) Glenn Snyder, Maurice Becker, Stanley Lutz, William Six, and Franklin Baker. (Courtesy of the Historical Society of Carroll County.)

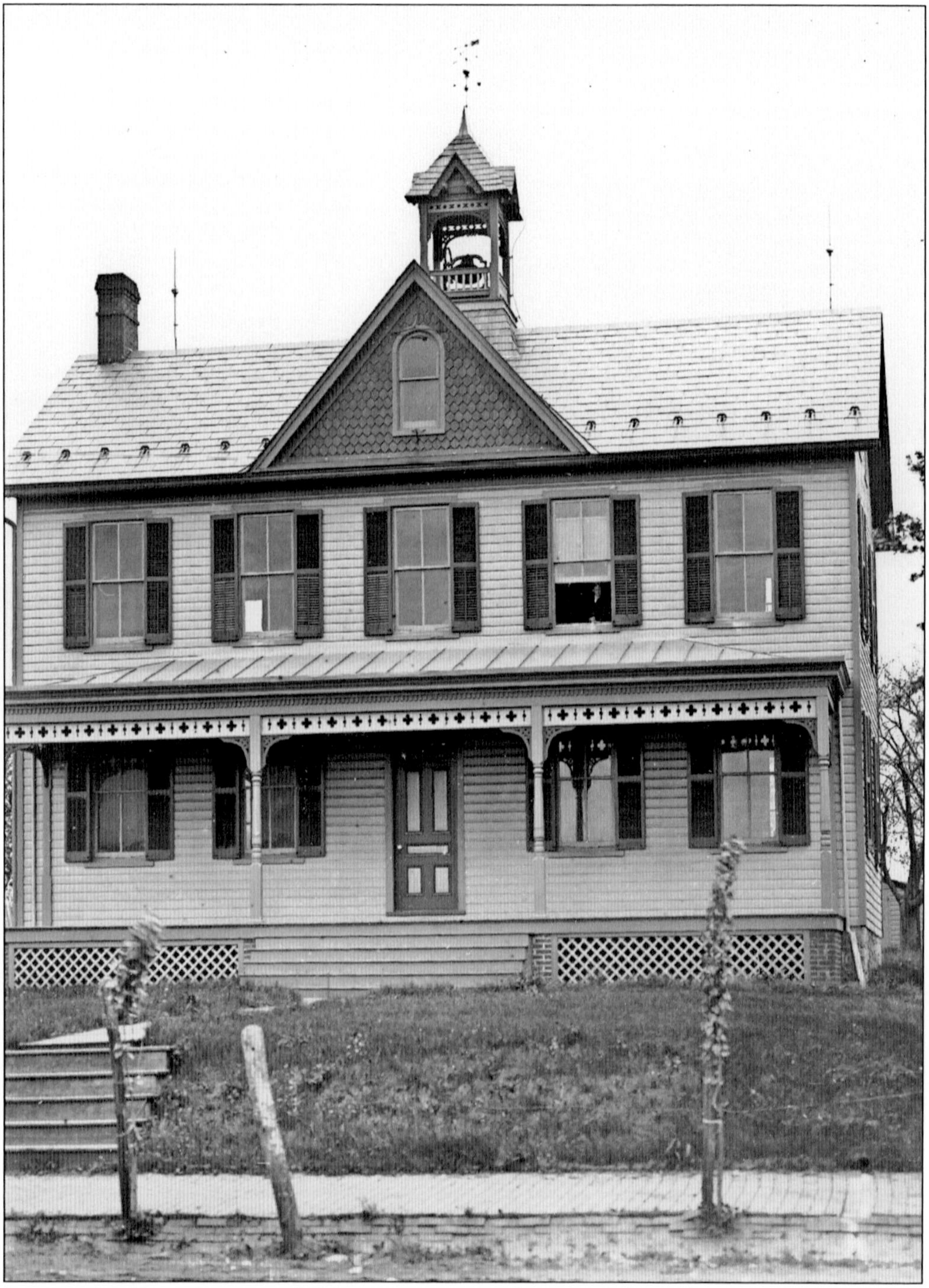

In 1894, Professor Springer of Baltimore opened a branch of the Milton Academy on West Baltimore Street. Prof. Henry Meier, a native of Switzerland, served as principal. Dr. F.H. Seiss, Dr. Clotworthy Birnie, and George H. Birnie served as lecturers at the school. (Courtesy of the Historical Society of Carroll County.)

The prospectus of the Milton Academy for the 1898–1899 school year presents an expense list. Tuition varies between $20 and $50, depending on the courses taken. The prospectus also advises, "Board for students may be obtained in very respectable families." (Courtesy of Dean Reindollar.)

MILTON ACADEMY. 19

Expenses.

The tuition ranges from $20.00 to $50.00 per year, according to the class and number of studies pursued. They are as follows:

Primary Department, (7 to 10 years)	$20.00.
General English Branches,	30.00.
Languages, each	5.00.
Geometry, Trigonometry, etc., each	5.00.
Physics, Astronomy, each	5.00.
Book-keeping,	5.00.
Office Routine and Book-keeping,	10.00.
Shorthand Writing,	5.00.

The tuition is payable in advance, at the beginning of each term, unless other arrangements have been made with the principal. A proportionate rebate will be made for prolonged absence on account of illness of student.

Board for students may be obtained in very respectable families, for $2.50 to $3.00 per week; or from Monday to Friday afternoon, for $2.00.

Those driving to and from school every day, may make use of the stable belonging to the Academy, free of charge.

For all further information, address

HENRY MEIER, Principal,
MILTON ACADEMY,
Taneytown, Md.

Shown here is a diploma from the Milton Academy in 1901. (Courtesy of the Historical Society of Carroll County.)

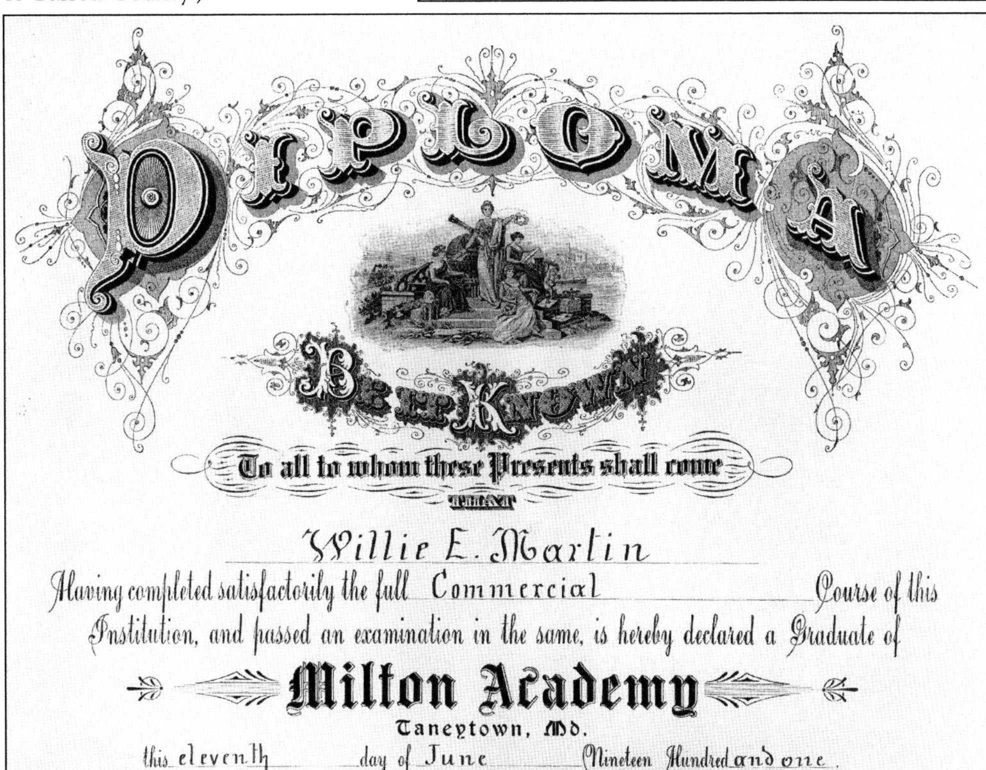

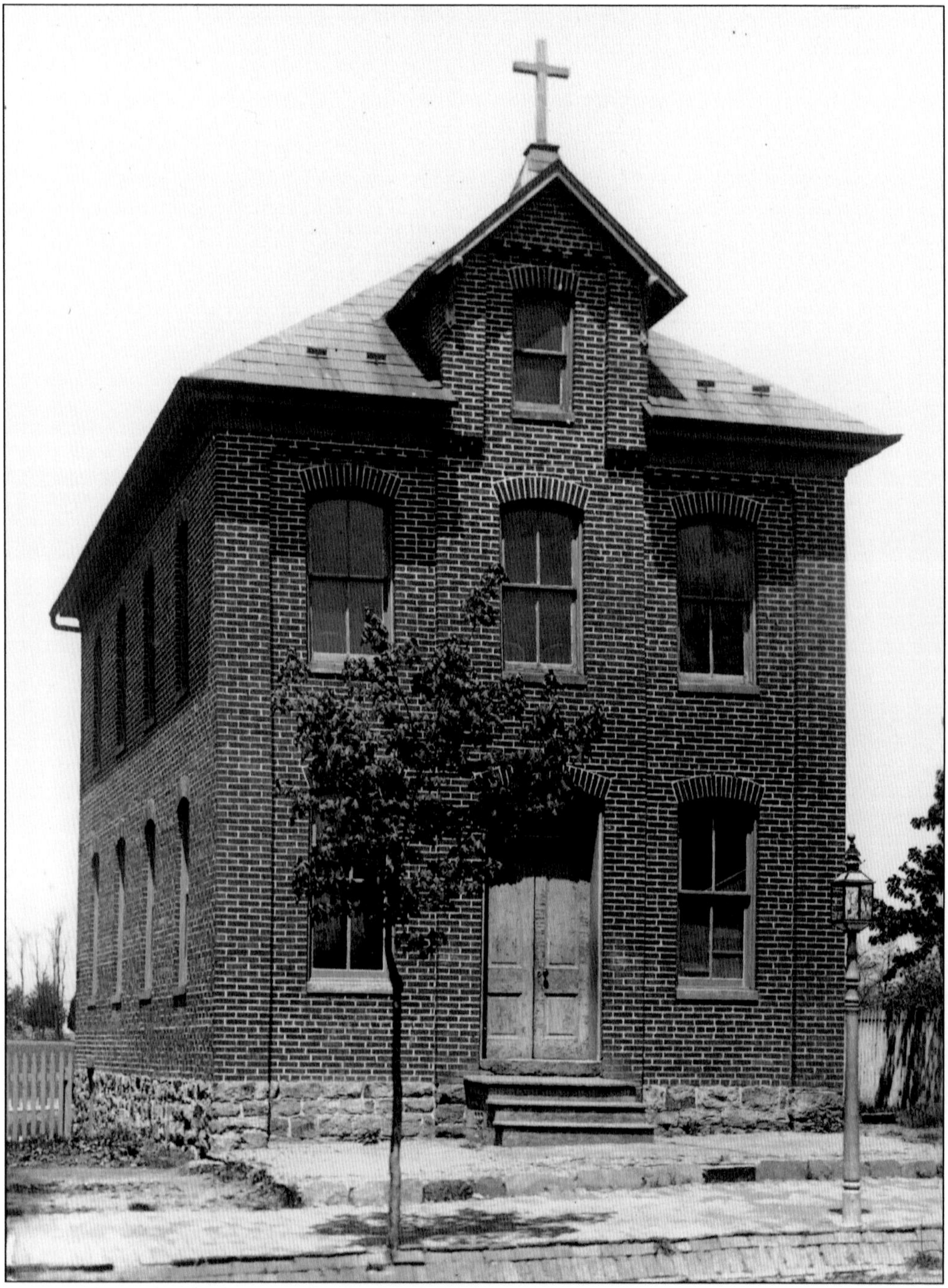

St. Joseph's School, the parochial school of the Catholic Church on Frederick Street, was established during the pastorate of Fr. John Delaney (1879–1890). George Arnold served as the first teacher. At the turn of the century, 20 students were enrolled and all grades studied in one room. In 1918, the School Sisters of Notre Dame arrived to teach. By the 1960s, enrollment peaked at 125 pupils. The school closed in 1971. (Courtesy of Michael and Susan Reifsnider.)

Staff and students of St. Joseph's School are pictured c. 1900. (Courtesy of Michael and Susan Reifsnider.)

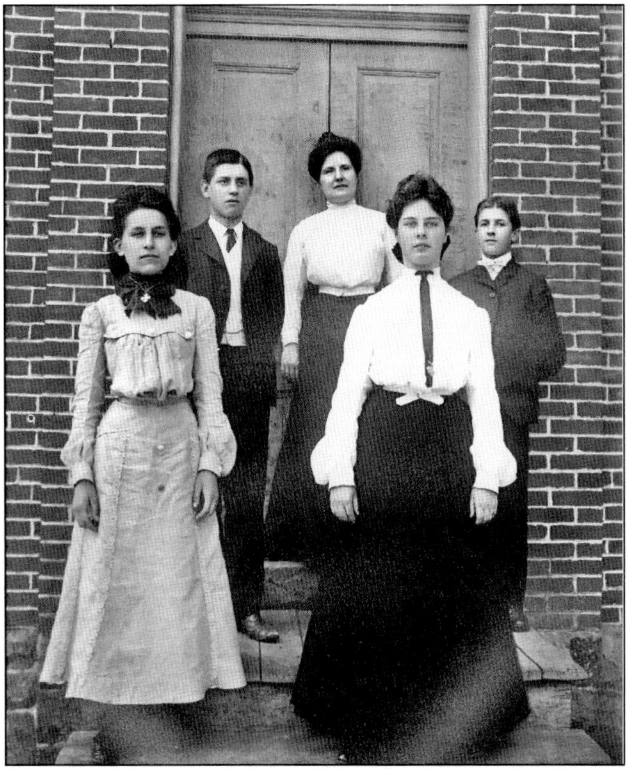

The students of St. Joseph's School stand at the front of the schoolhouse for this photograph taken c. 1900. Rev. Bernard J. Lennon stands at the back. (Courtesy of Michael and Susan Reifsnider.)

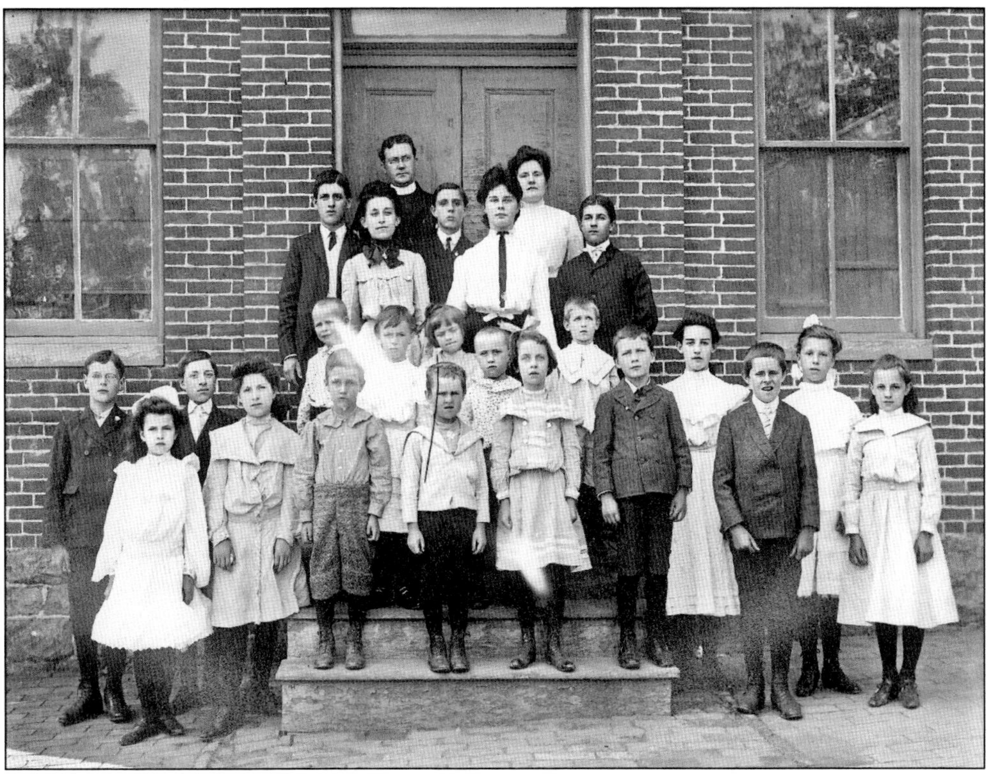

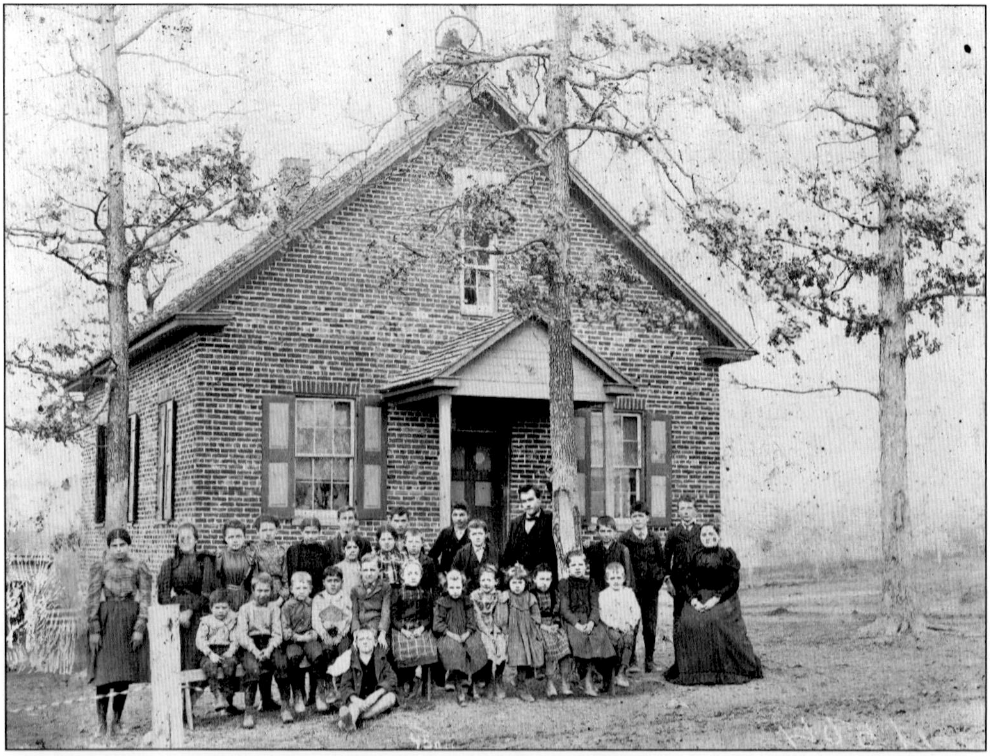

The students of the Otterdale School are pictured *c.* 1895. (Courtesy of Historical Society of Carroll County.)

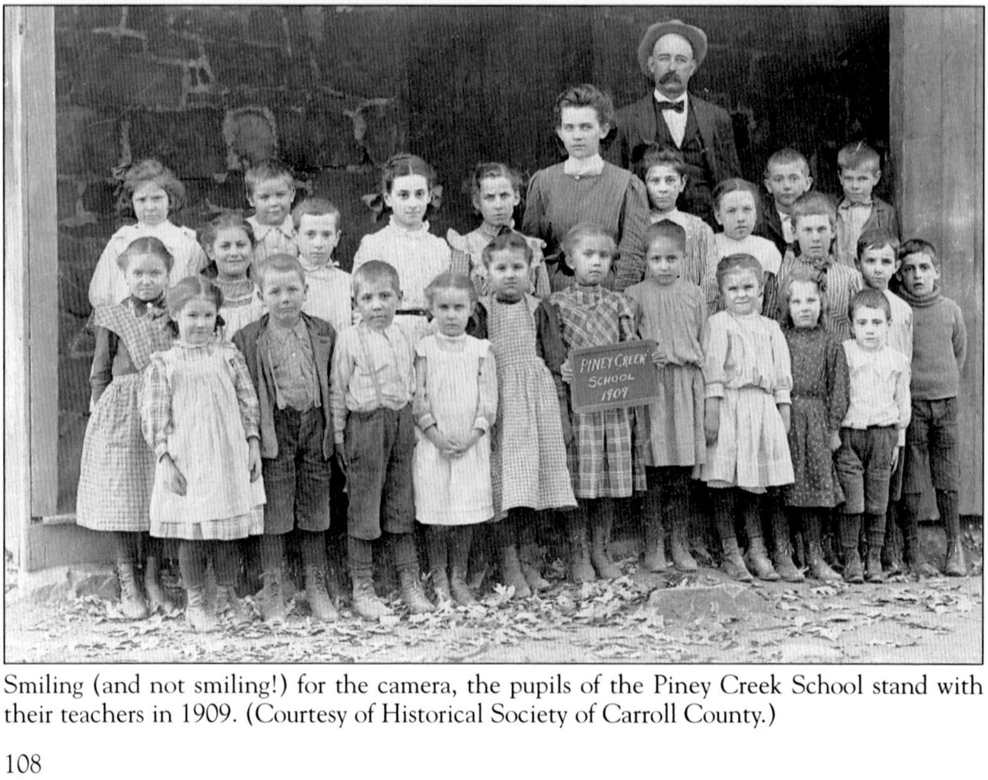

Smiling (and not smiling!) for the camera, the pupils of the Piney Creek School stand with their teachers in 1909. (Courtesy of Historical Society of Carroll County.)

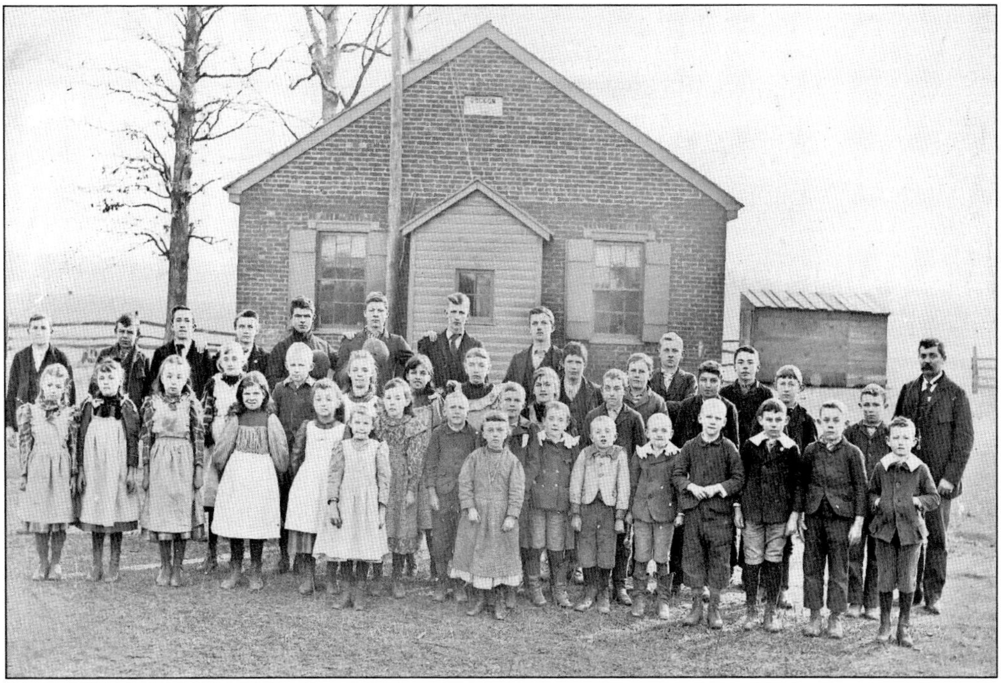

Standing outside of their brick school house, the students of the Oregon School lined up for this photograph in 1890. (Courtesy of the Historical Society of Carroll County.)

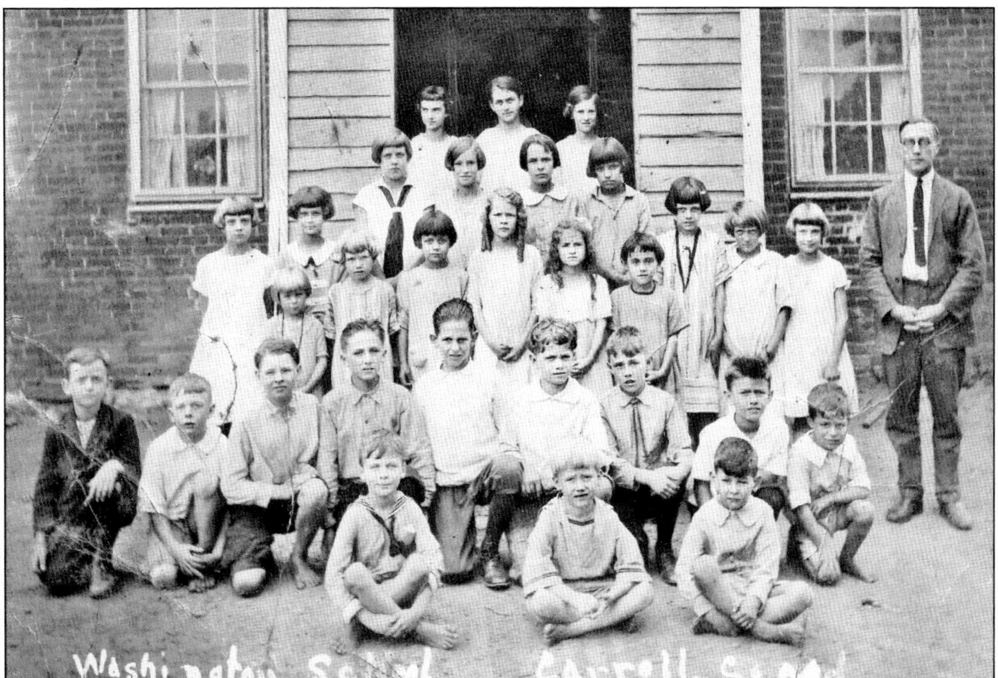

With the boys in the front and the girls in the back, the pupils of the Washington School stood still long enough to have their picture taken in 1925. (Courtesy of Historical Society of Carroll County.)

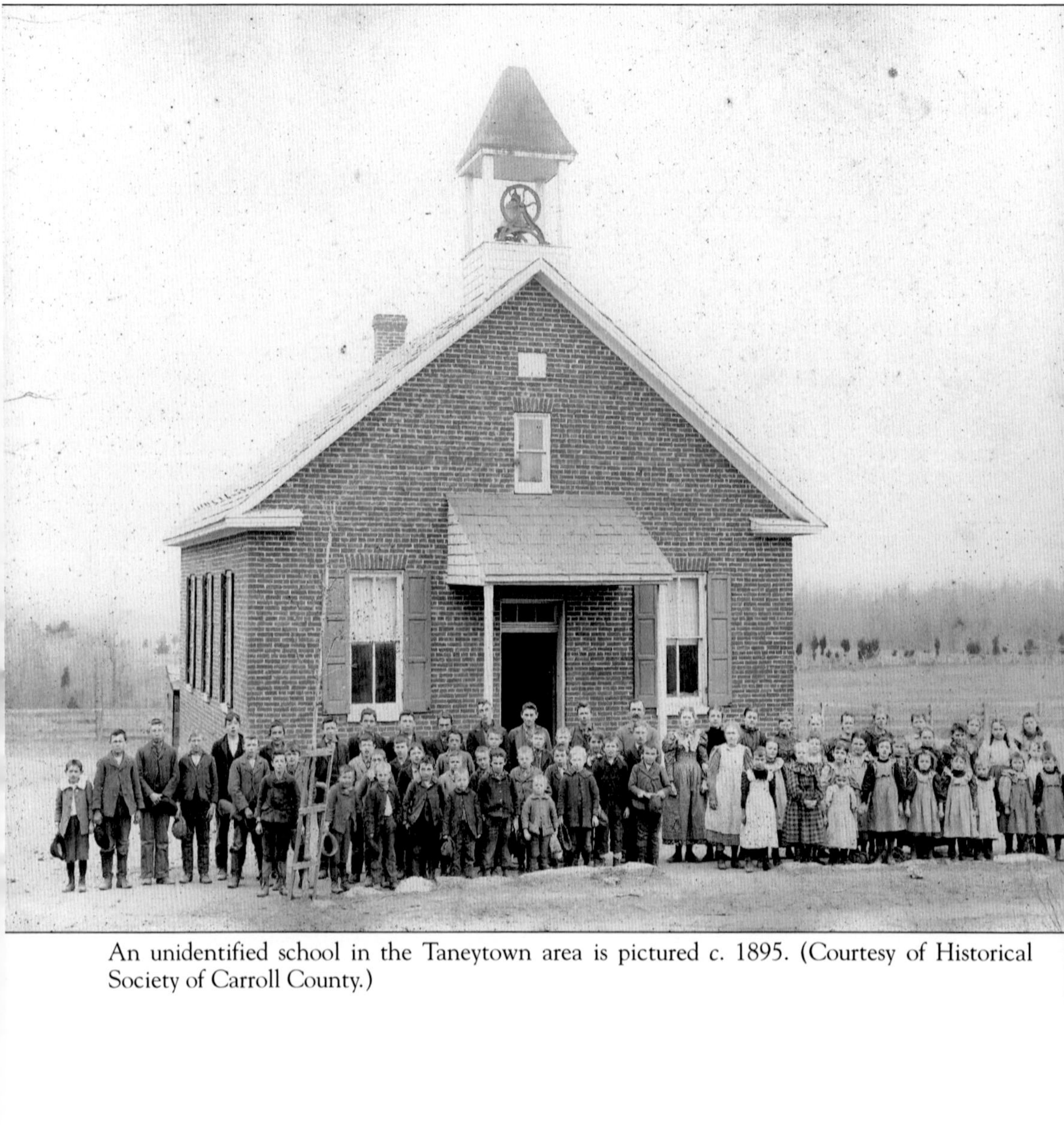

An unidentified school in the Taneytown area is pictured *c.* 1895. (Courtesy of Historical Society of Carroll County.)

Seven

EARLY BANKING

In an agrarian community like Taneytown, banks were important resources, enabling farmers to farm and merchants to maintain their businesses. By the late 19th century, two prosperous banks had opened in town, "although before either was established, many of our citizens would not believe that the town could support one bank." The Birnie Trust Company opened in 1884 and the Taneytown Savings Bank opened in 1887. Prior to this time it must be assumed that residents kept their money safely deposited under their mattresses and in their cookie jars!

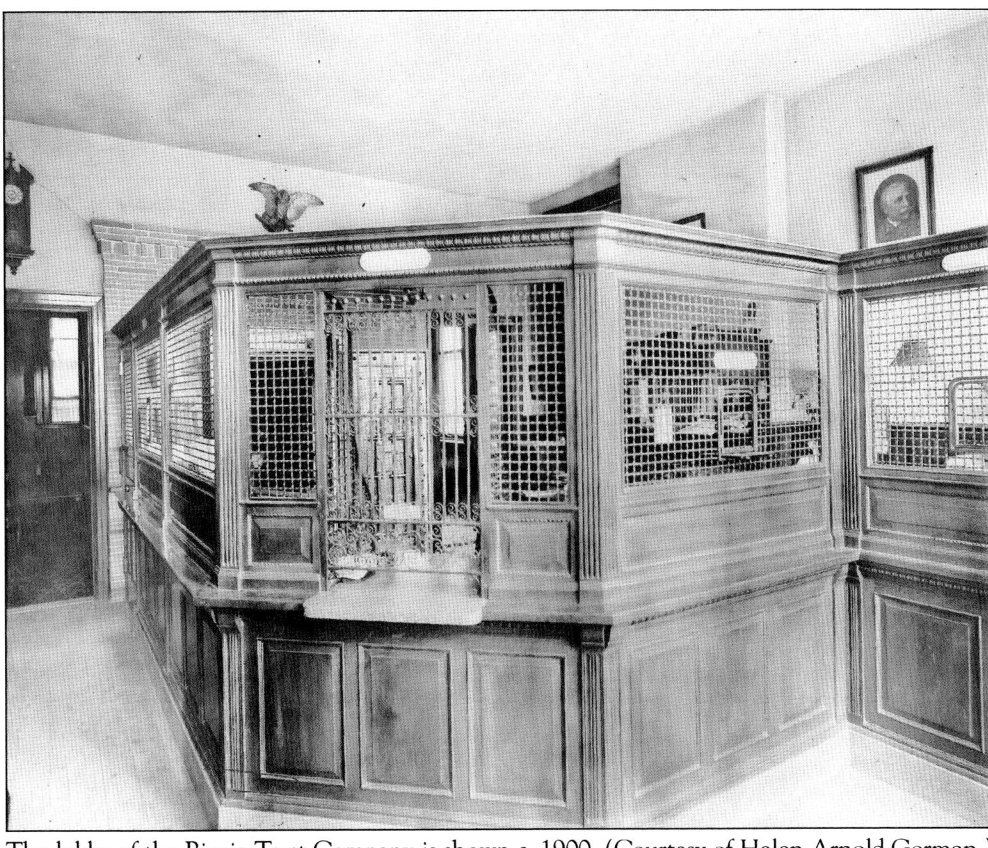

The lobby of the Birnie Trust Company is shown c. 1900. (Courtesy of Helen Arnold Gorman.)

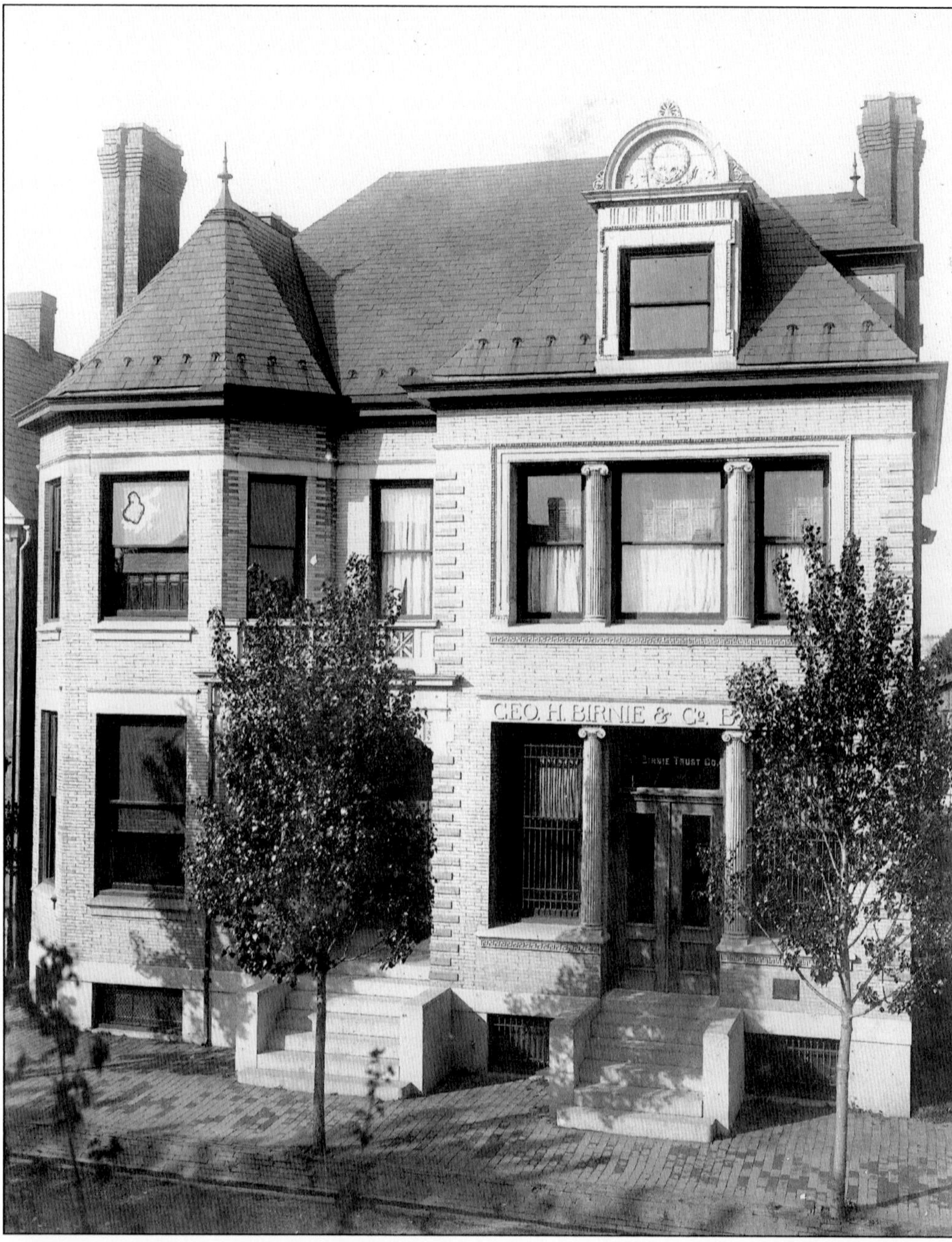

Founded in 1884 by George H. Birnie, with associates E.E. Reindollar and Dr. G.T. Motter, the banking firm of George H. Birnie & Company soon became known as the Birnie Trust Company. With a fine building erected about 1899, the Birnie Trust Company continued banking operations until 1966, when it merged with the First National Bank of Taneytown to become the Taneytown Bank and Trust Company. (Courtesy of the Historical Society of Carroll County.)

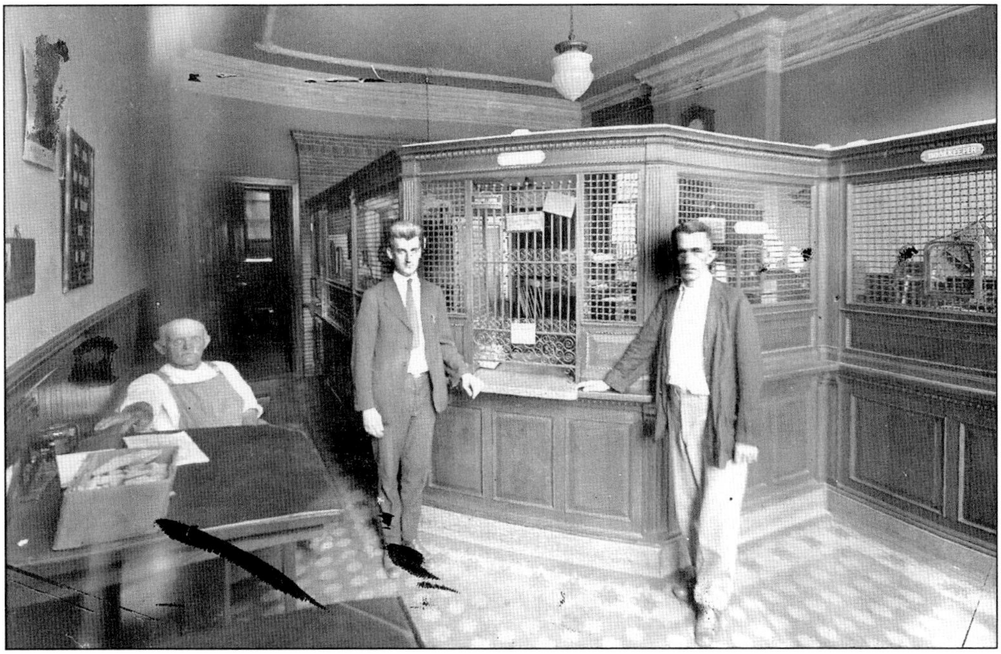

The following employees are pictured from left to right inside the Birnie Trust Company, c. 1920: Jerry Stauffer, custodian; Charles R. Arnold, assistant cashier; and G. Walter Wilt, cashier. (Courtesy of Helen Arnold Gorman.)

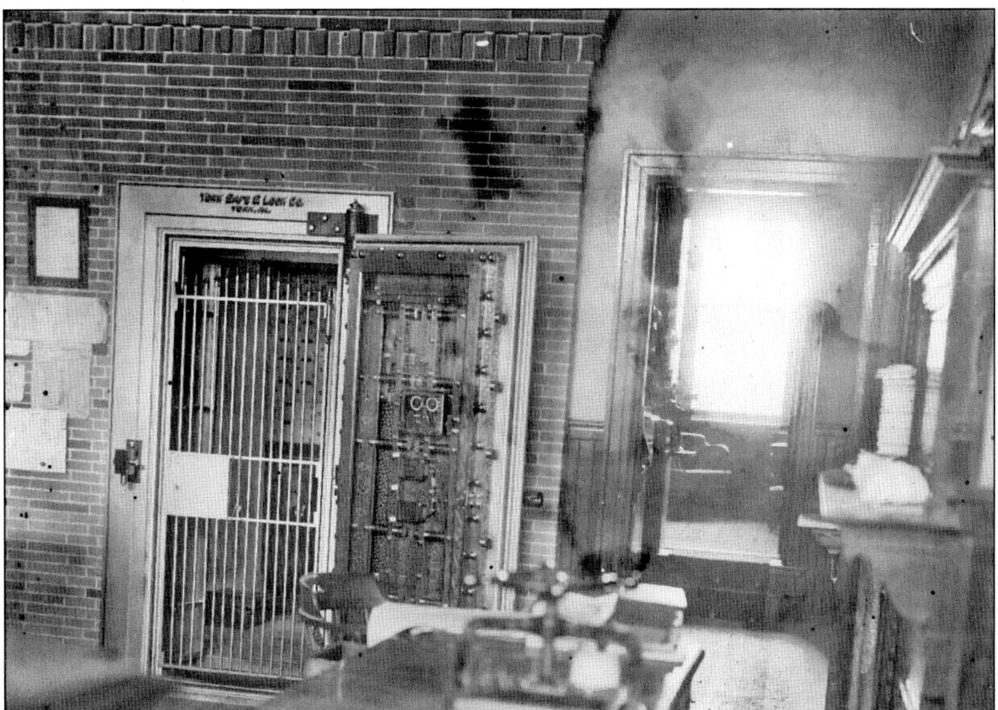

The massive vault of the Birnie Trust Company is pictured c. 1900. (Courtesy of Helen Arnold Gorman.)

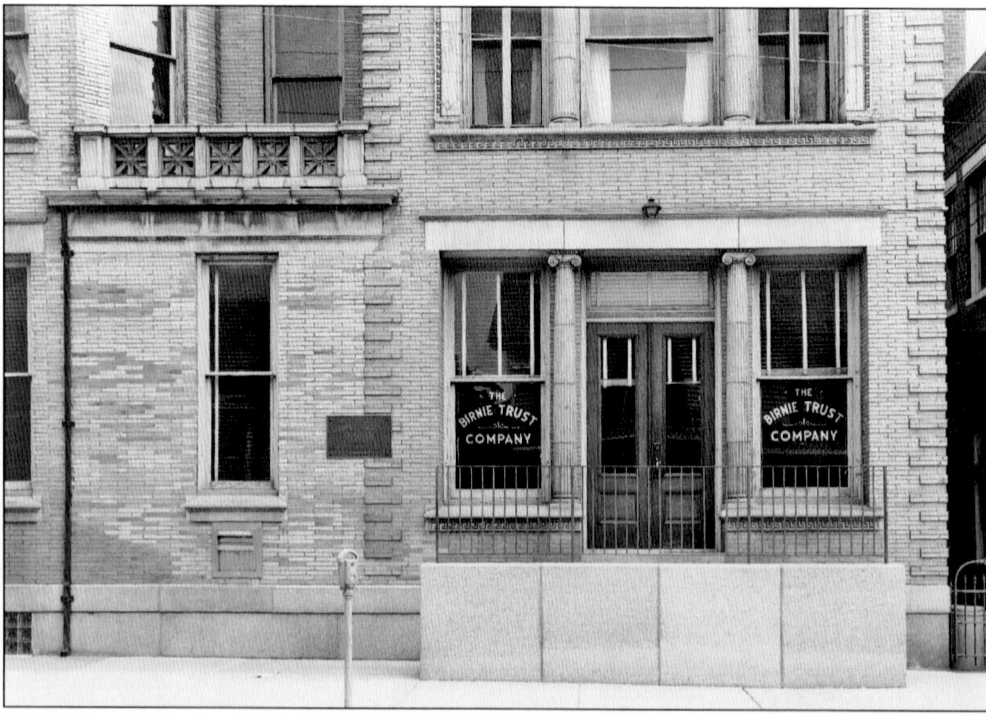

This photograph shows the newly renovated exterior of the Birnie Trust Company in 1959. (Courtesy of Historical Society of Carroll County.)

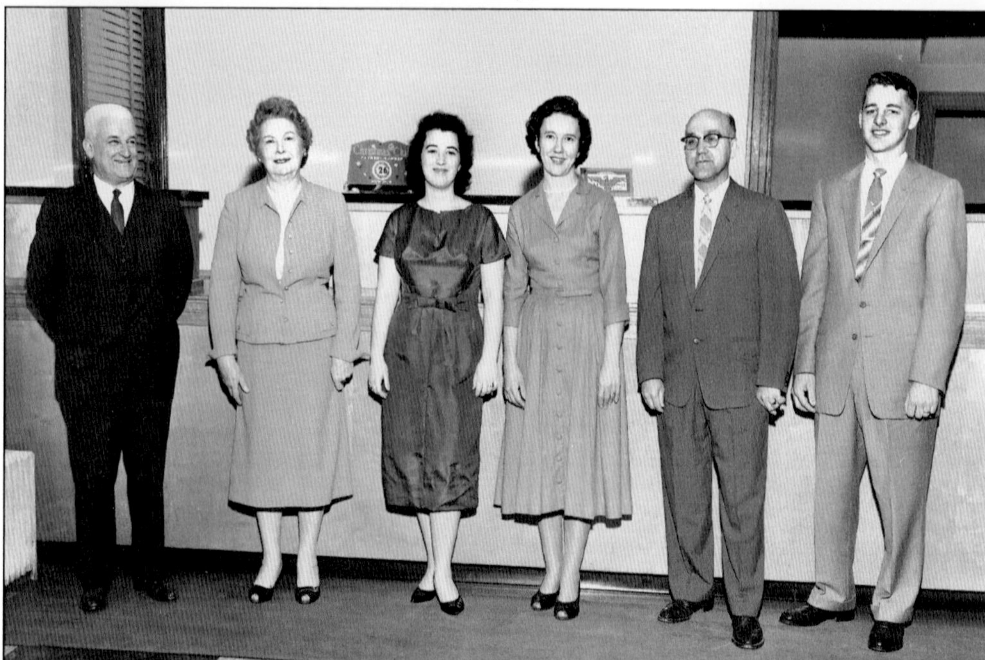
The employees of the Birnie Trust Company pose for a photograph in 1959. From left to right are Charles R. Arnold, Grace Smelser, Anne Breth, Emma Devilbiss, Murray Baumgardner, and Donald Lawyer. (Courtesy of Historical Society of Carroll County.)

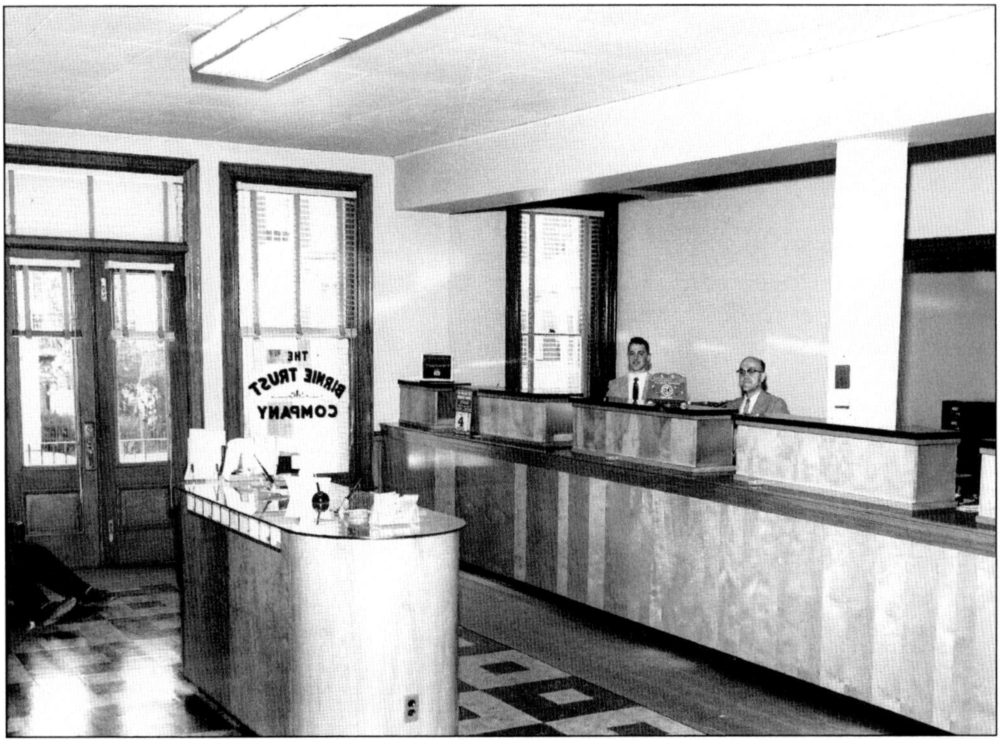

Donald Lawyer and Murray Baumgardner work behind the counter of the Birnie Trust Company in 1959. (Courtesy of Historical Society of Carroll County.)

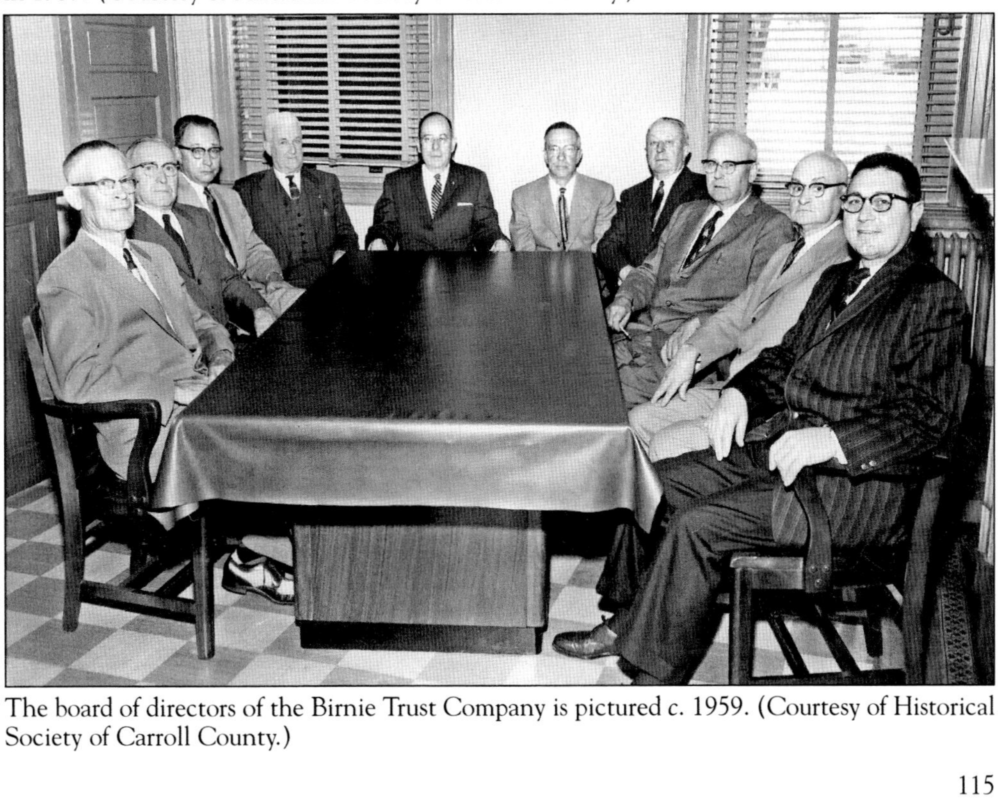

The board of directors of the Birnie Trust Company is pictured c. 1959. (Courtesy of Historical Society of Carroll County.)

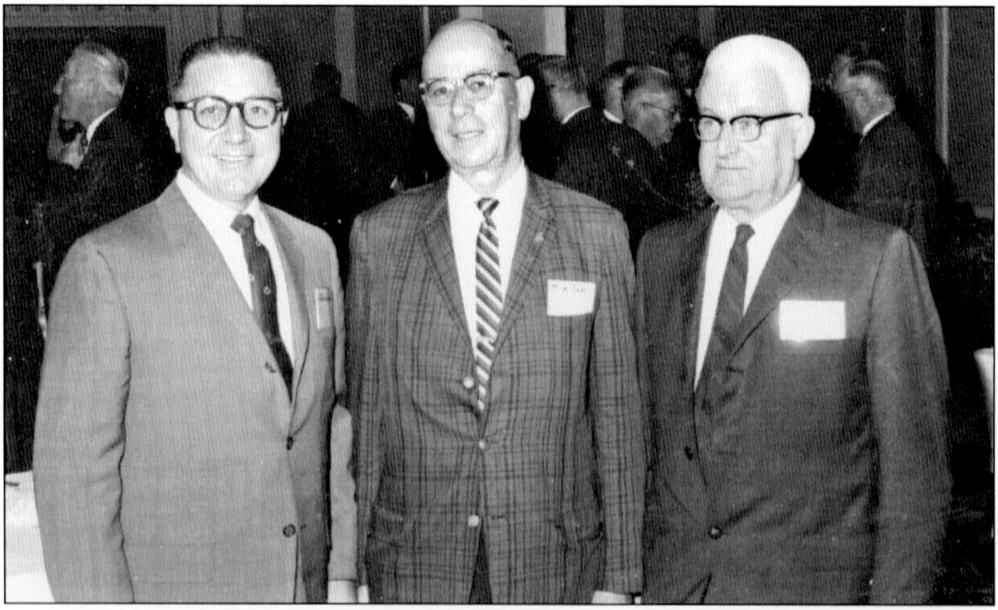

From left to right, James C. Baumgardner, Merwyn C. Fuss, and Charles R. Arnold are photographed attending a function on behalf of the Birnie Trust Company. (Courtesy of Helen Arnold Gorman.)

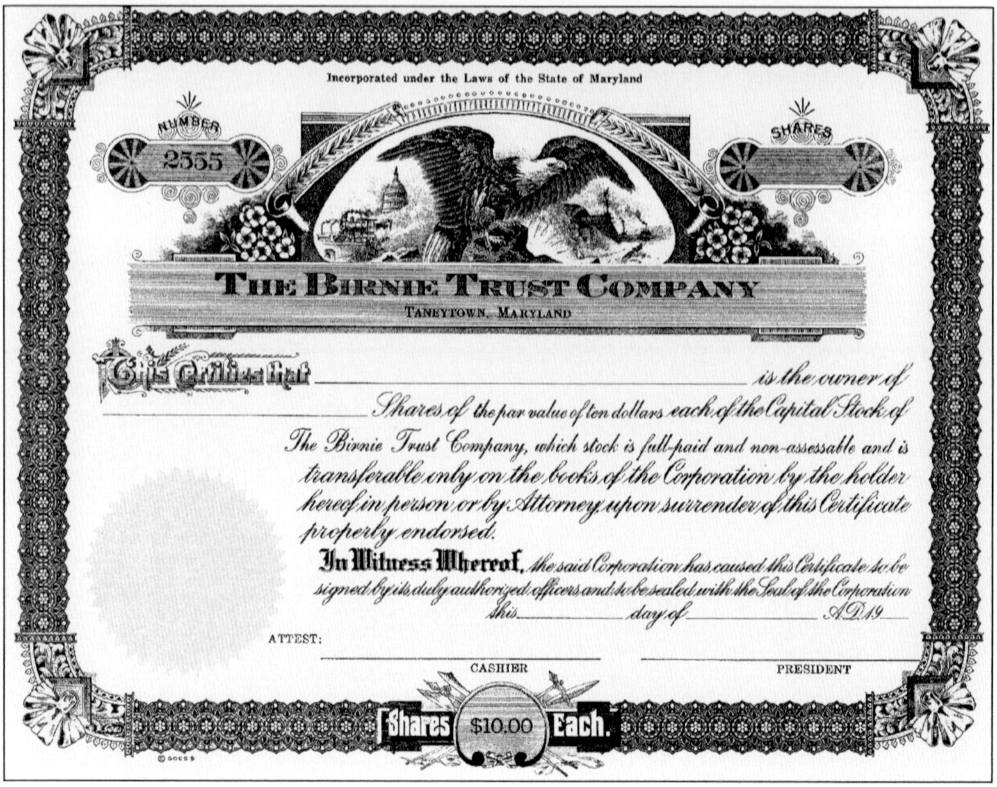

Incorporated under the Laws of the State of Maryland

NUMBER 2555

SHARES

THE BIRNIE TRUST COMPANY

TANEYTOWN, MARYLAND

This Certifies that ______________ is the owner of ______________ Shares of the par value of ten dollars each of the Capital Stock of The Birnie Trust Company, which stock is full-paid and non-assessable and is transferable only on the books of the Corporation by the holder hereof in person or by Attorney upon surrender of this Certificate properly endorsed.

In Witness Whereof, the said Corporation has caused this Certificate to be signed by its duly authorized officers and to be sealed with the Seal of the Corporation this ______ day of ______ A.D. 19__

ATTEST:

CASHIER

PRESIDENT

Shares $10.00 Each.

This is a stock certificate from the Birnie Trust Company, c. 1930. (Courtesy of Historical Society of Carroll County.)

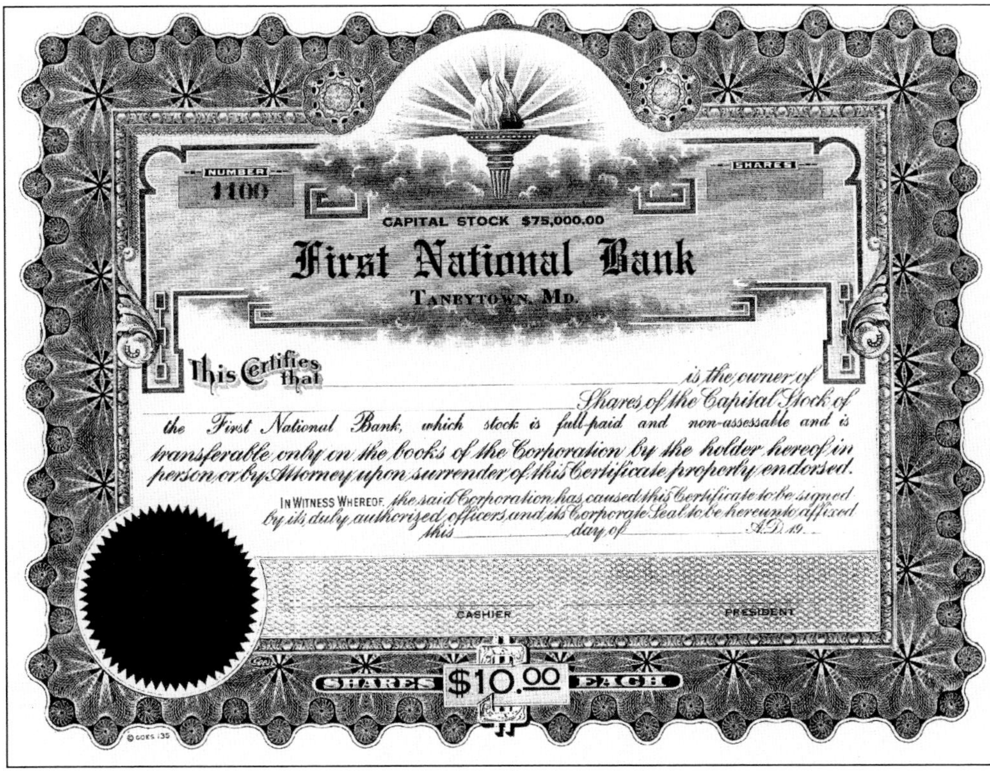

NUMBER 1100

SHARES

CAPITAL STOCK $75,000.00

First National Bank

TANEYTOWN, MD.

This Certifies that ______________________ is the owner of ______ Shares of the Capital Stock of the First National Bank, which stock is full-paid and non-assessable and is transferable only on the books of the Corporation by the holder hereof in person or by Attorney upon surrender of this Certificate properly endorsed.

IN WITNESS WHEREOF, the said Corporation has caused this Certificate to be signed by its duly authorized officers and its Corporate Seal to be hereunto affixed this ______ day of ______ A.D. 19__.

CASHIER

PRESIDENT

SHARES $10.00 EACH

Shown above is a stock certificate from the First National Bank, c. 1930. (Courtesy of Historical Society of Carroll County.)

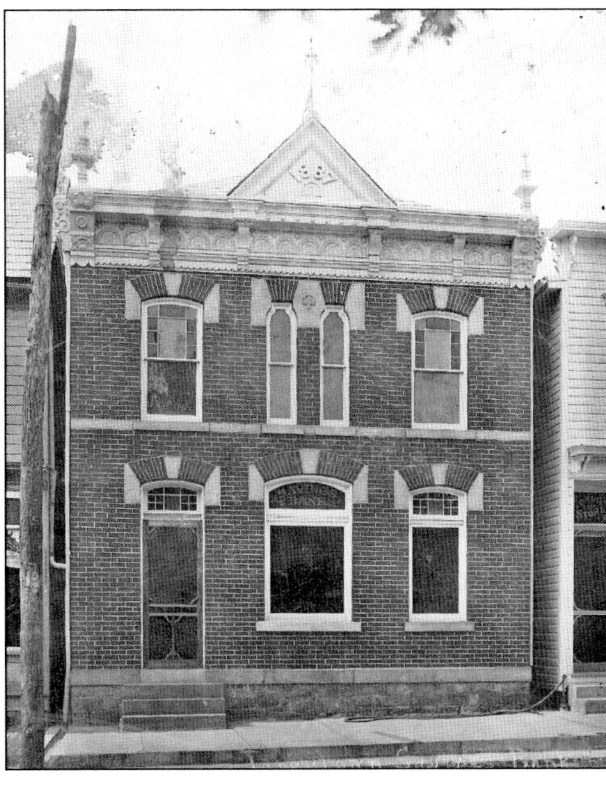

The Taneytown Savings Bank was organized in 1887; when it opened, Amos Duttera served as president and Henry Galt as treasurer. The elaborate pressed tin cornice and finials that adorn the top of the building are of architectural note. (Courtesy of Helen Arnold Gorman.)

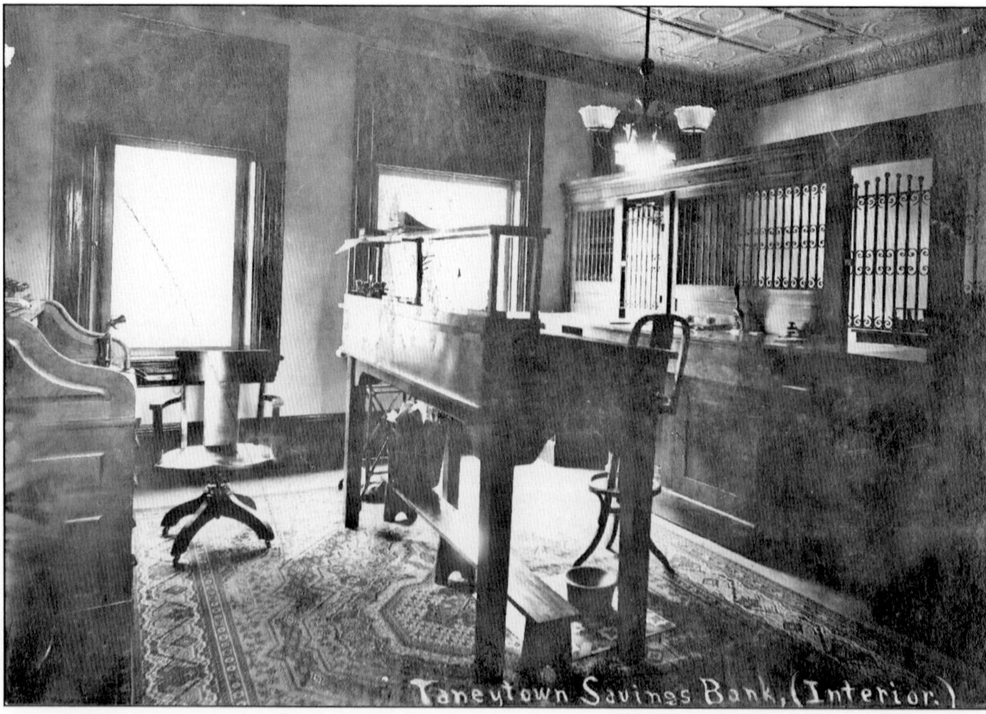

An interior view of the Taneytown Savings Bank from the late 1800s features the pressed tin ceiling, gas light fixture, and Oriental rug covering the floor. (Courtesy of Helen Arnold Gorman.)

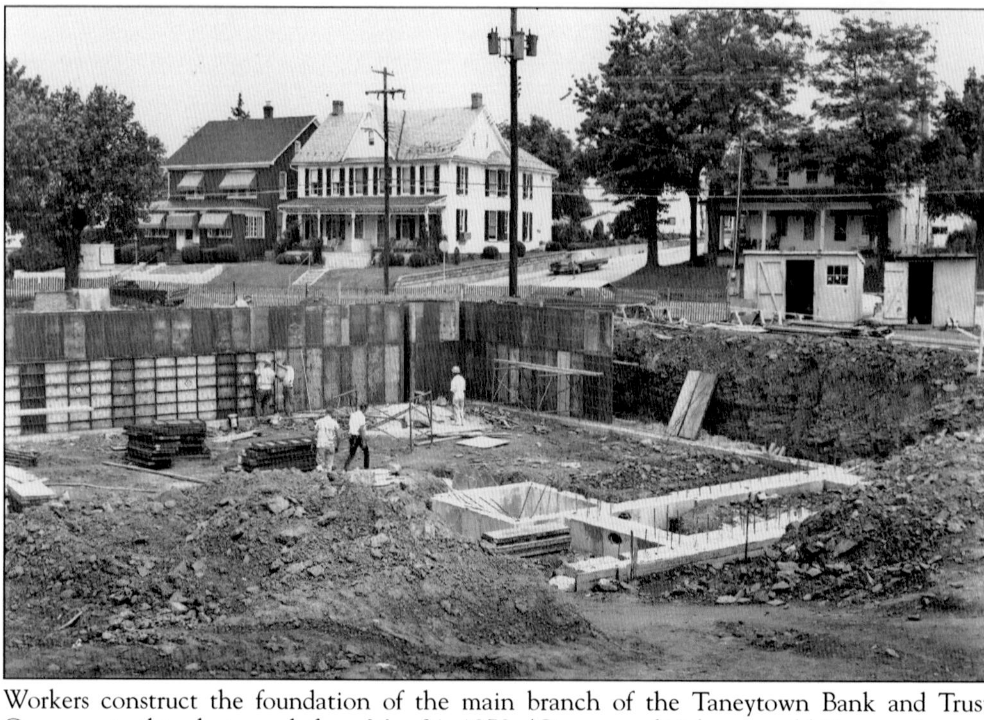
Workers construct the foundation of the main branch of the Taneytown Bank and Trust Company in this photograph from May 31, 1970. (Courtesy of Helen Arnold Gorman.)

Eight

MEMORIES

What is Taneytown? Upon reflection, there seems to be no clear-cut answer to this seemingly simple question. Certainly it is a place where the past and the present mingle freely. Events of decades past are mentioned in the same breath as the front-page headline of the day. Friends and family long since gone are remembered, their memories and stories kept alive inside the hearts of many.

No book could ever completely chronicle the story of Taneytown, simply because the story is not over. For generations to come, people will continue to live out their lives here, just as generations before have done. In the meantime, it is hoped that some of the images and anecdotes presented in this work will spark more conversation and lead to more stories and fond memories.

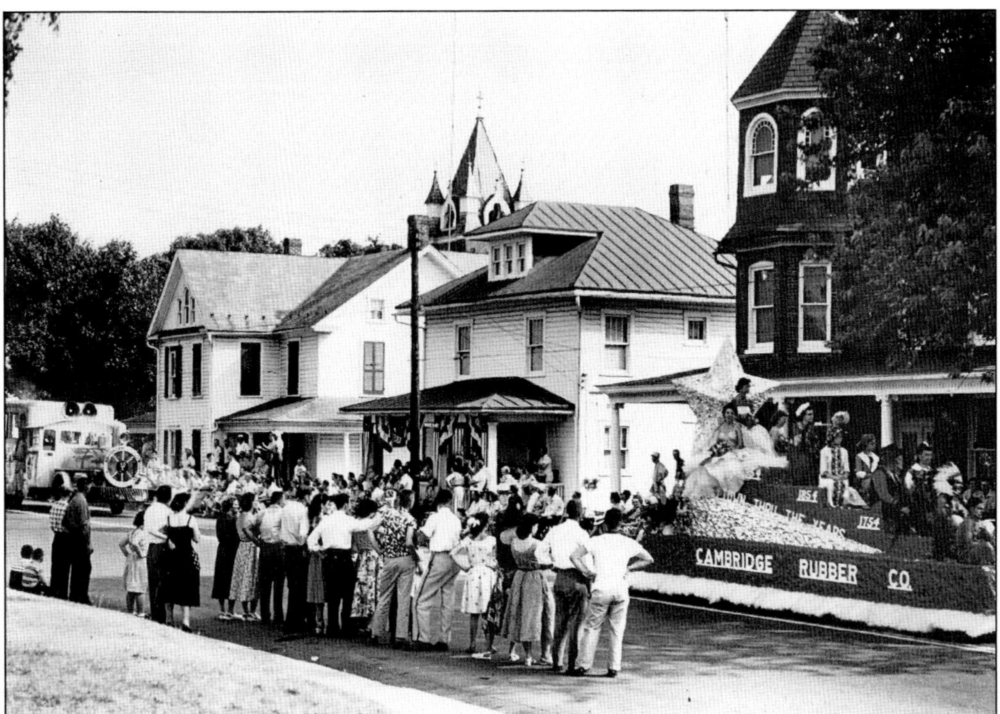

A crowd of onlookers views the Cambridge Rubber Company float in the mammoth parade held on July 31, 1954, to commemorate Taneytown's bicentennial. (Courtesy of George Naylor.)

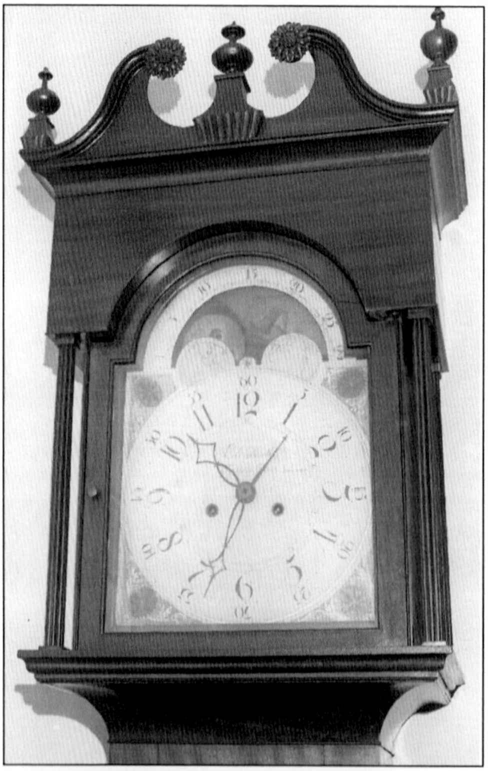

Clockmaker Eli Bentley worked in Taneytown during the late 18th and early 19th centuries. Many of his beautiful clocks still exist in the Taneytown area today and are cherished by their owners. This clock was made in 1815 for the Biggs family, who lived near Keysville. Originally purchased for the great sum of $95, the clock was donated by Victor Weybright to the Historical Society of Carroll County. (Photograph by Robert Porterfield, courtesy of the Historical Society of Carroll County.)

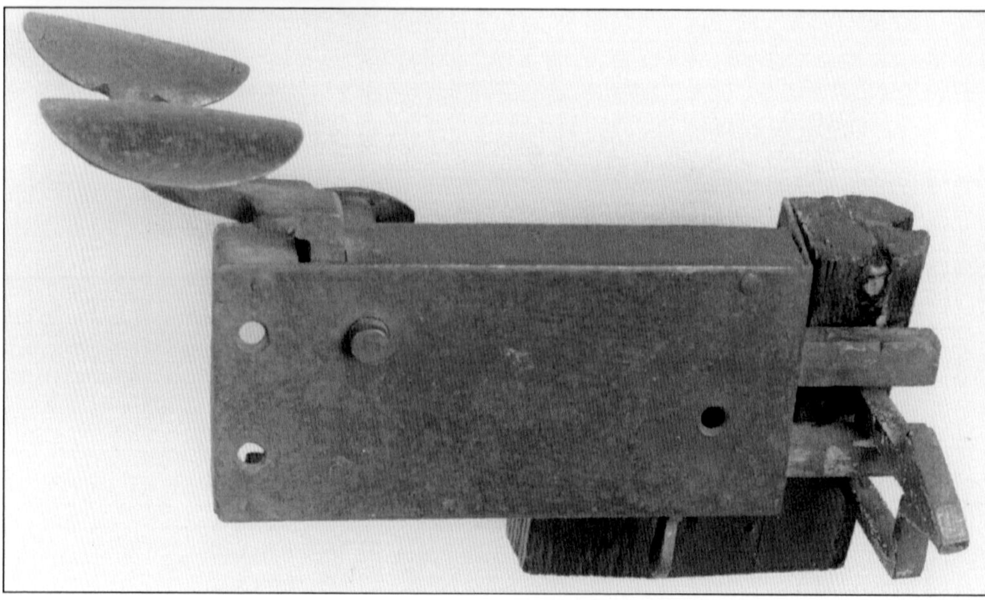

In July 1791, George Washington lodged overnight at the Adam Good Tavern. Local legend maintains that Washington chose to stay at the inn because he found its sign to be amusing. Because of a mistake in spacing made by the sign painter, the sign read, "A dam Good Inn." Although the tavern located on Frederick Street was torn down in the 1890s, this lock from the front door was saved, simply because Washington may have touched it. (Photograph by Robert Porterfield, courtesy of the Historical Society of Carroll County.)

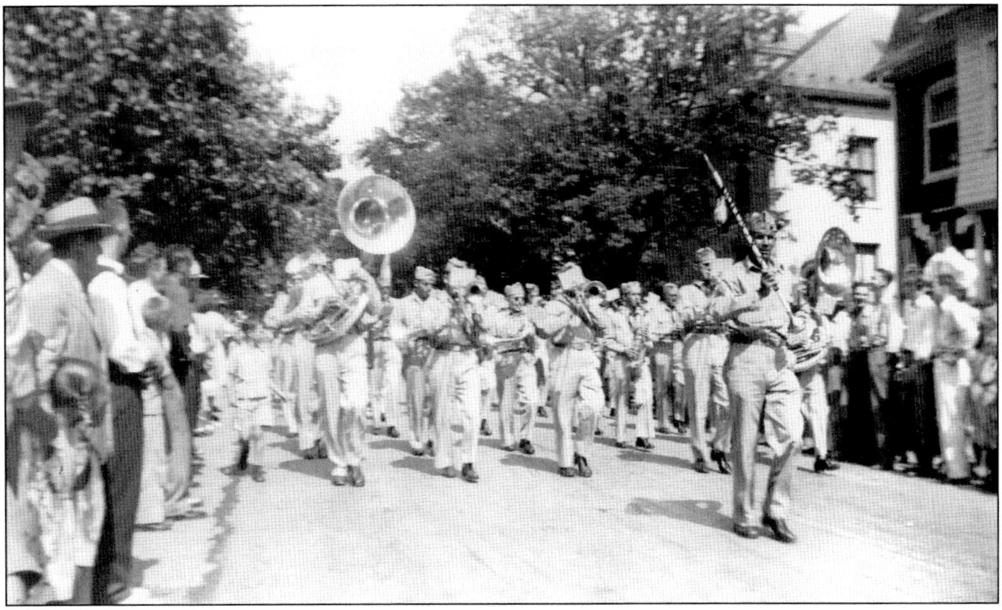

A band marches down York Street in a Memorial Day parade held after World War II. (Courtesy of Jean Brown.)

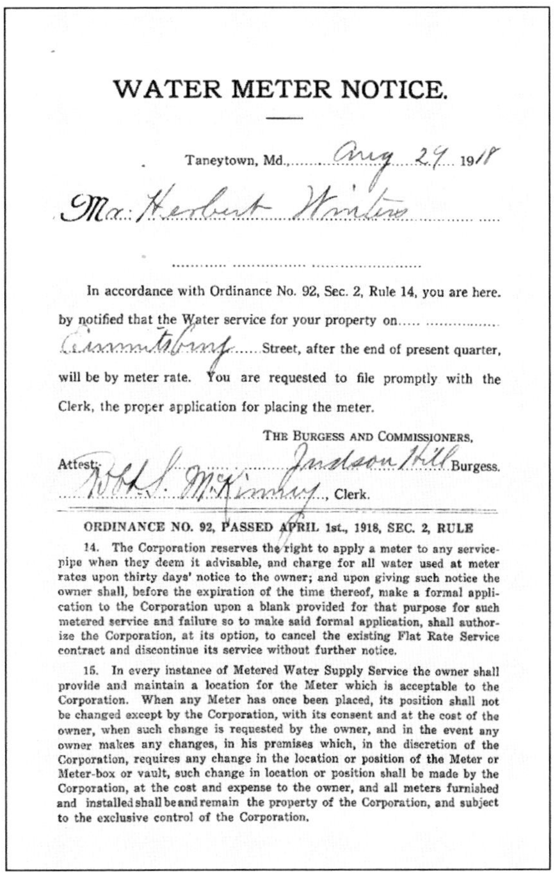

WATER METER NOTICE.

Taneytown, Md., Aug 29 1918

Mr. Herbert Winter

In accordance with Ordinance No. 92, Sec. 2, Rule 14, you are hereby notified that the Water service for your property on Emmitsburg Street, after the end of present quarter, will be by meter rate. You are requested to file promptly with the Clerk, the proper application for placing the meter.

THE BURGESS AND COMMISSIONERS,

Attest: Judson Hill Burgess.

Wm. S. McKinney, Clerk.

ORDINANCE NO. 92, PASSED APRIL 1st., 1918, SEC. 2, RULE

14. The Corporation reserves the right to apply a meter to any service-pipe when they deem it advisable, and charge for all water used at meter rates upon thirty days' notice to the owner; and upon giving such notice the owner shall, before the expiration of the time thereof, make a formal application to the Corporation upon a blank provided for that purpose for such metered service and failure so to make said formal application, shall authorize the Corporation, at its option, to cancel the existing Flat Rate Service contract and discontinue its service without further notice.

15. In every instance of Metered Water Supply Service the owner shall provide and maintain a location for the Meter which is acceptable to the Corporation. When any Meter has once been placed, its position shall not be changed except by the Corporation, with its consent and at the cost of the owner, when such change is requested by the owner, and in the event any owner makes any changes, in his premises which, in the discretion of the Corporation, requires any change in the location or position of the Meter or Meter-box or vault, such change in location or position shall be made by the Corporation, at the cost and expense to the owner, and all meters furnished and installed shall be and remain the property of the Corporation, and subject to the exclusive control of the Corporation.

In 1918, this notice was sent to the citizens of Taneytown, alerting them to the fact that water service would no longer be free. (Courtesy of the Historical Society of Carroll County.)

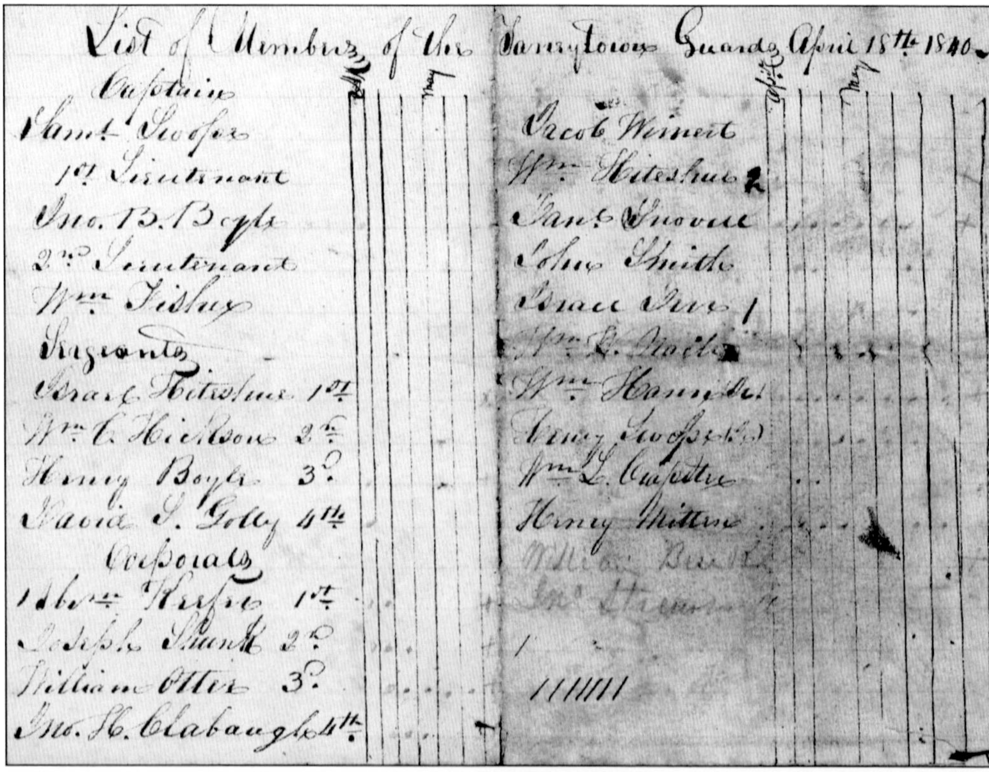

List of Members of the Taneytown Guards April 18th 1840

Captain
Saml. Swope
1st Lieutenant
Jno. B. Boyle
2nd Lieutenant
Wm. Fisher
Sergeants
Israel Hiteshue 1st
Wm. C. Hickson 2nd
Henry Boyle 3rd
David S. Golley 4th
Corporals
Abrm. Keefer 1st
Joseph Shunk 2nd
William Otter 3rd
Jno. H. Clabaugh 4th

Jacob Weinert
Wm. Hiteshue
Saml. [illegible]
John Smith
Israel [illegible]
Wm. [illegible]
Wm. Hamilton
Henry Swope
Wm. L. [illegible]
Henry Mitten
William [illegible]
Jno. [illegible]

This rare manuscript is the roster of members of the Taneytown Guards from April 18, 1840. Organized by Dr. Samuel Swope in 1838, the militia unit was well known for its precise drills and blue and white uniforms. (Courtesy of the Historical Society of Carroll County.)

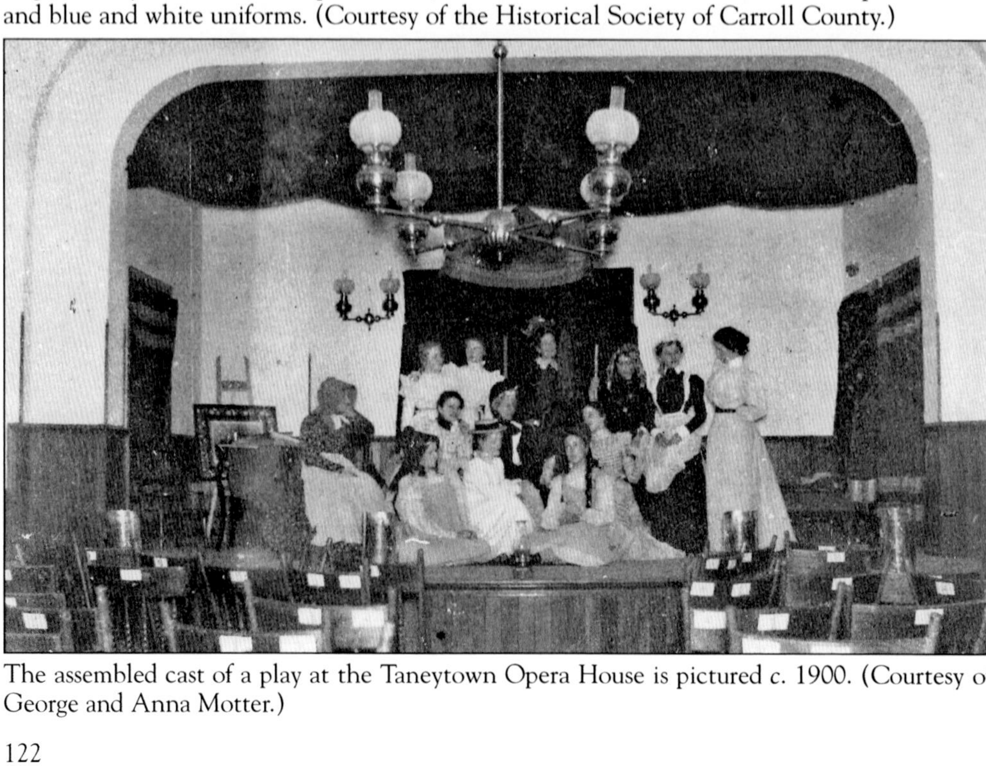

The assembled cast of a play at the Taneytown Opera House is pictured *c*. 1900. (Courtesy of George and Anna Motter.)

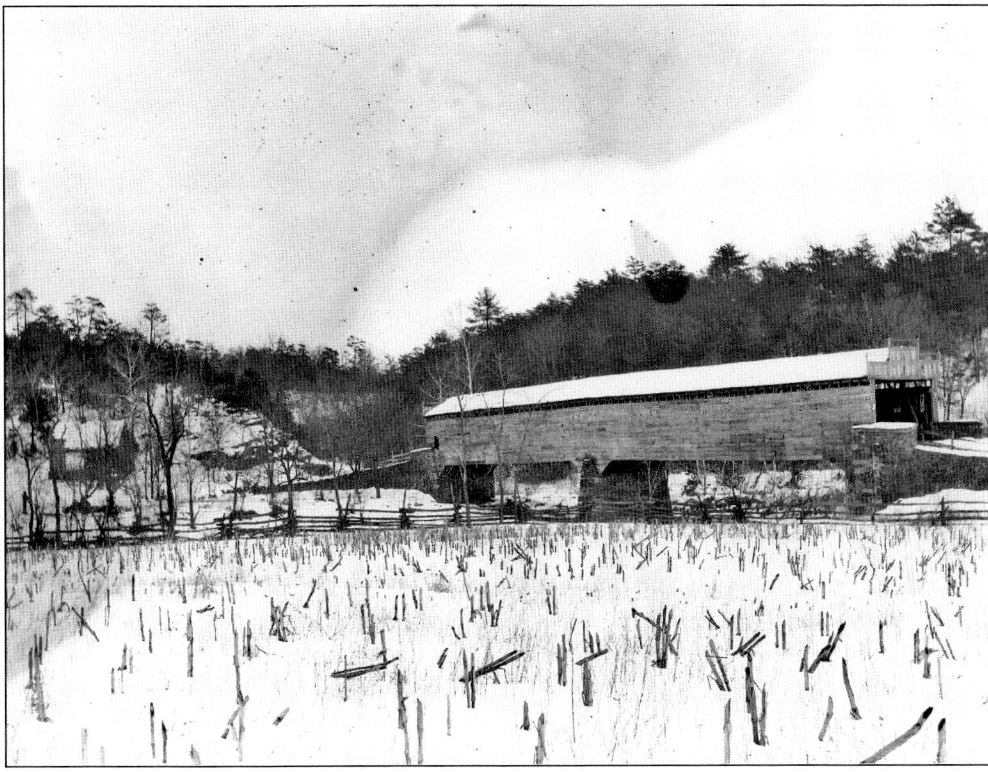

This covered bridge over the Monocacy River at Bridgeport was built in 1849 and continued in use until 1932. (Courtesy of the Historical Society of Carroll County.)

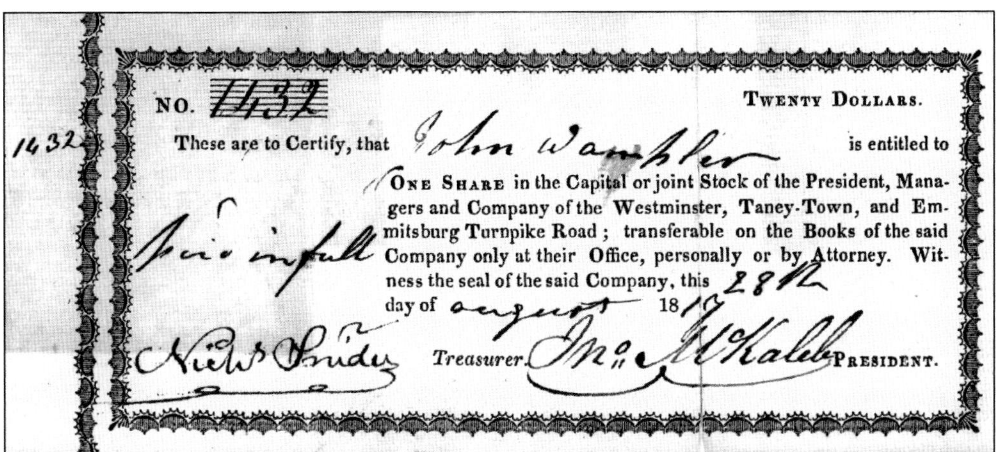

NO. 1432 — TWENTY DOLLARS.

1432

These are to Certify, that John Wambler is entitled to ONE SHARE in the Capital or joint Stock of the President, Managers and Company of the Westminster, Taney-Town, and Emmitsburg Turnpike Road; transferable on the Books of the said Company only at their Office, personally or by Attorney. Witness the seal of the said Company, this 28th day of august 1817

Paid in full

Nich's Snider Treasurer. Jno. McKaleb PRESIDENT.

In the early 1800s, local citizens sought to improve the quality of the roads leading from Westminster to Taneytown to Emmitsburg. They formed a company and sold stock with no government assistance. Although the plan to build a plank road was never realized, this rare stock certificate from 1817 survives. (Courtesy of the Historical Society of Carroll County.)

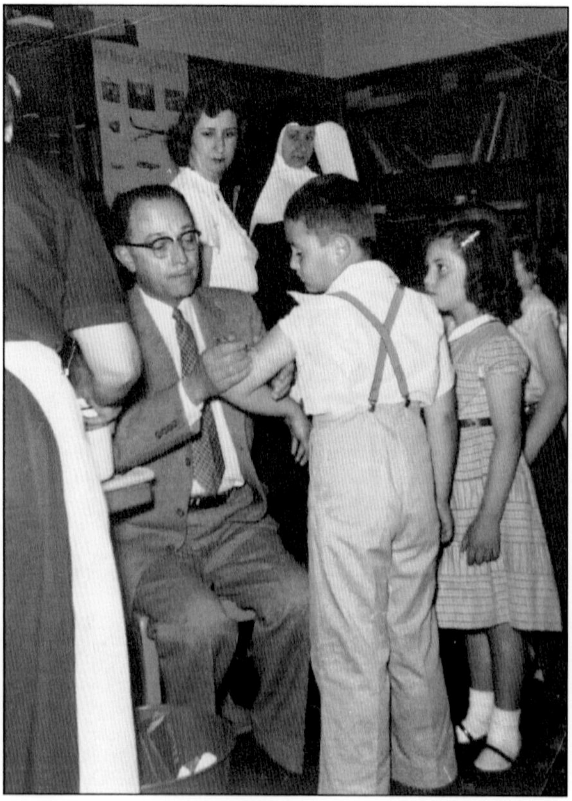

Dr. Robert S. McVaugh administers the first polio vaccine given in Taneytown at St. Joseph's School. (Courtesy of the Clem family.)

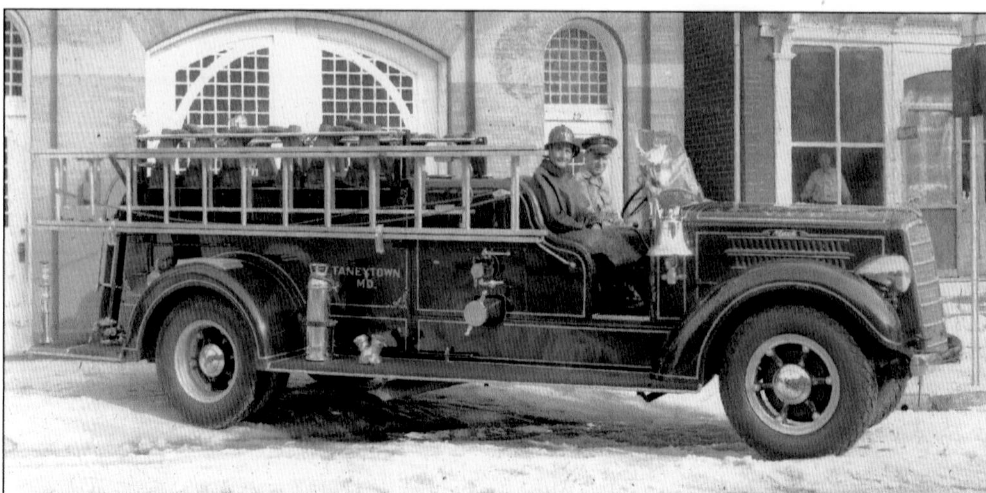

Meredith Gross and Dave Smeak pose for a picture in a Mack fire truck in front of the fire engine house in the 1940s. (Courtesy of George Naylor.)

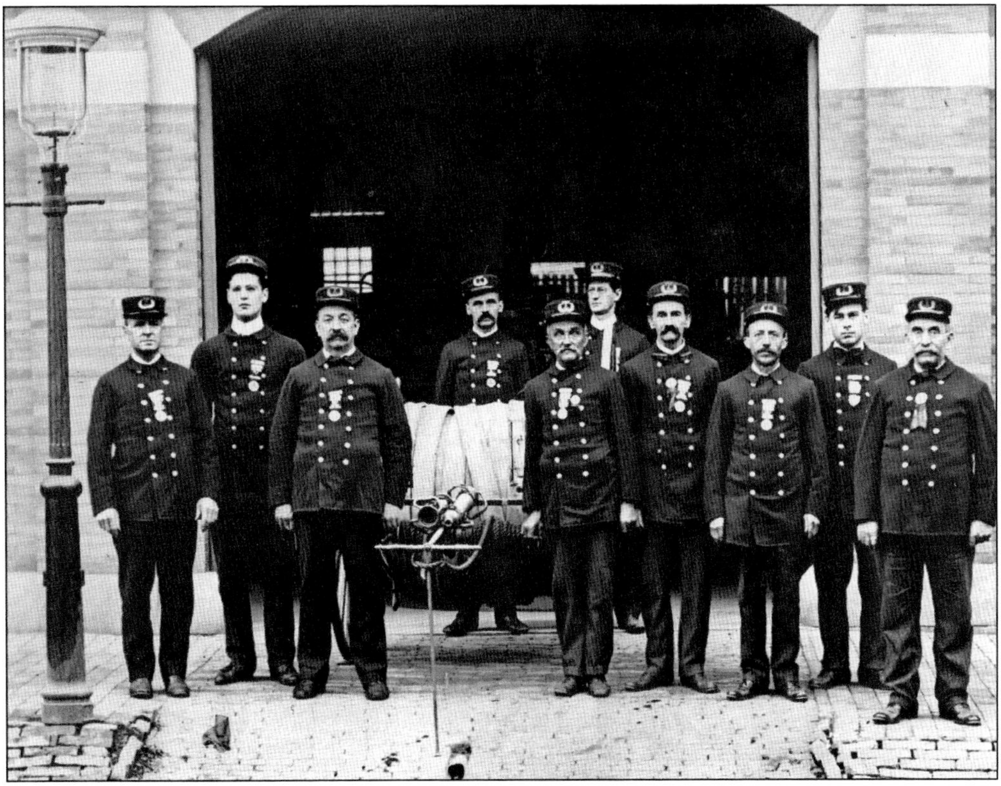

The charter members of the Taneytown Volunteer Fire Co. No. 1, which was organized in 1897, pictured from left to right, are James Galt, George Elliot, William E. Burke, Norman Hagen, Burgess S. Miller, Robert S. McKinney, Charles O. Fuss, G.F. Sherman Gilds, Walter Bowers, and Westley Fink. Charles Elliot is not pictured. (Courtesy of the Taneytown Volunteer Fire Co. No. 1.)

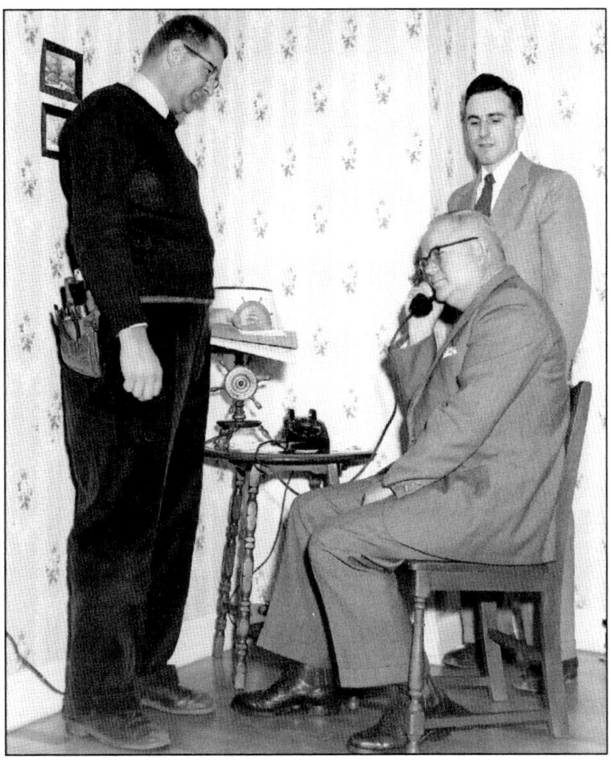

"Smokey" Morelock, Bob Klunk, and Mayor Raymond Perry preside over the installation of the 1,000th telephone in Taneytown, c. 1950. (Courtesy of the Clem family.)

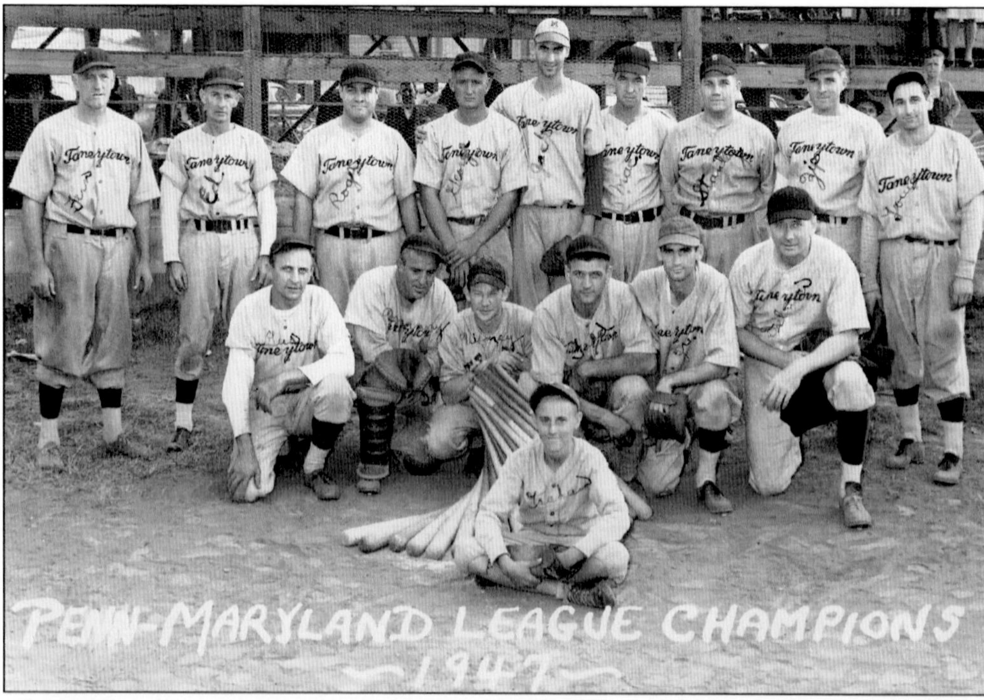

The Taneytown baseball team was the Penn-Maryland League Champions in 1947. The following team members are listed from left to right: (front row, kneeling) Gus Shank, Manny Wildasin, Wimpy Fritz, Fred Shank, Fern Hitchcock Jr., and Delmar Riffle; (back row, standing) Fern Hitchcock Sr. (manager), Ed Pulsun, Roger Blettner, George Null, Clarence Balon, Mack McNulty, Stanley King, Glenn Dayhoff, and Louie Crapster. The bat boy is Graham Wildasin. (Courtesy of the Clem family.)

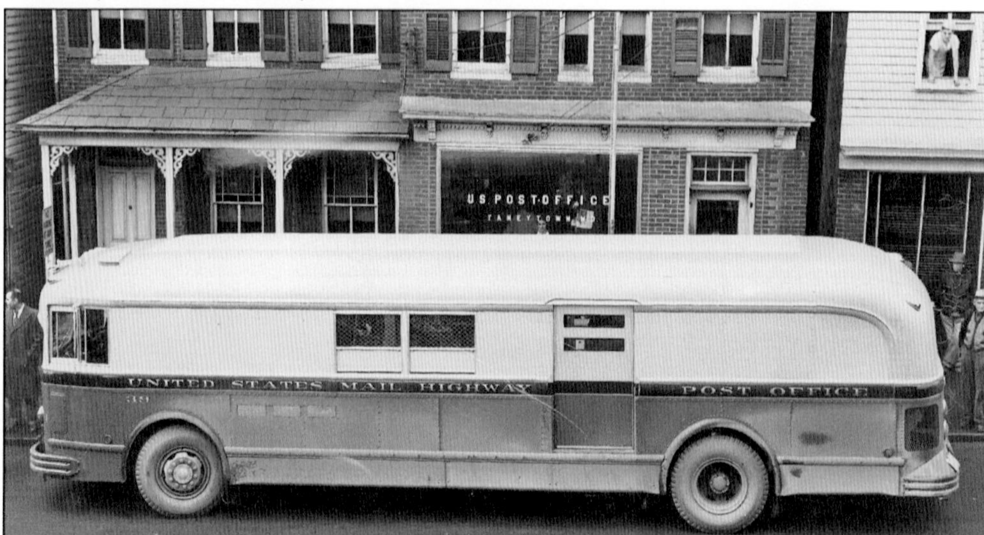

This photograph of the Highway Post Office was taken on the occasion of its inaugural run in 1949. Serving 27 towns between Lancaster and Washington, the Highway Post Office was designed to replace railway postal service to small, outlying communities and provide fast and dependable service. (Courtesy of Helen Arnold Gorman.)

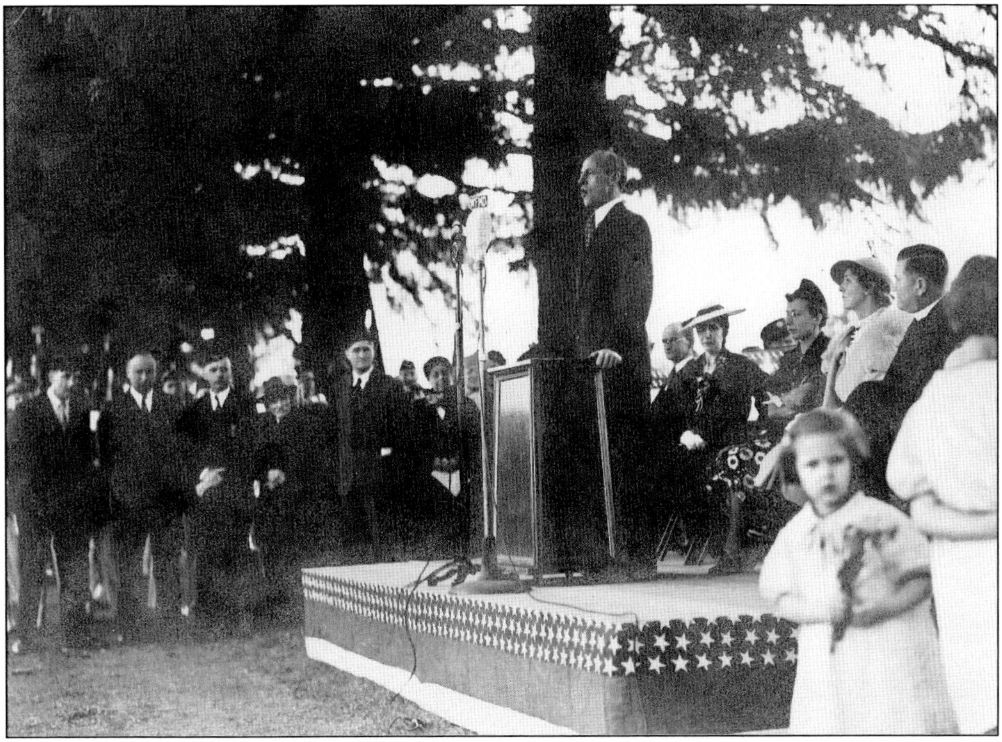

Sen. Millard E. Tydings addressed the crowd at the May 30, 1938, Taneytown Memorial Day observances held at the Taneytown Reformed Church Cemetery. Pictured from left to right are (seated) Dr. C.M. Benner, Mrs. Francis T. Elliott, Mrs. Louise Lancaster, Mrs. Millard E. Tydings, and Fr. Joseph F. Lane; (standing) Albert Smith, James C. Myers, B. Walter Crapster, James Salley, Louis Lancaster, and Rose Crabbs. (Courtesy of the Historical Society of Carroll County.)

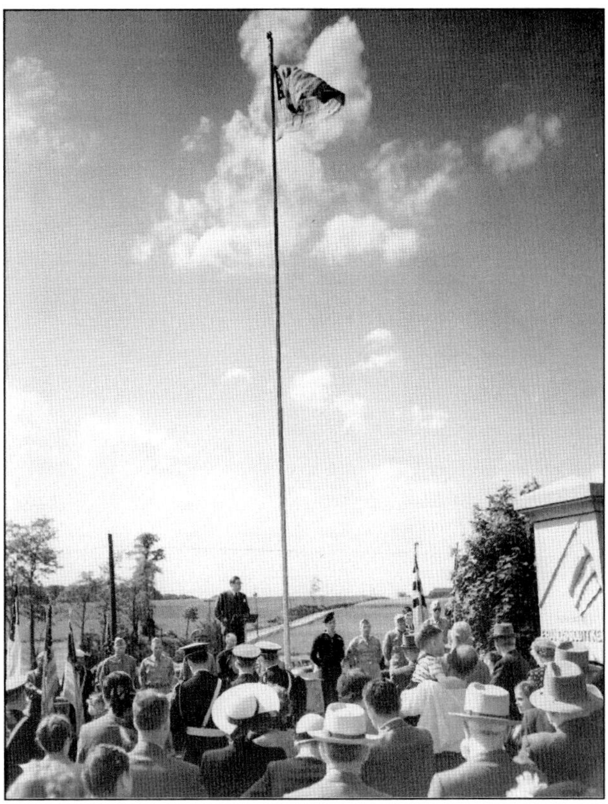

On Memorial Day 1949, a dedication ceremony was held at Terra Rubra for the flagpole donated by the Kiwanis Club of Westminster. Victor Weybright, who authored a biography on Key, addressed the crowd of 300. (Courtesy of the Historical Society of Carroll County.)

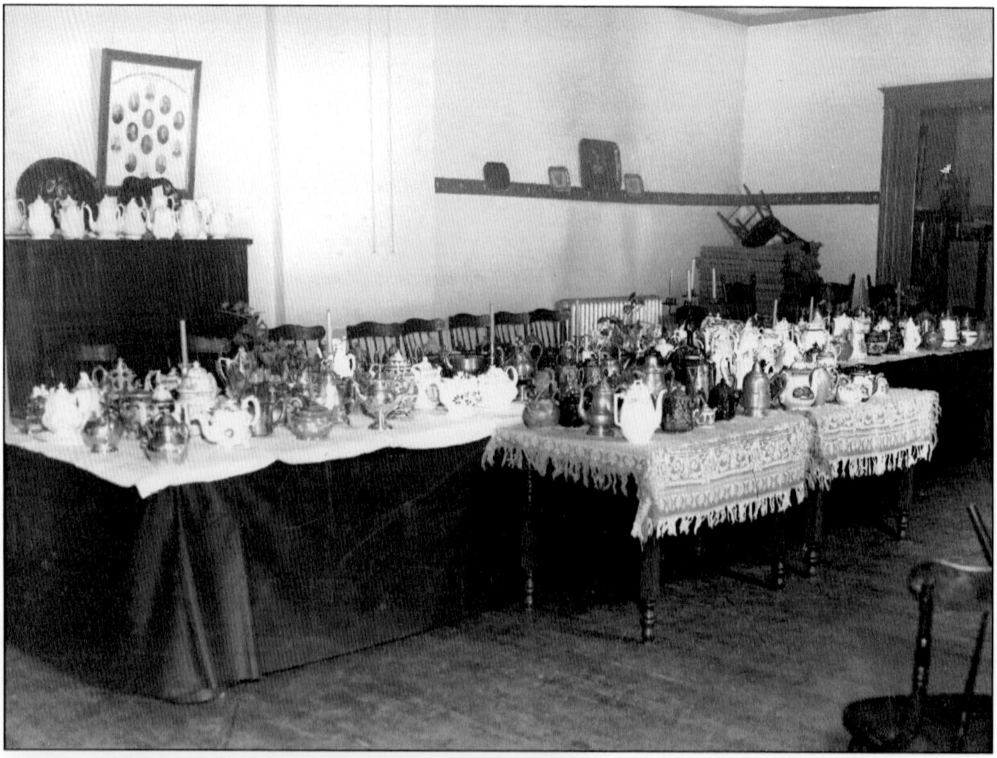

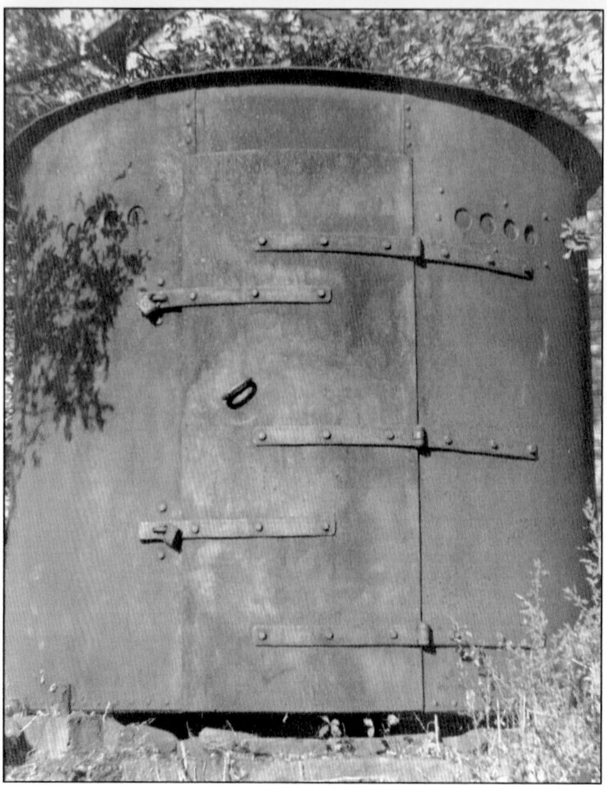

One of the earliest events sponsored to support the Historical Society of Carroll County was this exhibit of teapots held in the upstairs room of the fire engine house in Taneytown on January 18, 1946. (Courtesy of the Historical Society of Carroll County.)

The city jail was used for many years as a place of detention for offenders picked up when it was not convenient to take them immediately to the county jail or when it was desired to hold them temporarily for a hearing before the squire. Constructed of steel plates and weighing about two tons, "The Can" was donated to a scrap drive during World War II. (Courtesy of the Historical Society of Carroll County.)